MUSIC AND SOCIETY
SINCE 1815

By the same author

THE SOCIAL HISTORY OF MUSIC
From the Middle Ages to Beethoven

Music and Society
Since 1815

HENRY RAYNOR

SCHOCKEN BOOKS • NEW YORK

First published by SCHOCKEN BOOKS 1976

© 1976 by Henry Raynor

Library of Congress Catalog Card No. 76–1377

Printed in Great Britain

Contents

Introduction and Acknowledgements

Revolution at the end of the eighteenth century and reaction after 1815, with the consequent upheavals in European society and politics, left the musician and especially the composer without a recognised place in society or an understood social function; it seemed only too easy for the world to continue without him. Left without an audience, he had to challenge the 'great masters' for the attention of the public, and in doing so he had to write 'great' music, on a bigger scale than the masters themselves. The public was to be met, and if possible subjugated, in huge opera houses and large concert halls if the composer was to earn his living, so that orchestras and choruses had to grow if they were to be sufficiently imposing in auditoria built to hold thousands.

At the same time, both musical developments and social conditions created a specialised 'light music', taking away the 'serious' composer's traditional function as an entertainer and widening the gulf between him and his audience, compelling him to concentrate on huge sensations and often painful extremes of emotion. As European religion declined and composers dwelt almost exclusively on the tremendous and the intense, the 'serious' composer, like Berlioz and Wagner, began to find in art, and especially in music, the only safe repository of spiritual values.

The composer, dispossessed by social and political conditions of his natural audience, became conscious of the imperfections of the society by which he was surrounded and to which he wished entirely to belong; his cure for social imperfections could only be through music. The salvation of the nation, the brotherhood of man, the power of nature, the sanctity of art: these became the themes for the nineteenth-century composer. Therefore he was, in a sense that his predecessors had never been, concerned with politics; he became aware of, and sought to exploit and develop, national musical characteristics. He found, often enough, a definite political role to play.

These are the trains of thought which this book attempts to follow into the twentieth century as it considers the social and political pressures under which the composer functioned until the patterns of European society and culture were broken into fragments by two world wars, revolution, the continuous dehumanisation of life in an age of industrial mass production, advertising and mass communications.

The development of music in these conditions poses questions which tempt the historian to moralise; not even Gibbon could totally resist the temptation, while Macaulay, like Spengler and many others, accepted it gratefully. In so far as a wish to preserve inherited standards of excellence in music, in historical enquiry, in society and in its politics (matters in all of which inherited standards are anything but static or reactionary) tend to promote moralising, the author apologises in advance if he has unthinkingly yielded to a natural temptation and drawn too many morals.

I am deeply grateful to a multitude of friends who, in discussion or general conversation, or in correspondence, often without knowing that they were doing so, have guided my hand and suggested answers to problems while stimulating my attempt to probe the relationship between music and the world it inhabits, reflects, expresses and interprets.

I am specially grateful to Stainton de B. Taylor for putting at my disposal his researches into the musical history of nineteenth-century Liverpool.

To Martin Roth, Esq., for finding me a way through the quagmires and thickets of nineteenth-century European currencies:

To A. C. Stock, Esq., who has taken care that my translations from French shall be plausible:

To David Cairns, Esq., to Messrs Victor Gollancz, Ltd, for permission to quote from Mr Cairns's translation of the *Memoirs of Berlioz*:

To Messrs John Calder for permission to quote from *The American Symphony Orchestra*, by John H. Mueller:

To John G. Pattisson, Esq., of Messrs Barrie and Jenkins, for unfailing patience and encouragement:

And, as always, to Ellie, who has reduced German translations to accuracy, reprimanded verbosities and demanded the rationalisation of occasional stray pronouns.

HENRY RAYNOR

Reigate, Surrey: June, 1975

I

The Decline of Court Patronage

The Europe of the Old Regime, of the sometimes benevolent despotism and of the classic ideal, began its protracted dissolution with the outbreak of the French Revolution in 1789. As the old world dissolved, the system of musical patronage which had persisted since the renaissance dissolved with it, for though the Congress of Vienna set out in 1814 to revitalise the corpse of pre-revolutionary Europe, it could not restore the aristocratic wealth on which not only the social and political life of the eighteenth century had depended but which had also made possible its artistic achievements. In 1803 Beethoven's patron and friend Prince Lobkowitz had supported the orchestra which gave the first performance of Beethoven's *Eroica* Symphony; after 1812 Prince Lobkowitz was apparently satisfied to be an active member of the newly formed Vienna *Gesellschaft für Musikfreunde*.

As the huge aristocratic fortunes evaporated, a savage inflation and postwar depression after 1815 made the support of a paying audience essential to the satisfactory performance of opera and of large-scale orchestral music. Beethoven had developed the habit of addressing his symphonies and concertos to the general public; his successors followed him in this because his example set the fashion for larger and larger orchestras essential to satisfactory performances in auditoria large enough to permit the general public to hear a composer's message. The general public had to be invited because the special public to whom the court musician had addressed his communications assembled less and less frequently in princely salons and music rooms. Music and musicians turned to the general public for support because the traditional patrons were no longer able to play their traditional role in music with anything like their old lavishness. Patrons who before the revolution had created musical organisations to serve their individual taste found that they needed to make room for paying audiences to augment the subsidies they were able to grant to their orchestras and opera houses. Such subsidies, which in the past had come from the personal income of a royal or noble patron, began to come to music directly from taxation or indirectly from civil list payments to a ruler; orchestras and opera companies began to become, in fact if not in name, state or national musical organisations.

At the same time, the number of such musical organisations decreased during the Revolutionary and Napoleonic Wars and though the work of the

Congress of Vienna itself, which accepted its inability to put every clock everywhere back to 1788; it accepted, for example, the secularisation of ecclesiastical states and prince-bishoprics, the destruction of the Imperial Free Cities and the absorption of a number of smaller states by their larger neighbours; a hundred and twenty-one of the minor German states lost their old independence, and with it their traditional musical establishments.

Eichstätt, a tiny Prince-Bishopric between Nuremberg and Munich, can serve as an example. The city's musical history dates unsensationally back at least to 1293. The Eichstätt *Kapellmeisters* seemed to have maintained an unbroken tradition of complete mediocrity and the *Kapelle* they directed was never large or important; by the 1750s it had seventy-three singers, including those of the cathedral choir, and sixteen instrumentalists. These musicians were responsible for the cathedral services as well as for the Prince-Bishop's court concerts, *Singspiele* and what Joseph Gmelch, the Jesuit historian of music in Eichstätt, calls 'little Italian operas'. In 1799 the members of the *Kapelle* were chiefly responsible for the organisation of a concert society which met every week in the Black Bear Inn; the society had the collaboration of the city's *Stadtpfeifer* band and of local amateur musicians. Travelling virtuosi passing through Eichstätt and presumably hoping for an invitation to play before the Prince-Bishop, took part in its concerts. The city's geographical position suggests that such visitors may well have been both numerous and eminent, but Gmelch's history mentions none of them by name.[1]

With secularisation, in 1802, the city lost virtually all of its professional musicians except its *Stadtpfeiferei* and those directly attached to the cathedral; though some may have stayed in Eichstätt to earn their living as music teachers, some fifty lost their court employment. The local amateurs and the *Stadtpfeifer* kept the concert society going under the direction of the cathedral *Kapellmeister*. Events at Salzburg, where Leopold Mozart and Michael Haydn, as well as the rebellious younger Mozart, had been employed; at Bonn, where the Archbishop Elector had a claim on the services of Beethoven until he was driven from his capital by the French; at Groswardein, where Dittersdorf had been *Kapellmeister*; at Breslau where both Dittersdorf and Michael Haydn had served, and at Würzburg, a city with a musical history as unexciting as Eichstätt's, paralleled the musical history chronicled by Gmelch.

None of these cities had any influence upon the music of their age, for Mozart and Beethoven were the only composers of decisive influence to have worked in an ecclesiastical state, and of all the ecclesiastical states only Bonn could afford to finance music as lavishly as the royal courts, with a busy opera house and opera company. The disappearance of the ecclesiastic states and of numerous minor dukedoms, principalities and kingdoms

[1] Joseph Gmelch: *Musikgeschichte Eichstätts*. Eichstätt, 1912.

reduced the number of court establishments requiring professional musicians, but quite possibly made available the number of performers needed to organise music in the larger towns on the post-revolutionary, post-Beethoven scale. The extra demands made by Beethoven and his successors may well have absorbed many of the players whose occupation in the minor states had gone. It is impossible to estimate the hardships imposed on professional musicians by the political events of the post-revolutionary settlement. At the same time, however, the demands of amateurs, especially those of the rapidly rising bourgeoisie, for musical instruction offered considerable opportunities for employment to those who could earn their living as teachers. What has been called the 'democratisation' of music thus provided some alternative outlets for the abilities of musicians thrown out of employment by political readjustment.

The major states, which naturally retained their musical establishments, were forced to accept change. The concert remained a minor consideration in those cities, notably the political capitals, where opera was the traditional centre of musical life, as it was in every Italian city which could support a company even of the lowest standard. But even such institutions as the Imperial and Royal Opera, in Vienna, found themselves forced to depend upon supplies of money from which their box offices to augment the subsidies poured into them by the ruler or by the state. The Court Theatre in Munich, for example, was burned down in 1818 and reopened two years later under the new and significant title *Hof und National Theater*: it too had passed from the sole control of a monarch and become a theatre which, in spite of a heavy subsidy, needed to earn a considerable income from the sale of seats; whilst an Intendant appointed by the King from among his courtiers was its supreme authority. His control of the theatre did not cover its repertoire or any of its musical activities, and he interfered in its management only when it ran into difficulties.

The Dresden Court Opera became a public institution in 1814; Saxony's alliance with Napoleon I brought the Saxon Royal House, and the Opera House which had been its pride, close to dissolution as French power crumbled. But Prince Repnin, the Russian Governor of Saxony appointed by the victors, prevented the disbandment of the orchestra and opera company by placing them under public control. When the monarchy returned, under the Peace Treaty of 1817 and the coronation of Carl Friedrich I, the theatre again became the Court Opera, but its traditional title did not prevent its dependence upon paying audiences; the appointment of Weber two years later as *Kapellmeister* of a newly established German Opera to run in conjunction with the traditional Italian Opera under its *Kapellmeister*, Francesco Morlacchi, was a political and financial move designed to add to the popularity of a royal house suspected of lack of patriotism; at the same time, it sought to develop and exploit a new audience whose patronage would contribute to the heavy expenses of the theatre. German opera owed a great deal to Carl Friedrich's use of its popular appeal as a means of winning public support; the German audience's enjoyment of opera in its own language, too, eventually came to mean a growth of support for opera in general, sung as a matter of course in German translation.

The post-war settlement, therefore, opened a new era for composers; they no longer looked for a *Kapellmeister*'s post which would bring them in touch with an audience. It became their duty to serve but demanded that they found an audience from among the general, concert- and opera-going public. But at the same time it demanded a return to pre-revolutionary styles of government. Throughout central Europe and the Austrian dominions in Italy, and in the southern Italian Kingdom of the Two Sicilies, the aim of the authorities was to preserve and consolidate their restored power, ruling on eighteenth-century lines through nineteenth-century instruments of coercion. Anything that questioned official established policy was to be suppressed as prejudicial to religion, morality or good order. The composer's appeal to the public was not allowed to step outside narrowly drawn limits of what was politically and socially acceptable to an old regime conscious of the fundamental dangers of its position.

Austria, which in the eighteenth century had been the centre of progressive music largely because of the Imperial family's musical enthusiasm and the frequent presence at court of a nobility which accepted opera, concert and chamber music as social necessities no less important than dance music, became the centre from which reaction spread. Joseph II, who died in 1790, had been among the most liberal of benevolent despots. The revolution in France and its aftermath had withdrawn the liberalism which he had encouraged, and Francis I, who became Emperor in 1792, had been persuaded both by events and by his political advisers to suppress whatever in the circumstances of the day could be regarded as politically dangerous. In 1810 his Chief of Police, Baron von Hagen, had taught him that too rigid a suppression was itself politically dangerous because it closed safety valves, so that the Emperor had instructed his censors not to forbid works by scholars, even when they contained new discoveries, unless those discoveries were likely to have an adverse effect on religion or morals, or to encourage subversion. But the relatively liberal von Hagen was succeeded in 1815 by Count Sedlnitzky (the bogeyman of the revolutionaries in 1848), whose harsher repression grew from an utter fear of anything new as likely to lead to political or religious dissent or even to encourage criticism.

Repression, therefore, was already powerful in Austria when, in 1819, the conservative dramatist Kozebue was assassinated by a liberal student. As the universities were the centres of political unrest, Kozebue's murder led to concerted action among the German states led by the Austrian Chancellor, Count Metternich, whose policy dominated Europe between

Napoleon's overthrow and the revolutions of 1848. With King Frederick William of Prussia, Metternich evolved a policy of added repression for the entire German-speaking world and Austria's Italian possessions. Their Carlsbad Decrees, of 1820, extended the censorship to pamphlets, magazines and newspapers, previously exempt, and proposed a Pan-German Commission to enquire into conditions in the universities in order to prevent revolutionary teaching and activity within them. Metternich wished the commission to be empowered to withdraw suspected revolutionaries from their own states for trial, but Frederick William sensibly believed that a supra-national authority would create more problems than it could solve among German rulers jealous for their independence, while at the same time it would foment the disorders it was intended to stifle. Metternich, of course, disavowed any wish to interfere in the content of university education but only to preserve the discipline of students and their teachers; but in place of the Pan-Germanic Commission he proposed, each state appointed a special official to control political activity in its universities. Naturally, purely arbitrary lines were drawn between the legitimate teaching of philosophy, politics and history and what was officially regarded as their corruption into seditious criticism of existing practice. Similar lines were drawn between valid artistic expression and the apparent encouragement of disorder.

The result was that until after 1848 the intellectual life of Central Europe became almost dormant. Political and social circumstances encouraged the exploitation of national myth and legend in works like *Der Freischütz* and the German romantic opera represented by such works as E. T. A. Hoffmann's *Undine*. As it became impossible to compose the successors to such socially orientated operas as *Le Nozze di Figaro* and *Fidelio*, which reflected too precisely and with too cutting an implied criticism of existing political conditions, music, as a serious study, tended to concentrate on the past. Mendelssohn and the choral society movement began the rediscovery of the choral works of J. S. Bach, and the result of political repression was not merely the extension of the repertoire into the forgotten world of baroque composition but also the writing of a number of crucial, monumental works of what came to be known as 'musicology'. Such critical biographies as Carl von Winterfeld's *Johannes Gabrieli und sein Zeitalter* (1834), Otto Jahn's *Wolfgang Amadeus Mozart* (published between 1856 and 1859) and Chrysander's *G. F. Handel* (the three volumes of which appeared between 1858 and 1867) combated the idea, tacitly encouraged by the repression, that the arts are simply ornamental appendages to 'real life' by carefully linking the artistic achievements of their subjects to the conditions and society of their day.

The repression set out also to create an unbridgeable chasm between the 'safe' educated classes and the rest. In 1821 an Austrian newspaper reported an address by Francis I to teachers at the Lyceum in Laibach:

> I do not need savants but good honest citizens. Your task is to teach young men to be this. He who serves me must teach what I order him. If anyone cannot do this, or comes with new ideas, he can go, or I will remove him.[2]

Consequently, both education and the censorship grew narrower and increasingly obscurantist, and until after 1848 the view of what could be treated as specialised learned writing, or as purely creative artistic work, became too restricted to permit the publication of, for example, a medical book which, purely in passing, referred unflatteringly to the state of the roads in Carinthia. A poem by Franz Grillparzer nearly brought his dismissal from the civil service and his play *König Ottakars Gluck und Ende*, in 1825, described the resistance of King Ottakar of Bohemia against Rudolph of Habsburg in a way which seemed to suggest that the Habsburg was simply an earlier Bonaparte; it reached the stage in Vienna only after its author had almost despaired of its success and his own future. Schiller's *Piccolimini*, which deals with events in the Thirty Years War, was forbidden, and his *William Tell* was produced in Vienna only after it had been ruthlessly cut in an apparent attempt to disguise the fact that its hero was a Swiss rebel against Austrian rule. 'Musicians are lucky,' wrote Grillparzer in one of Beethoven's Conversation Books, 'they don't have to bother about the censors. But if only the censors knew what the musicians are thinking as they compose.'

Metternich's system not only utilised the Empire's large and efficient force of secret police; he himself set up a private force responsible to and reporting to him personally. In 1815 Beethoven was a disillusioned Francophile who had become a patriotic Austrian republican. He had risked arrest during the French occupation by his refusal to play to an audience of officers of the army of occupation; under the Metternichian regime he chose Schindler, a student revolutionary who had spent a year in prison for taking part in a political riot, as his secretary-confidant and his friends tried in vain to quieten the loud political complaints and criticisms he made in public places. Apparently Beethoven escaped arrest because he was a celebrated eccentric rather than a political opponent to be taken seriously. His Conversation Books made clear his eager interest in what officially passed as sedition: his enthusiasm for libertarian political theory and the enthusiasm for England which he based on a possibly exaggerated belief in the liberty of English political life. He talked proudly of the banned books which he owned and had read.

Between 1814 and 1819, when the repression at its height was joined by a disastrous post-war depression, Beethoven fell into a relative silence; he

[2] C. A. MacCartney: *The Habsburg Empire, 1790–1918*. London, 1968. p. 212.

ceased to compose any of the large public works on which his reputation was based and which had won him his great popularity. This silence is usually blamed upon ill-health, private unhappiness and the troubles brought upon him by his unfortunate nephew Carl. But it may well be that the dead weight of a detested political system had a great deal to do with his failure to complete large public works like the Mass in D, which he began in 1818 and could not finish for five years, and the Ninth Symphony, begun in 1817 but not completed until 1823. During these years of repression and poverty Beethoven's output consisted chiefly of a handful of songs and three piano sonatas—*Opp.* 90, 101 and 106; even the mighty *Hammerklavier* in B flat (the use of the German equivalent to 'pianoforte' in the titles of *Opp.* 101 and 106 seems significant in the intellectual and social climate of the immediate post-war years) is a private work, not addressed to the general audience which had greeted the meretricious *Wellingtons Sieg* with frenzy and had made the Seventh Symphony, composed in the hopeful days when Napoleon's power began to totter, into its favourite among his large-scale works.

After 1822, when the slow increase of prosperity slightly reduced the burden on the Austrian people, the large public works began again with the Mass and the Ninth Symphony. But even the text which Beethoven chose for the choral finale of the Ninth was dangerous in the age of Metternich and the political circumstances of Beethoven's day. Beethoven's vision of joy in a world where all men are brothers uses a poem which Schiller had originally intended to be an 'ode to Freedom' (*Freiheit*) but which the poet had tactfully changed to 'Joy' (*Freude*).

To attempt to analyse the effect of political repression on the music of composers who suffered it—Beethoven and Schubert were the most immediately affected—would be foolishly subjective. Beethoven was, in these difficult years, trying to solve the problems set by his guardianship of his nephew; he was, too, reaching a state of mind in which any decision outside those demanded by composition was becoming increasingly difficult to him. But his hatred of the political situation seems to have been a factor not only in his failure to continue the composition of public works but also in the sense of alienation from everyday concerns which bothered and baffled the friends who worked to arrange the performance of the Ninth Symphony.

Schubert was active in the Vienna of the same period, and most of Schubert's work was not addressed to the general public. Without a patron, unable to find a church post or to keep the only position in the Imperial Opera which was ever offered to him, Schubert seems to us to be an entirely unpolitical personality, but his death in 1828 removed the last major composer Austria had produced before the repression or was to produce until the rise of Bruckner. The city's musical prestige and its long tradition continued to ensure that Vienna would act as a magnet to composers from outside

Austria, but until after the revolution of 1848 Austrian composers, in the words of Stendhal, turned away from serious considerations and devoted themselves to the 'sweet sensuality' of light music, the operas of Rossini, the development of the waltz and the exploitation of nostalgia. 'In Vienna,' wrote Stendhal, 'sensual pleasures, less likely to trouble the Government, took possession of the people.'[3]

The post-war period was one in which amateur orchestras flourished and amateur choral societies were founded, all, according to the authorities, fraught with political dangers. The choral societies in particular seemed to be not far from active sedition because choirs were run on democratic lines, the members themselves electing directors and committees of management, working with an enthusiasm and success, which, the Austrian and German authorities believed, could easily be applied to political ends; for any efficient democracy, even in music, implied a criticism of autocracy. Metternich himself said that he would have liked to prohibit choral societies, but he left them in existence not as a useful safety-valve for the public spirit of their members but because action against them would draw attention to the dangers they represented. Nevertheless, throughout Austria and Germany such organisations had to submit to careful police control.

Because repression was inescapable, even so unpolitical a musician as Schubert was influenced by the situation. The strict control upon the lives of students and the intelligentsia which followed the assassination of Kozebue involved Schubert directly. His close friend and sometime schoolfellow Johann Senn (two of whose poems, *Selige Welt* and *Schwannengesang*, Schubert made into *Lieder*) came under police suspicion because of his regular meetings with a group of fellow intellectuals in a Vienna inn. In 1820 the police searched his lodgings, confiscated many of his papers and arrested him, together with the friends, Schubert amongst them, who were in his lodgings at the time. Senn was imprisoned for fourteen months but the composer escaped with no injury but a black eye after a night in gaol.[4] Schubert, a friend arrested and the censorship interfering in the libretti of his operas *Die Verschworenen* and *Der Graf von Gleichstein*, did not live outside the world's troubles. In 1824 he enclosed a poem of his own, *Complaint to the People*, in a letter to his friend Franz von Schober; the poem bemoans the inactive, insignificant life of 'the youth of the present time'. 'Me too,' he writes, 'these times are fast to ruin bringing' while the people creep about 'sick and decrepit', dismissing the ideals and actions of youth as 'mere dreaming'.[5]

[3] Stendhal: *Letters on the celebrated composer Joseph Haydn*, by 'A. C. Bombet'. English translation, London, 1817. Letter 1.

[4] O. E. Deutsch: *Schubert, a Documentary Biography*. London, 1946. pp. 128–9.

[5] *Ibid*. p. 375.

Metternich's intelligence system operated effectively outside German-speaking Europe, and as national feeling grew in Italy, the Austrian authorities gripped their subject provinces as relentlessly as they could. Berlioz, a student at the French Academy in Rome after his success in the Prix de Rome in 1831, wrote from Rome to Charles Duveyrier, professional librettist and editor of *Le Globe*. Duveyrier was a social reformer, a follower of Saint-Simon; that probably is why Berlioz's letter fell into the hands of Metternich's police: 'among schemes for the political reorganisation of society, I am convinced that the plan of Saint-Simon is the most effective and most thorough,' he wrote. '. . . I believe that there is nothing to prevent my uniting my voice and my efforts with those of others for the amelioration of the conditions of the largest and poorest class of people.'[6] The official response to this letter, probably found by a Metternichian agent as it made its way across the Austrian territories to an addressee known for his journalistic support of liberal policies, was a letter from Metternich to Count von Lutzow, the Imperial Minister in Rome, in which a copy of Berlioz's letter was enclosed:

> I take the liberty of sending you the enclosed letter, which came to me through a secret channel and must therefore be for your personal information only. My reason for sending this copy to you is that I should like to point out to Your Excellency the dangerous tendency towards fanaticism indulged in by its writer, a disciple of Saint-Simon and, apparently, a student at the French Academy in Rome. I am sure, my dear Count, that you will think it suitable to inform the Papal authorities of this young man's views and to warn students who are subjects of his [Austrian] Imperial Majesty resident in Rome of his dangerous influence, warning them against contact of any kind with this young man. Should M. Hector Berlioz, on his departure from Rome, visit the Imperial Embassy to ask for a visa into the Austrian states, Your Excellency will, of course, be obliged to refuse his request.
>
> Metternich.[7]

The July Revolution in France in 1831 had, naturally, stimulated the discontent of Italians against their Austrian overlords so that any French student would be an object of interest and suspicion to the Austrian authorities in Italy, but the modern reader cannot but admire a spy network which found its way so far down the political scale that it examined the correspondence of obscure music students.

Even in France itself it was possible to plunge accidentally into political hot water. In 1844 Berlioz and Isaac Strauss (whom Berlioz called 'the

[6] H. Berlioz: *Correspondance Générale*. Flammarion, Paris. Letter of 28 July 1831. p. 476.

[7] André Espials de la Maistre: *Hector Berlioz and Metternich*, in *Oesterreichische Musikzeitschrift*, 1953, *Heft* 12. Quoted in Georg Knepler: *Musikgeschichte 19 Jahrhunderts, Band* 1. p. 303.

Maestro of the fashionable balls') planned a three-day festival to salute the
end of the Exhibition of Industrial Products. The musical events would
take place in the Exhibition's vast Hall of Machines. The Minister of Trade
accepted Berlioz's proposal, but the Commissioner of Police refused his permission until the composer persuaded the Minister of the Interior to order
the police to sanction the festival. Berlioz recruited a huge choir and
orchestra and drilled his battalions to perfection in a series of rehearsals.
The final concert included music by Beethoven and a hotch-potch of
'modern' works, and a vast, frenziedly enthusiastic audience left Berlioz
with a net profit of 800 francs and an urgent summons to attend the office
of the Commissioner of Police. He had, he was told, 'secretly added to the
programme a piece of music calculated to arouse certain passions which the
government is endeavouring to suppress'.

The offending item was a chorus from Halévy's *Charles V*; it had
a crudely nationalistic text apparently condemning the policy of friendship
with England which Louis Philippe was sedulously fostering at the time,
and it won the loudest applause of the afternoon. Berlioz explained that
Halévy, nettled at being the one important French composer left out of the
programme, had persuaded his publishers to approach Berlioz and have the
omission remedied; Berlioz had chosen the offending chorus because it was
both effective for the huge number of performers and easy to prepare; although it had not been included in the preliminary announcement of the
concert which had been submitted to the police, it had not been 'secretly
added' to the programme because it had been advertised for a week on the
festival posters. 'Nevertheless,' wrote Berlioz, 'from that time a censorship
of programmes was established, and today you cannot sing a romance by
Berac or Mlle. Peyer in a public place without a licence from the Ministry
of the Interior countersigned by a Superintendent of Police.'[8]

The censorship did not directly affect the composer of instrumental
music except in so far as it imposed an atmosphere of intellectual sterility
on European life, and this naturally affected composers. It was, however,
the composer of operas who had to tread carefully; it is noticeable that
Weber and his German successors were little concerned with the political
and social realities which had been the basis of *The Marriage of Figaro*
and *Fidelio*. Weber's *Der Freischütz*, in 1821, is not far from being
the operatic equivalent to the 'Gothic' novel which had become popular in
Britain at the end of the eighteenth century set in a German society of folk
tales and folk superstitions; the same spirit animated, and the same substance gives a foundation to, such works as Marschner's *Der Vampyr*, of
1828, as well as the operas of E. T. A. Hoffmann. The other strand
of popular nineteenth-century opera with which the composer could deal in

[8] Hector Berlioz: *Memoirs*; translated and edited by David Cairns;
London, 1969. p. 365.

safety was the historical romance; Weber's *Euryanthe*, produced in Vienna in 1823, was an early example of the vast number of operas set in a remote and largely unreal past as well as in a strange country; these works choose history as a starting point but have less interest in the interpretation of historical reality than in the use of history as a source of sensational stories.

Historical romance was a manifestation of a new spirit in the arts which stretched a considerable distance beyond music. It was in part a result of Scott's novels and their remarkable vogue throughout Europe, but it grew as well from the historical, or pseudo-historical, plays of Schiller, in which history is subservient to dramatic effect and Schiller's enthusiasm for what he felt ought to have happened. Rossini composed his *Elisabetta, Regina d'Inghilterra*, in 1814, the year before Scott began his literary career with *Waverley* and sixteen years before he handled the same situation as Rossini's opera in *Kenilworth*. History allowed the censored composer to deal with serious subjects in settings which would not disturb his political overlords. In Italy, opera was the essentially popular form of theatre, and a scrupulous attention to historical truth was no more essential to the composer of romantic opera than it is to the creator of a cinematic historical epic. Often enough, 'historical romance' in opera lies outside the boundaries of 'real' history, as it does in Bellini's *Norma*, a work which, although it deals with the struggles of a subject people to gain their freedom, seems to have annoyed none of the authorities who were adept in finding a contemporary significance in any dramatisation of the careers of historical personages in a genuinely historical setting. Actually, it is perhaps *I Puritani* which gives the most truthful reflection of the romantic composer's attitude to history; the events it describes did not happen, but history might have been more enjoyable if they had done so, as though a strange romance about a cavalier's engagement to a puritan girl, and the danger to their happiness of his attempt to rescue a persecuted queen from her rebellious subjects, has more dramatic vitality than the actual struggle of the English Civil War.

Donizetti and his librettists plundered European history for plots which, romanticised out of reality, directed attention to things which, if they had ever happened, would have happened a long time ago and preferably a long way away. *Pietro il Grande, Anna Bolena, Lucrezia Borgia, Rosamunda d'Inghilterra, Maria Stuarda, Belisario, Roberto Devereux* and about half a dozen other Donizetti operas take plots not from a nation's history but from the myths which spring up around the actual history of every nation; it is clear that the composer who set *Emilia di Liverpool* in its heroine's hospice for travellers in the mountains near Liverpool was not prepared to have his romantic aspirations and emotions crushed by a too slavish observation of mere physical reality; it was emotional reality which he looked for.

The attractions of England and English settings to the Italian composers of romantic operas who had never visited the British Isles is a fascinating aspect of the romantic outlook which it is hard to explain. The Tudor period in particular, with its melodrama, its richness of character and setting, its brutalities and splendours, was especially dear to them; it offered them not only the baffling figure of Elizabeth—a heretic but a glorious heretic, adored, feminine and unmarried—but her rivalry with her beautiful, catholic, persecuted cousin. It had, perhaps, a special relevance to an Italy aching for independence because it emphasised the national spirit and independence of England. It is hard not to think, too, of Italian composers and librettists fascinated by the huge and successful heresies of Henry VIII and his younger daughter while they were heartbroken at the tragedy of Mary Queen of Scots as they saw it through the distorting filter of Schiller's play. Schiller, after all, gave the world the essential unhistorical scene which the theatre demanded—the confrontation of Mary with Elizabeth.

Even more than in Italy, opera in Austria was a source of political danger. Revolutionary passions might too easily be inflamed by music linked to a dangerous story. Count Sedlnitzky's police kept dossiers on all the artists, writers and composers active in the Empire, noting their political allegiances and any record they had of activities which might imperil the Empire. The activities of the censors ran to almost hilarious extremes. Meyerbeer's *Les Huguenots*, historically one of the most important of operas, could not be seen and heard by the Austrian public because the strife between catholics and protestants in sixteenth-century France might direct their sympathies in the wrong direction, so that *Les Huguenots* could not be produced in Vienna until it had been fitted out with a new libretto and had become *The Ghibellines of Pisa*, in which thirteenth-century rebels were identified by their singing of Luther's hymn *Ein feste Burg ist unser Gott*. There was a period, after the battle of Solferino, when the word 'Rome' was forbidden on the Austrian stage, so that a production of *Tannhäuser* in 1859 sent its hero for absolution to the Pope simply '*dort*' (there), and the forbidden name was avoided.

Verdi, whose historical melodramas cannot be mistaken for historical fantasy and whose plots were often uncomfortably close to the realities of nineteenth-century, unliberated Italy, found that the Austrian censorship had strong teeth and a natural readiness to bite. Almost by accident, with the chorus of exiled Hebews in *Nabucco*, Verdi became the mouthpiece of Italian nationalism; the sufferings of his own country made possible the lament in the opera which won not only tears but the lasting devotion of Italian audiences. Verdi's choice of libretti, too, was not simply the need to find sensational plots in old, unhappy, far-off things and battles long ago. *La Battaglia di Legnano*, in 1848, sailed dangerously close to the wind by dealing with the defeat of the Emperor Barbarossa by the Lombard League in the twelfth century—a dangerous subject in the days of Italy's struggle for independence, and Verdi knew that the opera might be unacceptable to the authorities in its original form. He wrote to his librettist, Salvatore Cammarano: 'If the censor should not pass it, do you think that, with the title and locale *etc.* changed, all or most of the text could be retained?'[9] Even in Verdi's years of galley slavery—the period of ten years from 1842 in which he wrote at least an opera a year—a complete opera was too considerable an enterprise to be put at risk by a cavalier attitude to the prejudices of the censorship. *La Battaglia di Legnano* was produced in Rome in 1849, but then it disappeared from the stage to reappear as *L'Assedio di Haarlem,* an opera about the Dutch resistance to the Spanish occupation of Holland in the sixteenth century. Both composer and librettist were careful, in *Luisa Miller,* to avoid the dangers of a straight adaptation of Schiller's *Kabale und Liebe*; the danger of Schiller's critical attitude to life in a minor German court of the eighteenth century evaporated, however, when the courtiers and officials turned into the gentry and peasants of a Tyrolean village.

The censorship was moral and religious as well as political, so that *Stiffelio,* in 1850, had to be changed from the story of a priest whose moral character had some doubtful aspects to a story about a politician whose private life impeded his usefulness. It was *Rigoletto,* however, and *Un Ballo in Maschera* which caused most perturbation both to the composer and to the censors who had to deal with his work, simply because both operas reflected harshly upon monarchy and envisaged circumstances in which the assassination of king might be a laudable, heroic action. *Rigoletto* is a version of Victor Hugo's *Le Roi s'amuse,* and the censors condemned it for 'revolving immorality and obscene triviality'. These flaws in its character disappeared, however, when Victor Hugo's king was turned, on the advice of the censorship, into a mythical Duke of Mantua. *Un Ballo in Maschera* is an adaptation of Eugene Scribe's play *Gustavus III* and deals unequivocally, if with less than total historical accuracy, with the character of the Swedish king and the assassination plot against him. Not only did the libretto suggest that a king could be morally reprehensible; at the same time it sympathised with his murderers. Verdi refused to accept the censors' advice that the plot be transplanted to the middle ages or the early renaissance; such a period, he declared, would not suit his music, and a plan to transfer the action to sixteenth-century Pomerania still left the plot hinging upon the assassination plan; the presence in the *dramatis personae* of a fortune-teller treated not as a charlatan or as a figure of fun but as a character with real dramatic power and validity was, compared to this, a minor if dangerous feature of the work. Eventually, to save the opera's life, eighteenth-century Sweden became Massachusetts shortly before the War of American Independence and the morally unstable king was transformed into a mere Governor-

[9] Giuseppe Verdi: *Letters*; selected, edited and translated by Charles Osborne. London, 1971. p. 55.

General of the colony, a mythical Riccardo, Earl of Warwick.

If these Verdian problems suggest nothing to us more than the absurdity of a short-sighted, repressive political censorship, they at least show the frustrations to which a great dramatic composer was subject. But their effect went deeper: the only way in which a composer in the first half of the nineteenth century could establish himself financially and win a reputation was through opera. The censorship meant that he was either to risk a series of headlong collisions with the authorities or to accept that his work could never be more than a pleasant decoration of the surfaces of life and to work in a vacuum where political and social realities no longer applied and the relationships of his characters were falsified by their removal from social reality. The deliberate stultification of opera closed one of the doors to success to the composer, and its effect can be seen in the failure of the German opera houses between the death of Beethoven and the rise of Wagner to produce a single work not necessarily on their level but even on the lower level of Bellini and Donizetti.

Virtuosity was the only other direct road to success, a term which in this connection is synonymous with acceptance. A Liszt, a Paganini and a Mendelssohn (the latter a universally gifted young man with a considerable family fortune and no essential need to earn a living) could win acceptance through their superlative quality as instrumentalists. There was, of course, another and more indirect route to acceptance—that through criticism. The 'democratisation' of music, the opening up of both opera house and concert hall to the general public and popular taste, enhanced the importance of the critic who, like Berlioz, could write with wit and elegance as well as musical knowledge. Berlioz disliked writing criticism in spite of his superlative gifts as a writer. Schumann, probably the most gifted and lucid of writers on music in the Germany of his period, was probably the most powerful advocate the mid-European romantic composers ever found. The direct routes to success and acceptance, open in the eighteenth century to every fertile, hard-working composer, was effectively closed to all but the most obstinately gifted of his successors in the early nineteenth century.

2

The Romantic Composer

The political readjustments of the early nineteenth century and the declining fortunes of the aristocracy left the composer in search of a social function. This meant that he was left without an actual audience with whom to communicate. Published music increasingly provided the surviving court orchestras with works by composers who had already established their reputations so that orchestras had little need for a *Kapellmeister*, an all-round composer who could provide music whenever it was needed for church, opera house, Milord and Milady's private music-making and whatever concerts were to be given; they needed a conductor whose abilities as an executant and administrator were of more immediate consequence than his possession of interesting creative gifts. That being so, how was the composer whose secondary gifts as executant or conductor were less developed than his creative ability to find the audience which, by its approval of his work, gave him both his social function and the power to earn his living?

Spohr, born in 1784, and Weber, two years younger, adapted themselves to the new situation. Spohr undertook his first concert tour as a violinist when he was only fourteen, became leader of the Duke of Gotha's orchestra in 1803 (he had already been a member of the Duke of Brunswick's orchestra, suffering from an unmusical Duchess), and continued his career as a soloist during his periods of leave, incidentally gaining an impressive reputation as a conductor. From 1812 to 1815 he conducted the orchestra of the Theater an der Wien, and in 1817 took over the direction of the Frankfurt Opera. In 1822 he became Court *Kapellmeister* at Cassel, where he spent the rest of his life. The bulk of his compositions were in no way connected with his official duties: his violin concertos were the stock-in-trade of his concert tours; his symphonies were written for the German musical festivals or for organisations he conducted outside Cassel, three of them for the Philharmonic Society in London; his oratorios were commissioned by the German Festivals or for English organisations—*Calvary* for London and *Der Fall Babylon* for the Norwich Festival; the last six of his eleven operas were first produced in Cassel, but their composition was not demanded by his contract there. He was, officially, a conductor, who composed as and when it pleased him to do so.

Weber was a successful concert pianist in his teens; at the age of eighteen he became director of the orchestra at Breslau, an institution like the

Gewandhaus Orchestra in Leipzig, run by the wealthier citizens of the town; but an eighteen-year-old conductor has little power to exert authority over older and more experienced musicians. In 1807 he became secretary to the brother of the King of Württemberg, a position which made it possible for him to draw attention to his compositions and seemed likely to secure the production of his opera *Silvana* (the third opera he had written but the first to have any opportunity of being brought to the stage). Unfortunately Weber fell foul of the autocratic, unmusical King Friedrich. His experience of a luxurious court bleeding a poor country with limited resources and little intellectual life caused, first, his arrest for insolence (he directed an old woman looking for the Court washerwoman to the King's private room) and then his exile after a financial muddle for which his father, not he, was to blame. For a time he lived in Mannheim and then in Darmstadt as a free-lance pianist and composer before undertaking another concert tour in 1811. Two years later he settled down in Prague as director of the theatre orchestra.

Weber was an efficient administrator and, born into a theatrical family, one of those musicians gifted with a clear sense of what is effective on the stage, not only in singing and acting but in design, décor and the minutiae of production. In 1817 he accepted the post of *Kapellmeister* of the new German Opera at Dresden, where his duties were to create a company and direct its performances. Any additions he might make to its originally very limited repertory were only incidental to his primary duties as a conductor-administrator.

The speediest way to success was unusual ability as a soloist. Chopin, an unusual personality of great charm, with an original style of composition which demanded an unusual and magical style of performance, founded his career on the success he won in Paris, where the revolution of 1830 took the aristocracy out of the centre of musical patronage as it took them from the centre of government; the bourgeoisie which replaced the old ruling class was touchingly eager to believe what the intellectuals told it so long as it was told nothing disturbing. Chopin, with the support of powerful critics and, in Germany, of Schumann, the critical voice of rebellious youth, was able to live comfortably, not as a frequent giver of concerts and recitals but on the profits of his publications and on the proceeds of his lessons to the very well-to-do. Liszt, handsome, phenomenally gifted, with a personality like a firework display, dazzling everybody with whom he came into contact, discovered, as Paganini had discovered before him, that the musical world was his for the taking. Brahms was a redoubtable pianist who, by putting his own works into his concert programmes, could convince publishers that his music could become profitable and supplied them not only with piano pieces but with songs, exploiting the growing amateur market.

The position of the composer who had no marked abilities as instrumentalist, conductor or administrator was far less profitable. Schubert's life was contemporary with the second half of Beethoven's, and it shows very clearly what the new situation meant to a composer of supreme genius who could not impose himself on the world as soloist or conductor. The situation was unprecedented: from any worldly point of view, no career was ever so unsuccessful as Schubert's, but to write of him as a neglected genius is hardly accurate. His songs and piano music were known to a rather influential circle of friends in the minor aristocracy and the upper bourgeoisie of Vienna. The well-known picture by his friend Moritz von Schwind includes not only the composer but a number of identifiable people who have gathered to listen to his music. They include not only Vogl, the leading bass of the Imperial Opera who introduced many of Schubert's songs to the Viennese public, but other well-known singers. A group of writers includes Grillparzer and Mayrhofer; there are members of the official class and, present at least in spirit is Schubert's pupil Karoline von Esterhazy, whose portrait hangs on the wall. Von Schwind's picture, painted some years after Schubert's death, assembles the people who at one time or another attended his musical evenings and none of them seems to be a nonentity. It is, of course, significant that despite the eminence of some of those who attended such musical evenings that the events were 'Schubertiaden', named after the composer and not after some eminent friend.

The essential fact was that the musical situation of the early nineteenth century provided no way in which Schubert could earn a living. He was indisputably the greatest Central European composer of the generation which followed Beethoven. His education, at the Cathedral Choir School and the Imperial Seminary, was superior to that which Haydn had received at the Choir School some three-quarters of a century before. He had become, it seems, a respectable pianist and violinist and a promising conductor, but he was never the type of virtuoso who could accumulate a fortune by tramping round the international celebrity circuit. As a boy he had composed songs and piano music, chamber works for his family and friends, and orchestral music for the school and other amateur orchestras; he had composed other orchestral works before he reached his First Symphony, in 1813, when he was sixteen, and seven operas before he was twenty. In 1816, the year of his Fourth and Fifth Symphonies and about a hundred songs (Gretchen am Spinnrade, Der Erlkönig and Heidenröslein had been composed a year earlier, in the excitement of his first discovery of Goethe's poetry), he left school and became a schoolmaster, though he soon fled from that uncongenial occupation. His salvation from that time onwards depended upon his either securing a church appointment or a success as a composer of operas, and from this date his church works and later operas were composed to stake his claim to any suitable vacancy. In 1818 the Kärntnerthor Theater management commissioned Die Zwillingsbrüder, which was kept unproduced for eighteen months by Joseph Weigl, whose *Schweizerfamilie* was so popular that his influence in the theatre, where he was *Kapellmeister*, was unassailable; Weigl had no intention of encouraging young men who might undermine his popularity. *Die Zwillingsbrüder* ran for six reasonably successful performances and earned its composer 500 florins, about £20 in the English money of the day.

Die Zwillingsbrüder seems to have convinced the opera management that Schubert could be useful. It commissioned an aria and a duet from him to be added to Hérold's *La Clochette* when it was produced in Vienna as *Das Zauberglöckchen* and then set him to work on the incidental music for *Rosamunde*, the play by Helmina von Chezy. A year later, in 1822, his opera *Alfonso und Estrella* was commissioned when its composition was almost complete, but in spite of the commission it was not produced. *Die Verschworenen* and *Fierrebras* were both composed in 1823. *Die Verschworenen*, a one-act work, ran into trouble with the censors because its title, 'The Conspirators' (apparently as much of the work as the censors read), suggested that it might have a dangerous political theme; actually, it is based on Aristophanes' *Lysistrata*. Rechristened *Das Häusliche Krieg* the censorship sanctioned its production, but it had not been commissioned and it remained unproduced. The librettist of *Fierrebras*, Josef Kupelweiser, was secretary to the Directors of the Kärntnerthor Theater and the work was announced in the press as a forthcoming attraction, but Kupelweiser left the theatre staff before the production was due, and the opera's hopes departed with him. In the last year of his life Schubert worked on the sketches of yet another opera, *Der Graf von Gleichen*, which he apparently abandoned because the censorship objected to its libretto.

Schubert's failure in the Opera House had nothing to do with the quality of his music. His *Lieder*, for example, are essentially and effectively dramatic in the sense that they paint a situation or create a character within a dramatic situation; the operas, apart from their wealth of music, are as stageworthy, to say the least, as anything by the successful composers whose works were seen in Schubert's Vienna; but within the Kärntnerthor Theater the power struggle, which became inevitable when opera ceased to depend upon the will of an all-powerful patron, was waged with the odds heavily against any newcomer who threatened to become a dangerous rival to established composers. Schubert had one champion within the company, Vogl, who was instrumental in securing for him the commission for *Die Zwillingsbrüder*; the delay in its production Schubert himself blamed on the machinations of the resident powers. 'In spite of Vogl,' he wrote, 'it is impossible to outwit such *canaille* as Weigl, Treitschke *etc.*'[1] Obviously the

---

[1] Letter of 19 May 1820 to Anselm Huttenbrenner. In Deutsch: *op. cit.* p. 117.

belated production established the composer's claim to consideration and led to his work on *Das Zauberglöckchen* and *Rosamunde*.

This measure of success, not unpromising for a young man in his early twenties, seems to have prompted his application in 1821 for a post as composer or conductor at the Opera. He was supported by impressive testimonials from a Court Secretary, Ignaz von Mosel, from the Court Music Intendent Count Moritz Dietrichstein, from the Court *Kapellmeister* Salieri and from Weigl, *Kapellmeister* of the Opera. Perhaps because Schubert, at twenty-four, had no professional experience of work in the theatre, his application brought him only the offer of work as a coach; this at least provided him with a foothold in the theatre on which an ambitious, practical, determined young man could have based a career, but the accounts of the Kärntnerthor Theater record only one payment to Schubert for undertaking duties as a coach; in April 1821 he was paid 50 florins (about £2) for coaching a young singer in the part of Dorabella in Mozart's *Così fan Tutte*. According to Leopold Sonnleitner, nephew of Joseph Sonnleitner, director of the Theater an der Wien, librettist of the original version of Beethoven's *Fidelio* and one of the founders of the *Gesellschaft der Musikfreunde*, Schubert was unable to observe rehearsal times, 'punctuality and the mechanical nature of the work were vexatious to him'. 'Schubert,' he wrote, 'was extremely fertile and industrious in composing. For anything else that goes by the name of work he had no inclination.'[2] It seems that Schubert's casual attitude to what he must have regarded as boring hack-work closed the door on any hopes of more valuable or creative work as a member of the theatre staff. According to Anton Schindler, Beethoven's friend, confidant and dogsbody, Schubert applied again, five years later, when he was twenty-six, for a conductorship at the Kärntnerthor Theater, and was asked to write a lengthy *scena*, with orchestral accompaniment, for the soprano Nanette Streicher and chorus. The music proved to be too difficult for the soloist, but in spite of entreaties Schubert refused to make any alterations and stormed from the theatre taking the score with him.

If twentieth-century readers regard such an action as a demonstration of unshakable artistic integrity, in 1826 it would have seemed to be no more than a rudely unprofessional tantrum and another reason for keeping Schubert out of any responsible post in the theatre. Schindler's account of the incident, however, was not published until 1857, and though many people who would have been involved in the actual event were still alive to read what Schindler wrote and not one challenged his veracity, no Schubert work of sufficient bulk to be the *scena* has survived, and Schindler is known to have been an unreliable biographer.

Though Schubert's dealings with the Opera were a series of disappoint-

---

[2] Quoted in Maurice J. E. Brown: *Essays on Schubert*. London, 1966. pp. 130, 132.

ments, they were the most profitable of his ventures, though that says very little. He earned occasional fees as a pianist and accompanist at private and public concerts; between 1818 and 1824 about 1000 florins came to him from lessons, and the rest of his income was earned by his publications; Deutsch reckons his total earnings during his professional career of more than twelve years as 7638 florins, and to this should be added some 350 florins paid to him by the Kärntnerthor Theater the details of which were not available when Deutsch compiled his list.[3] During Schubert's lifetime his publications included one of his string quartets, the E flat Piano Trio, three of his piano sonatas, one of the duets for violin and piano, a group of works for piano duet, a large number of smaller piano pieces, some part songs, one Mass, three slighter, motet-type church works and a hundred and eighty-seven songs.

Derisory as are these earnings—some £350 for his entire life's work— some of Schubert's music became well known. Some of his church works were heard outside Vienna as well as in some of the city churches, so that in 1825, during a holiday in Upper Austria, he could write to his parents: 'I find my compositions everywhere, especially at the monasteries of St. Florian and Kremsmunster.'[4] Some of his songs were heard at concerts in Vienna, especially at the chamber concerts, or *Abendunterhaltungen*, of the *Gesellschaft der Musikfreunde*, where the A minor String Quartet, the Octet and several of his part songs were performed. Schubert was apparently held in high regard as a composer by the *Gesellschaft*, which in 1826 elected him to membership and awarded him 100 florins for his services to the Society. These, apparently, were simply his readiness to hand over works for performance; apart from this reward, such performances would earn a composer nothing.

Schubert's only public concert of his music, on 21 March 1828, brought him a net profit of 192 florins, not quite £8. Its programme consisted of the first movement of the String Quartet in G major, five songs sung by Vogl, the Serenade for soprano and female voices, one of the Piano Trios, the duet *Auf dem Strome* and the *Schlachtgesang*, for double male-voice choir. Several musical periodicals from outside Vienna—for example the *Allgemeine Musikalsiche Zeitung* of Leipzig, the *Abendzeitung* of Dresden and the *Allgemeine Musikalische Zeitung* of Berlin (all of which, with other periodicals, from time to time reviewed Schubert's publications enthusiastically)—noticed the concert with enthusiasm; the Berlin paper noted the 'numerous audience' and the 'resounding applause' with which the music was received and mentioned that several items were encored.[5]

[3] Deutsch: *op. cit.* pp. 932–3. Brown: *op. cit. Schubert and the Kärntnerthor Theatre.* pp. 127–38.

[4] Deutsch: *op. cit.* Letter of 25 July 1825. p. 757.

[5] Deutsch: *op. cit.* pp. 756–7.

Of Schubert's orchestral music, only the two Italian Overtures were heard during his lifetime at professional concerts, and these, with the *Rosamunde* Overture, were published in piano duet form, but towards the end of his life he was beginning to negotiate for the publication of other orchestral works. But if his music was known in Upper Austria, his fame must have been spread by his published music; the monasteries may have added his Mass in C and a group of Offertory motets to the repertoire after these works, the first of Schubert's church music to reach print, had achieved publication, but that was not until two months after he had written to tell his parents that his music was known in St. Florian and Kremsmunster. It is, of course, possible that the C major Mass, one of his other early Masses or some of his miscellaneous pieces had reached the monasteries in manuscript copies. His symphonies, to all intents and purposes, were unknown; the Sixth was played by an amateur orchestra in 1817, when it was new, but the incomplete Symphony in E (No. 7), the 'Unfinished' B minor (No. 8) and the 'Great C Major' (No. 9) remained unknown until long after Schubert's death.

Thus, without any system of copyright and no acceptance of any performing right, it was possible for Schubert to have a more than local reputation and a considerable local following but remain unable to earn a living. Schubert could dispose of piano music and songs to the publishers, but what he received from publication could hardly be described as a living. His published works were addressed to the amateur market, and his supply of songs seems to have outstripped the publishers' capacity for issuing them. Schubert's publication did not benefit him as effectively as Beethoven's publication of works of all kinds, including deliberate pot-boilers for amateurs, benefited their composer; but Schubert never had the aristocratic patronage which eased Beethoven's way in his early years in Vienna and enabled him to gain international recognition while still a young man.

The German song, when Schubert began to compose, had little to show for itself except the seventy or so songs of Beethoven which are the true precursors of the German *Lied*. Though *Lieder* were Schubert's most effective material for publication, his songs were outside the conventions of his age and tradition. Any age of great song-writing, like the Elizabethan period in England, depends upon the existence of an extensive body of lyrical poetry to serve as its raw material, and before Schubert's day German lyric poetry barely existed. Goethe was born in 1749 and Schiller ten years later; Schubert discovered the poetry of Schiller when he was fourteen, in 1811, and the works of Goethe four years later; in the year of his death he discovered the poetry of Heine, his exact contemporary. Schubert's appetite for song texts devoured lyrics by a number of minor poets whose work varies from the effective to the merest composer-fodder.

Carl Loewe, born a year before Schubert and outliving him by more than forty years, was a reasonably successful composer of operas, and he also left a collection of three hundred and sixty-eight songs, mostly in ballad style and many of them extremely attractive. To compare Loewe's songs with Schubert's is to discover the novelty of the Schubertian *Lieder* style, not only in its command of an unprecedently rich harmonic vocabulary but also in its economical creation of situation and character and, chiefly, in the chamber-music-like perfection of the balance of its two equal partners.

Mendelssohn and Schubert were prolific *Lieder* writers, as was Brahms; Hugo Wolf is accepted as a master on the basis of his songs alone. The *Lied*, that is to say, was established by Schubert, and it offered challenges to vocal style, literary insight and musicianship which are hardly the simplest way of catering for the taste of the amateur public. Schubert's dedication to *Lieder* was a matter of emotional compulsion rather than the not-unpraiseworthy desire to turn an honest penny or two whenever he needed it. The impulse which created German lyrical poetry led to the flowering of *Lieder*, which shows a new sensitivity to words among the composers of the early nineteenth century.

A little later Wagner was to write of the necessary fertilisation of music by poetry. By the time that Schubert died, not only had this new sensitivity created the *Lied* but Berlioz had embarked on the early concert overtures in which his musical impulses were drawn into focus by works of literature— *Waverley*, *King Lear* and *Rob Roy*. The *Fantastic Symphony* was performed less than eighteen months after Schubert's death. The new alliance between literature and music was to develop in the 1840s into the symphonic poems in which Liszt adapted the techniques of symphonic development to as close a parallel as can be achieved to narrative style in order to communicate his sense of the emotional significance of stories and poetry.

To declare any essential connection between the composer's new awareness of literature as a musical stimulus and the search for new audiences forced upon him by social and political conditions, would be to state more than we can ever have sufficient information to know. But it may well be that subconsciously—for no composer of programme music has suggested that his approach to literature was a deliberate attempt to create a community of feeling with an audience which might otherwise find it difficult to come to terms with what he had to communicate—the romantic composer realised that the shared experience of literature was a means of approach to listeners otherwise hard to reach.

Berlioz, whose programme music does not deal in narrative but in the expression of his emotional response to literature, lacked an audience sympathetic to his aims and familiar with his idioms, the type of audience which Mozart and Beethoven could expect for their concerts; and while there is no objective evidence that programme music was his means of finding a starting point from which he and his audience could begin a co-operative exploration of new musical territory, the history of the *Fantastic Symphony* suggests that its sensational programme was devised to put the audience into a frame of mind in which each listener could understand an exceedingly original musical conception. The symphony's main theme, its '*idée fixe*', is the final version and expansion of the melody of a song written in his teens; the grotesque, lurching *Marche au Supplice* was composed, two or three years before he thought of the symphony, for the unfinished opera *Les Francs Juges*; it is cyclically related to the symphony by the simplest scissors-and-paste method; the March is interrupted and the melody of the '*idée fixe*' inserted immediately before the movement's closing bars. Obviously this music had not previously been associated in Berlioz's mind with a sensational story about unrequited love, drugs and opium nightmares. The work was finished as neither more nor less than a strange musical experience when Berlioz, aware of the new romantic interest in drugs and their effect on the human mind (de Quincey's *Confessions of an English Opium Eater*, for example, was published in 1821), added a story 'about' the symphony to guide the listener through its unusually hectic emotional world. The story is not the point at which the experience starts but that at which the symphony ends.

'The fertilisation of music by poetry', then, can be seen as a happy coincidence in which the composer's new literary interests could appear as the ally of his own art, capable of establishing a means of communication between composer and audience. In Berlioz's mind, programme music was the use of familiar, appropriate literary ideas to define the type of purely musical communication he had to make. It was Liszt, Liszt's disciples and Richard Strauss who went further to re-create literature in music.

Berlioz was a considerable prose writer and as such responsible for a great deal of the essential mythology of the romantic age. The great composer, it seemed to him, is inevitably misunderstood and neglected, inevitably condemned to defend himself against the attacks of philistines and ignorant obscurantists; he is inevitably lonely because the world cannot understand originality. When Berlioz conducted in the Redoutensaal in Vienna, standing where Beethoven had stood, his mind was full of the sufferings of his heroic predecessor but not particularly attentive to the facts of Beethoven's career.

> It was in this large and handsome hall [he writes] that Beethoven first performed his masterpieces, now worshipped throughout Europe but at that time received by the Viennese with contempt. Count Michael Wielhorski told me that he was one of an audience of fifty which in 1820 heard the Symphony in A performed! The Viennese were busy going to Salieri's operas. Puny creatures! A giant had risen among them but they were happier with dwarfs.[6]

[6] Berlioz: *op. cit.* p. 375.

To ask why Berlioz did not mention the performers of the Seventh Symphony at this notably inauspicious concert, whether the orchestra and conductor were professionals or whether this was one of the Viennese concerts at which an amateur orchestra gave an optimistic sight-reading to the work, or to have expected him to remember that the Seventh Symphony had been enormously popular at its first performance in 1812 and repeated several times at Beethoven's own concerts would have been as pointless as reminding him that in 1820 the Viennese might well have been listening to Rossini's operas but that Salieri had composed nothing for the theatre for about twenty years. The point of his outburst is that by the time Berlioz reached Vienna, in 1845, it had become necessary for him to see the great composer as a sacrificial victim offered up to the self-seeking meanness of an academic establishment and the mean-minded narrowness of an inartistic general public.

Berlioz's sufferings were real enough. Henry Chorley read Berlioz's articles and occasionally quoted them in his own music criticism; he referred several times in his *Music and Manners in France and Germany* (1841) to Berlioz as an obviously important but apparently difficult composer, but admitted that during his visits to Paris he had tried unsuccessfully to hear some of Berlioz's work. He noticed that in spite of its reputation for obscurity, Berlioz's music had a great influence in Paris and described him as 'the idol of the younger critics'.[7]

All Berlioz's major works were greeted with excitement: the single performance planned for *Romeo and Juliet* and the *Symphonie Funèbre et Triomphale* turned by public demand into three performances. *Benvenuto Cellini* and *The Damnation of Faust* were his only real failures.

'The Overture was extravagantly applauded,' wrote Berlioz of the first performance of *Benvenuto* on 10 September 1838, 'the rest was hissed with exemplary precision and energy'.[8] Berlioz knew, of course, that he had not insured the opera by buying the support of the singularly efficient claque of the Paris Opéra. *Benvenuto Cellini* is an unorthodox work, making few concessions to the conservative, restricted taste of the Paris public. *The Damnation of Faust* was played on two successive Sundays in the November of 1846. The whole venture—fees, rehearsal costs, publicity, ushers and attendants, box office staff—was undertaken at his own risk. He had to pay excessive rent for the Opéra Comique, the only suitable auditorium available. None of his singers was a star, only members of the theatre's regular company. Paris was in the grip of a financial depression and there had been rioting in the streets; further to deter the audience, the weather was execrable. 'For all the number of people who came,' wrote the defeated

[7] Henry F. Chorley: *Music and Manners in France and Germany.* 3 volumes. London, 1841. Vol. 2. p. 301.
[8] Berlioz: *op. cit.* p. 245.

composer, 'it might have been the most footling opera in the company's repertoire.'[9] The 'progressive', Berliozian critics applauded; the opposition, realising the extent of the catastrophe—the number of unfilled seats— decided that they had heard the last of an unruly perverter of public taste. Berlioz rescued himself from the debts he had incurred by a concert tour in Russia and made a vow, which he was unable to keep for very long, never again to mount a concert in Paris.

If two disastrous failures seems comparatively little foundation for the ironical despair of the Berlioz of later years, the mere practicalities of his success provide a reason for it. His first concert, in 1829, which included the *Waverley* and *Francs Juges* Overtures, the *Dance of Sylphs* from the *Eight Scenes of Faust* and the *Resurrexit* of his early Mass as well as Beethoven's E flat Piano Concerto, made him a net profit of about 150 francs (about £3). He hired a hall, paid copyists, orchestra, choir and conductor, under- took the management of publicity and the box office, and what was left over was for his own use. Critical acclaim and widespread heated discussion are not capable of supporting life. Almost all Berlioz's successes were won at concerts which he himself financed; the choruses he used were the profes- sional choruses of the theatres; he undertook months of work for a negligible financial reward. For *Romeo and Juliet* the hall was sold out so that he issued corridor tickets for the overflow. Part of the débâcle of *Faust* was that the rent of the Opéra Comique was 1600 francs and the copyists' fees were enormous, so that he came to believe that the venture would justify itself only through a success as crowded as that of *Romeo*. It was the finances of the performance, not its reception by the audience, which were ruinous.

This is the context in which Berlioz's sense of failure can be understood; it explains his bitter, ironic desperation at his unwanted though successful career as a critic; it explains the perhaps apochryphal story of the dream symphony he dared not write. He woke one morning, shortly before his wife's death, clearly remembering a Symphony in A which he had been com- posing in a dream; he could remember its entire first movement, an *allegro* in two-four time, and was going immediately to write it down.

> I suddenly thought: 'If I do, I shall be led on to compose the rest. My ideas tend to expand nowadays, so this symphony could well be on an enormous scale. I shall spend three or four months on the work [I took seven to write *Romeo and Juliet*], during which I shall do no articles, or very few, and my income will diminish accordingly. When the Symphony is written I shall be weak enough to be persuaded by my copyist to have it copied, which will immediately put me a thousand or twelve hundred francs in debt. Once the parts exist, I shall be plagued by the temptation to have the work performed. I shall give a concert, the receipts of which will hardly cover the costs—that is inevitable these days. I shall lose what I haven't got, and be short of money to provide for the poor invalid, and no longer able to meet my personal

[9] *Ibid.* p. 416.

expenses or pay my son's allowance on the ship he will shortly be joining.' These thoughts made me shudder and I threw down my pen, thinking: 'What of it? I shall have forgotten it by tomorrow.'[10]

He dreamed the symphony again on the following night, suffered and overcame the same temptations, and then the music left him for ever.

There was little prospect of Berlioz earning regular sums of money through the publication of his works; only a handful of songs and vocal ensemble pieces with piano accompaniment was likely to appeal to the amateur public, and the huge scope of his most popular works precluded their having any extensive sale in print. But to set against this there was the great prestige of his huge ceremonial works, the *Messe des Mortes*, the *Symphonie Funèbre et Triomphale* and the *Te Deum*. The first two of these were official commissions. The Minister of the Interior, de Gasparin, commissioned the *Requiem* in 1836 as part of a plan to restore the prestige of French religious music by commissioning new works and sponsoring their performance. Unfortunately the Director of Fine Arts—'he was unable to concede real merit to any music except Rossini's,' complained Berlioz—was not musically adventurous so that for a time he doubted the possibility of the commission ever becoming more than a verbal promise which might easily be dishonoured. Nevertheless, the confirmation of the commission arrived and its performance was planned for the ceremony commemorating the dead of the Revolution of 1830. Then de Gasparin fell from power, and Berlioz, writing in the tradition of French ceremonial music at its most grandiloquent, planning music to saturate a lofty, resonant building, had already had parts copied and rehearsals in progress when the musical part of the commemoration was cancelled.

The problem of how to extract his own fee of 4000 francs, about £80—he considered it 'niggardly for the occasion but was not prepared to haggle'[11]—but also the copyists' fees and the cost of the rehearsals took second place for a time to the necessity of arranging a performance of the work. The death of General Damrémont in Algeria gave the Ministry of the Interior an opportunity to push the *Requiem* on to the Ministry for War; the Ministry for War was ready to accept financial responsibility for a performance but not for the composer's fee. Cherubini, whose own *Requiem* was customarily sung at such ceremonies, then had to be bribed by the rank of Commander of the Legion of Honour to surrender his right. The performance was a great musical success, so that Berlioz at last had time to address himself to the question of his unpaid fee, but it was not until six weeks after the performance and eighteen months after the

[10] *Ibid.* p. 470.
[11] Hector Berlioz: *A Selection from his Letters*. Selected, edited and translated by Humphrey Searle. Letter of 17 April 1837 to Adèle Berlioz, p. 64.

granting of the commission that, by threatening to publish the details of his negotiations with the two ministries, he extorted the money for which he had worked.

The commission for *Symphonie Funèbre et Triomphale* in 1840 to commemorate the tenth anniversary of the July Revolution came to a composer already made suspicious by the shoddy treatment he had received over the *Requiem*, so that the rumour that the musical part of the celebration was to be cancelled after he had written the first movement of the *Symphonie* left him prepared for the worst. The rumour was false, however, and the composition and rehearsals went ahead as planned. Berlioz had been offered 10,000 francs for the composition and the expenses of its performance; these included the copying of parts and the selection and rehearsal of orchestra and choir. The ceremonial went against the music; the first movement made little effect as it was played on the march to the *al fresco* ceremonies in the Place de la Bastille, and the dismissal of the National Guard from the Square during the second movement effectively destroyed the work's impact. Fortunately, the management of the Salle Vivienne, where the rehearsals had taken place, booked two further performances after the spoiled première, and from these Berlioz collected a respectable fee, so that his profit from the work was 2800 francs; it obviously paid Berlioz not to act as his own impresario.

The *Te Deum* was written without a commission, and after its completion in 1849 Berlioz had considerable difficulty in arranging its performance in conjunction with an event of sufficient magnitude; even an appeal to Napoleon III for support did Berlioz no good. In 1855 it was played at the closing ceremonies of the Paris Exhibition, with orchestral and choral forces matching Berlioz's demands and 200 drums in the final apotheosis.

Nothing that Berlioz did enabled him to secure a way of life in which he could devote himself to composition. His salary as Assistant Librarian and then as Librarian of the Conservatoire was, like most musical salaries, minimal, and his concert tours, successful as they were, did not bring him enough money to make him secure. A concert in Gotha, in 1855 for example, brought him 300 thalers (about £45), but though it was obviously cheaper to mount a concert in Germany with an established orchestra than to follow his Paris custom of assembling and drilling an *ad hoc* body of performers for each of his concerts, his tours in Germany, Austria and Russia were financed by himself and taken at his own risk; it was only in England that he conducted as the result of definite invitations with his fees guaranteed. Thus, despite his detestation of journalism (a detestation which must as often as not have been modified by his pleasure in a job superbly done) he could never escape the uncongenial demands of a secondary career followed with an honesty that closed against him the doors of many whom he treated with uncompromising disdain. Even his foreign tours had to be material for articles—racy, sardonic and witty—invaluable as accounts of musical conditions in the mid-nineteenth century.

Schubert and Berlioz, outside the system, demonstrate the near-impossibility of a free-lance career. Mendelssohn, whose music exactly met the taste of nineteenth-century Europe, was a member of a wealthy family even before he could live comfortably from his achievements as composer and conductor. Liszt, when his days of virtuoso touring ended, became *Kapellmeister* at Weimar with a conventional *Kapellmeister*'s salary of 400 thalers a year. This was about £100 in the English money of the period. The leader of the Opera orchestra at Leipzig, in the 1820s, also earned 400 thalers; the various section-leaders earned 200 thalers and the rank-and-file players a mere 150. For rehearsals they were paid eight groschen, with 16 groschen for dress rehearsals. The entire orchestra cost the Leipzig Opera about £900 (6000 thalers) a year, even when extra rehearsals were called, but it played for a hundred and ten operas and a similar number of plays.

Salaries in the court orchestras were not appreciably higher; a court orchestra consisted of *Kammermusiker,* seniors whose positions were permanent, and *Accessisten,* probationers, who waited until death or promotion among the higher ranks emptied a space which they could fill; their salary until they joined the ranks of the *Kammermusiker* was round about 150 thalers a year. Therefore orchestral players everywhere, however onerous their orchestral duties, were willy-nilly teachers in order to earn enough to survive. Both Berlioz and Charles Hallé described their hardships when the 1848 revolution in France scattered their wealthy pupils and closed the theatres. Hallé wrote:

> In Paris by far the greatest part of a Musician's income was invariably derived from teaching; and so it was with Chopin, Heller, many others and myself; but from the day after the Revolution, the pupils disappeared, and at the end of the week I could only boast of one. . . . The audience at our third concert did not number fifty people, although every place was subscribed for.[12]

Hallé, like Berlioz, found himself in England and settled there, to England's great musical advantage. Berlioz returned to Paris, though not by design, on the day that the National Assembly voted a grant to enable the theatres to reopen.

> Inadequate relief, [he wrote] above all to the musicians! A first violin at the Opéra was lucky if he earned 900 francs a year; he lived by giving lessons. It is hardly to be supposed that he could have saved on a very brilliant scale. Now their pupils have gone, what is to happen to such people?[13]

[12] C. E. and M. Hallé: *The Life and Letters of Sir Charles Hallé.* London, 1896. p. 92.
[13] Berlioz: *op. cit.* p. 45.

Naturally, a *Kapellmeister*'s salary was not commensurate with the skills he was expected to employ or the amount of work he had to face. Spohr, at Cassel, was paid 2000 thalers (not quite £300) with six to eight weeks' leave in a year in which he could follow his international career as violinist and conductor. His duties included the direction of the Court Opera and occasional court concerts as well as the administration of the entire musical establishment. In addition, he formed and directed an amateur choir and established regular orchestral concerts for the townspeople.[14] His publications and the fees he received from external engagements augmented his salary.

Weber's yearly salary at Dresden was 1500 thalers (about £220), equal to that of Morlacchi, *Kapellmeister* of the parallel Italian Opera in Dresden. But when Weber drew up the outline of the German opera company he was engaged to establish he noted that the first soprano would have to be paid 5000 thalers, the second soprano, the first and second lyric tenors and the dramatic tenor would each command a salary of 2000 thalers, while two additional woman singers could not be expected to accept engagements at less than 1500. Singers were more expensive than *Kapellmeisters*, though the proceeds of Weber's operas added to his exiguous earnings and in 1820, when he was offered the post in Cassel which Spohr eventually accepted, the Dresden authorities offered an extra 300 thalers a year to keep him in the city. To prevent jealousy between the two Dresden companies, Morlacchi's salary rose by the same amount.

The great success of *Der Freischütz* made it possible for Weber to demand more money from theatres eager to produce his operas. The original production of *Der Freischütz* brought the composer 80 Friedrichs d'or from the Berlin Opera in 1821, to which another 40 Friedrichs d'or were added before the first performance; a Friedrich d'or was worth about sixteen shillings in the English money of the time. When *Der Freischütz* reached its hundredth performance in Berlin, a hundredth performance signifying an epoch-making success, the management offered Weber an honorarium of 100 thalers; this he regarded as an insult, pointing out that the theatre had already made about 30,000 thalers from his work. But Vienna paid him 300 Friedrichs d'or for *Euryanthe*, but out of this sum he had to pay the cost of travel to and life in Vienna during the rehearsals of his opera. Covent Garden offered him £500 for *Oberon*; in addition he was offered £225 to conduct four orchestral concerts and there was a suggestion of an additional concert for his benefit. Until Weber realised that the cost of living in London was far higher than in Dresden or Vienna, he felt that fees so munificent would make him a rich man. But though he stayed in London as the guest of Sir George Smart, he had occasionally to spend money, and dinner with a friend—soup, fish, mutton cutlets with beans,

---

[14] Spohr: *op. cit.* Vol. 2. p. 141.

and beer—cost him all of six shillings (21 groschen, 4 pfennigs), he pointed out in a horrified letter to a friend.

Lortzing, born in 1801, composed operas which were an immediate success in the German theatres, but he kept their scores in his own hands to avoid the sale of his rights to theatres which could then cut and mangle his works before hiring scores to other theatres, hoping to mount performances from which the composer would receive no fee at all. He refused an offer made by Leipzig Opera in 1840 for his opera *Hans Sachs*:

> I cannot allow my opera for the fees your manager declares he paid Marschner—though I doubt it, because Ringelhardt used to pay 100 thalers for every opera by Marschner—for I should be ashamed to tell people about it when I get 30 thalers from the smallest company. I had to pay more than 16 reichthalers in copyist's fees for *Zar und Zimmermann*. So simply for your sake I shall drop three Friedrichs d'or and be content if your manager finds that price satisfactory. The fee I mention is paid by any municipal theatre of importance.[15]

Zar und Zimmermann is one of the permanent successes of the German theatre, and Lortzing's scale of fees for it ranged from 10 to 20 Louis d'or, according to the size and prestige of the theatre wishing to produce it; a Louis d'or of the 1840s was worth approximately £1. But for *Der Wildschütz*, a great success in 1842, he could extract no more than 6 Friedrichs d'or from the theatre in Coburg. Lortzing's operas were played repeatedly all over Germany while their composer wore himself out with overwork in small theatres with inferior companies.

The publication of a successful opera—unsuccessful operas remained unpublished unless their composer was rich and foolish enough to publish them at his own expense—made little difference to the composer's financial well-being. Marschner's *Der Vampyr*, a great success in Leipzig in 1828, was one of the most successful operas inspired by popular 'gothic' horror stories; Marschner sold it outright for 220 thalers. Lortzing, departing from his usual custom, offered his *Caramo*, produced in 1839, to Breitkopf and Härtel for 100 Friedrichs d'or, a price which the publisher thought excessive, although Lortzing was by that time a very popular composer.

Unlike Beethoven, who had made a not inconsiderable income from publishing his works, other composers had not yet learned how to exploit publication to their own advantage. They were unwilling, or unable, to write pleasant pot-boilers for amateur players and thus ensure the publisher of the profit on their minor works which would pay for the symphonies and concerts which would enhance their prestige. Spohr reached print when he was in his early teens and ready to hand over his music for a number of complimentary copies to impress actual and potential patrons.

[15] Hans Gal: *The Composer's World.*

Those composers who could publish their music in England could expect higher fees than they could obtain on the continent, but those fees were the result of the higher cost of living in England, where food prices had made Weber wince. Ewer and Ewer had offered Mendelssohn £250 for the English rights in *Elijah,* and after the composer's death had added £100 to their offer for the sake of the composer's widow. But the fantastically popular *Elijah* had the weight of the large English choral societies to guarantee a profit for the publisher.

> One of the greatest difficulties in the early days of music publishing [wrote William Boosey] was to know how adequately and fairly to pay a composer and mitigate one's losses in case of failure. Many instances occurred of the purchase of valuable copyrights, at the price of a mere song, in works which often resulted in a very big profit for the publisher. The English firm of Chappell gave £100 for all the publishing rights in Gounod's *Faust,* which was a great and lasting success, so they paid £1,000 for his next opera, *Mireille,* which was a total failure.[16]

Until later in the century, when a workable system of international copyright was worked out, and the paying of performing rights accepted as a matter of justice to the composer, publication could be a way of augmenting a composer's income but was a way of earning a living for only a very few who had seized the public imagination. Brahms made a respectable income from publication by virtue of the small pieces on which his relationship with publishers was based; so long as he supplied them with music that was immediately profitable, they would deal with large-scale, less profitable works for the prestige they gained from the handling of major symphonies and concertos although elaborate full scores were extremely expensive to produce and the market for them was necessarily limited. Publication could, for a composer whose style was original, be a positive danger. Berlioz, whose major works would have been a doubtful source of profit, decided that the *Francs Juges* Overture in print did him only harm; it was played by conductors who had no real understanding of his demands and performed travesties of his intention, so that he wrote to Schumann:

> I am afraid I should lose the esteem of musical people for ever if, by premature publication, I exposed my symphonies, while they are still too young to travel without me, to the risk of being mutilated even more than my overture.[17]

It is less than fair to the publisher to regard him always as an un-

[16] William Boosey: *Fifty Years of Music Publishing.* London, 1931. pp. 23–4.
[17] Hector Berlioz: *Letters,* translated by H. Dunstan. London, 1882. pp. 131ff.

Burlesque of a literary or dramatic composition; any debased likeness vt. imitate grotesquely

scrupulous money-grubber. In 1831, at the request of Wagner's teacher, Breitkopf and Härtel published a piano sonata by the young Richard Wagner; they paid the eighteen-year-old composer a mere 20 thalers, but at least they took the trouble to encourage an unknown beginner whose efforts were unlikely to bring them much return. Simrock paid Dvorak 300 marks for the first set of *Slavonic Dances* in 1878, when Dvorak was completely unknown in Germany. The dances became extremely popular and Simrock did very well out of his generosity; eight years later Dvorak refused the same sum for the D minor Symphony (No. 7), but Simrock doubled his offer while urging the composer to write some more Slavonic Dances.

Judged simply as a source of profit, Simrock found, Dvorak was a doubtful blessing; when he received the score of the G major Symphony (No. 8), in January 1890, the publisher wrote to the composer explaining the economic facts of life:

> If only I did sufficient business with your symphonies to be repaid for my enormous expense! But this is far from being the case as I am thousands down on them. . . . If the performances are successful, the composer always thinks that his work will sell well. You were successful here over Bülow's performance of your D minor Symphony, but subsequently not a single copy, not even a piano version, was sold.[18]

Neither performance nor publication replaced the loss the composer had suffered when the old system of patronage broke down, musical employment no longer was offered to him and he was left to find his own audience. He could become a popular hero adored by audiences wherever he appeared but still, like Berlioz, be involved in a hopeless struggle with intractable economic realities.

While the composer was left to depend upon his ability to find the audience for whom his music was intended, social and political circumstances made it difficult for him to do so. The educational policies fostered in the period of repression—from 1814 to 1848 and for some considerable time, in some states, afterwards—deliberately cut as many of the means of communication as possible between the intelligentsia and the common people. The man of culture had no direct access to communication with a working class brought up, according to the dictates of Francis I, to be simply good, honest citizens who knew their place and were contented with it. The composer found himself confronted by a social system which demanded that he found his audience but denied him the facilities for doing so. For the first time, the composer was edged into a position not simply dissatisfied with society but actively hostile to it. The social situation drew composers to the 'progressive', liberal side in politics.

[18] John Clapham: *Antonin Dvorak*. London, 1966. pp. 16, 19ff.

> I think that there is a big difference between revolution and reform. Reform is what I look forward to in all things—life, art, politics, road-making. Reform is intended to get rid of ill-usage and tries only to remove everything which hinders progress.[19]

The words are those of Mendelssohn, not, on the surface, the fieriest or most discontented of nineteenth-century composers. Since Beethoven had poetically embraced the millions in the exaltation of the Ninth Symphony, it was to the millions that the composer spoke, and to cry like Mendelssohn for reform was to look for a political and social system which ceased to divide him from his audience. He did not need to rationalise his aspirations in this way; to be aware of the educational system of Germany and Austria—or for that matter of Britain—in the 1830s and to speak for reform was to make unavoidable implications about the musical situation.

In 1848 Schumann, who was influenced by the writers who became known as 'Young Germany' and who married the emotionalism and un-worldliness of the Romantic Movement to the liberal ideal of freedom, ceased to write in a strain similar to Mendelssohn's because in 1848 he could not avoid the sight of the eggs being broken as they went into the omelette, and he drew back from the prospect of violent change with his social principles in ruins; if the alternative to repression was destruction, death and the end of the cultural traditions which had created him, the result could only be despair and withdrawal for social concern. Heine, the poet with whose lyrics Schumann most identified himself, spoke for him: to remake the world on juster lines would remove the poets and musicians; utilitarian potatoes would replace laurels and roses. His *Buch der Lieder*, Heine suggested, would come in handy in a greengrocer's shop for any tradesman who wanted to wrap up his cabbages. Lortzing, composing his 'revolutionary' opera *Regina* in 1848 (the work was not seen on the stage for fifty-one years), introduced striking workmen into his cast of characters, but even he wrote of them from a respectable, middle-class angle; they were the agents of destruction and anarchy acting in the names of freedom and justice. While the social situation drove the artist into the progressive, liberal camp, the revolutionaries drove him out again into a no-man's-land where all political action became pointless if it was not wicked. The artist may love freedom in theory, but he cannot exist without tradition.

The case of Wagner, in Dresden, is the extreme example of the artist driven into political action. Wagner believed art to be the only possible unifying force in an age which had lost the inspiration of religion and in which politics were only unprincipled expediency; the arts would bring back the true spiritual values with which conventional religion had lost contact. United by music into the *Gesamtkunstwerk*, which would bring

[19] Felix Mendelssohn: *Briefe aus dem Jahren 1833–1847*, edited by V. J. Rietz. Leipzig, 1864. pp. 72–3. Letter to Rebekah Dirickler.

together poetry, the dance, drama, painting and design in the service of
music, the arts would regenerate the shoddy, cheap-jack nineteenth century,
returning it to the path of truth and salvation. In his powerful but illogical
mind—for Wagner was a clear thinker only about music and musical
problems for all the power and fertility of his imagination—Wagner could
see no other hope for the world and felt it to be his destiny to provide the
means of salvation.

Dresden, where he was *Kapellmeister* and where, despite his known
financial unreliability, he had a good deal of official support and encouragement, was to be the point from which regeneration spread. He drew up
plans to reorganise and reform music in Dresden; his schemes were clear,
sensible, economical and fundamentally unpolitical. They would not only
have made Dresden a city in which music of all kinds could be heard at its
best; they would have improved the desperate lot of singers and instrumentalists in court employment. They were dismissed without discussion.
Wagner found new ideas irresistible: he was aware of the teachings of
socialists, communists and anarchists, and new ideas were attractive to him
to the extent that they seemed to have clear musical consequences, so that
if his mission of salvation was hindered by corrupt or old-fashioned
courtiers who stood in the way of his duty, the revolution would aid him
and was therefore to be supported. Into the sketches for *Siegfrieds Tod*,
the single opera which eventually developed into the monumental *Der
Ring des Nibelungen*, went Wagner's revolutionary fervour roused by the
obscurantism of the Saxon establishment: Siegfried, the redeeming hero,
owes something (as Bernard Shaw pointed out in *The Perfect Wagnerite*)
to the powerful figure of Bakhunin, the anarchist leader.[20]

To think of Wagner, the revolutionary activist of the Dresden barricades
of 1849 as an anarchist, socialist or communist would be to give him
command of a system of ideas which he seems never to have envisaged. The
revolutionary Wagner who was driven into exile with a price on his head
was simply a revolutionary composer looking for the society which would
make it possible for him to realise his mission, not a dedicated rebel who
happened incidentally to be Court *Kapellmeister* and composer of three
unusual operas which were refining and developing Meyerbeer's style of
grand opera. Wagner always had a typically German devotion to the idea
of leadership; actually, through his belief in music and its regenerative
power, he felt himself to be the leader in whom he most devoutly believed.
In 1863, faced with a failure so total that he seems for the first time to have
realised it as disaster, he was saved by Ludwig II of Bavaria, and his subsequent royalism was never really inconsistent with his revolutionary past.
The artist–philosopher–king Ludwig, a strange, handsome boy in his teens,
would lead the work of regeneration, himself led by the composer-

[20] G. Bernard Shaw: *The Perfect Wagnerite*. London, 1898. p. 48.

philosopher Wagner who could forge the redeeming *Gesamtkunstwerk*. Who nominally led was an irrelevancy so long as Wagner himself led the leader, the composer–philosopher–poet–vegetarian–anti-ecclesiastical– anti-semite designing the world of the future. It says everything for the power of Wagner's personality that his extra-musical doctrines were taken seriously by serious thinkers for nearly half a century.

The mere composer, with no elaborate if tangled philosophy to expound, had few other roads to explore except those which enabled him to create sufficient excitement to be taken notice of. The nineteenth century became the age of continual expansion. Wagner's attempt at a simple, economical repertoire opera became the five-hour gorgeous agony of *Tristan and Isolde*. Everyone's orchestra, except that of Brahms, became larger, everyone's palette more gorgeously coloured, everyone's symphonies longer and more demanding until, at the close of the century, we reach Strauss's *Ein Heldenleben*, Mahler's Eighth Symphony and Schoenberg's *Gurrelieder*. Sensation and extreme emotional intensity became necessities, and the startling thing about how much of the most sensational nineteenth-century music is the extent to which composers turned sensationalism to valid musical ends.

The composer in the nineteenth century, a man with no recognised, essential social function, could accept that he was an outcast, wandering through life in bohemian ineffectuality, or he could think of himself as the prophet of a new age in which his value would be recognised; he could see himself as, in Shelley's phrase, an 'unacknowledged legislator of the world'. But he could find no clear line of action outside music to which he could dedicate himself. Reform, opposed by repressive authority, led to revolution: it was the nature of authority to oppose reform. Revolution, if successful, would overthrow the traditional world of music which provided the centres from which the composer could preach his necessary, disregarded doctrines. The only escape from alienation, therefore, in a corrupt, philistine world is the fellowship of art itself, which must therefore direct its attention to the visionary and ideal rather than the practical. These are the ideas which pervade the serious music of the nineteenth century until they reach their conclusion in Schoenberg's statement that audiences are necessary to make music sound well; in an empty hall, music does not make the proper effect; in other respects, audiences are simply a nuisance.[21] The composer can only find his own, sympathetic, ideal audience, cultivate his own garden and withdraw himself from a world in which his aims and ideals are irrelevant.

[21] Arnold Schoenberg: *Letters*, Faber, London. Letter of 23 February 1918 to Alexander von Zemlinsky.

3

Musical Standards
in the Early Nineteenth Century

Our mental pictures of early nineteenth-century music-making are perhaps more glorious than the reality ever was. We think of Haydn at Esterhaza, with all the materials and trained personnel necessary to a composer ready to his hand and the approval of a musically-minded prince to stimulate his work. In Vienna Joseph II was at least a knowledgeable connoisseur of music, and in Munich the Elector Theodore was interested enough to attend the dress rehearsal, as well as the première, of Mozart's *Idomeneo*. On Friday mornings in the 1790s Prince Lichnowsky listened to chamber music played by the best instrumentalists he could find in Vienna, giving his protégé Beethoven the opportunity to write and hear works composed for these morning concerts. Prince Lobkowsky, an enthusiastic bass ready to take part in public performances, had his own orchestra, and in 1803 it gave the first performance of the *Eroica* Symphony, probably unaware that it was opening a new age. There were many patrons, of course, like Dittersdorf's first employer, Prince von Hildburgshausen, active and benevolent but, reading between the lines of Ditterdorf's *Autobiography*, with less than superfine musical tastes. There was a considerable number of lesser nobility involved in the life and work of Mozart and Beethoven.

Nevertheless, it is unlikely that any of the concerted music which such devoted patrons heard would have seemed to us to be played in a satisfactory way. Outside the opera house, where the co-ordination of so many diverse functions made rehearsal obligatory, performances seem to have taken place with the minimum of preparation. Mozart's concerts in one or other of the Viennese theatres seem to have been rehearsed, as was the first of the concerts in 1781 in which Mozart collaborated with Phillipp Martin in the Augarten Pavilion in Vienna, but not even Leopold Mozart's letters from Vienna during his visit in 1785 mention any rehearsal for the subscription concerts which his son was giving during the visit. Even Mozart seems to have taken for granted a system which put concert programmes on to the platform with at best the minimum of rehearsal. In 1781 he wrote to his father that on the previous day he had played a solo and accompanied the arias at a concert given by the Archduke Maximilian, Archbishop Elector of Cologne, who had instructed him to arrive after the guests were assembled, and caustic as Mozart could be about the musical tastes and demands with which he was confronted, he

mentions this unprepared performance as a matter of course.[1] He seems
not to have been worried when his own music was played unrehearsed, for
he mentions that the violinist Franz Mendel played his music a sight
better than any other violinist in Vienna.

When Spohr, as director of the orchestra at the Theater an der Wien,
took part in the concert in 1814 when Beethoven conducted *Wellingtons
Sieg* and the Seventh Symphony, he gave a shocked account of Beethoven's
eccentricities as a conductor, his disappearance behind the desk at a
pianissimo, during which, apparently, his arms were held motionless across
his chest, his leaps into the air at a *sforzando* and so on. If Beethoven had
conducted a rehearsal, such antics would have been equally noteworthy
then, so the implication is that either there was no rehearsal or that
Beethoven had been satisfied to take over a performance prepared by someone else, or that Spohr was altogether too eminent an instrumentalist to be
asked to rehearse.[2] None of these dubious ways of preparing a performance
would have seemed particularly negligent to the composer, who in 1818
wrote a hurried note to Carl Czerny asking him to play the last two movements of the Concerto in E flat (the *Emperor* Concerto) at a concert 'the
day after tomorrow' without mentioning a rehearsal; Czerny, of course,
knew the work—he had given its first performance—but Beethoven's letter
simply explains that two of the 'hymns' (by which he apparently means
movements from the Mass in C) could not be adequately rehearsed in time
and the Concerto movements were intended to take their place. It seems that
choirs needed rehearsal but that distinguished instrumentalists did not.[3]

In 1819 Franz Xaver Gebauer, the organist of the Augustinerkirche,
added a 'Concert Spirituel' to the end of his weekly choir practice; at this,
he conducted choir and orchestra through choral and orchestral works
played at sight, without any preparation at all. As Gebauer's programmes
included Beethoven's symphonies in spite of their unusual difficulty, the
results must have been unusually unsatisfactory. Beethoven, nevertheless,
attended some of them, for in 1821 he wrote to the publisher Sigmund
Anton Steiner asking for two tickets for what (in Emily Anderson's translation) he describes as 'lavatory concerts'.[4]

Spohr's *Autobiography* offers interesting testimony as to the court concerts in which, as a youth, he played either as soloist or as orchestral
musician to the German nobility. When he was fourteen he was invited to

---

[1] Emily Anderson: *The Letters of Mozart and his Family.* London,
1936. Letter of 17 November, 1781.
[2] Spohr: *op. cit.* Vol. 1. p. 186.
[3] Emily Anderson: *The Letters of Beethoven.* London, 1961. Vol. 2.
p. 775.
[4] *Ibid.* Vol. 2. p. 935.

play before the Duke and Duchess of Brunswick. The Duke himself was a violinist, but the Duchess played cards, so that the orchestra, stationed on a thick carpet to deaden the sound, was never allowed to reach *forte* and trumpets and drums were omitted from any score they tackled. 'One heard therefore the words "I play", "I stand" and so forth, much louder than the music.'[5] Appointed to the court orchestra, there was an evening when young Spohr grew over-excited by the music and forgot the embargo on *fortes*; his arm was 'seized by a lackey who whispered, "Her Highness sends me to tell you that you are not to scrape so vigorously." '

In 1807 Spohr played at Stuttgart to the King of Württemberg, who throughout the performance played cards at a table from which a semicircular segment had been removed to accommodate his corpulency; the episode is one of the few in the *Autobiography* which indicated that the earnest, high-minded Spohr actually had a sense of humour.

E. T. A. Hoffmann, the novelist–composer, animated the generation of Schumann, the generation following his own, by his writings. Hoffmann, the archetypal German romantic, invented an ardent, imaginative and daring musician, *Kapellmeister* Kreisler, to represent the new and exploratory world of music confronted, baffled and stultified by meaningless traditions and conventions, his imagination, learning and seriousness disqualifying him from success. Kreisler, who came to fictitious life between 1820 and 1822, experienced among the German provincial bourgeoisie private concerts as bizarre as those Spohr experienced at Brunswick and Stuttgart. As a local *Kapellmeister*, Kreisler could never escape these often hilariously painful events designed with snobbish inanity to allow the vain to show off their more or less imaginary talents.

When all the eating and drinking have finished at the Röderleins' dinner, Kreisler discovered, the seniors settle down to cards while the younger guests rush to the two young Misses Röderlein, who try in vain and with no real determination to escape the invitation to sing, pleading colds and lack of practice. It is possible, for Kreisler, who is their teacher, to guess what the songs and arias they attempt are meant to be. Their performance gives the card players, from the far end of the room, opportunity to join in. ' "*How much I loved, how happy I was!*" . . . "Pass!" "*When I never knew the pains of love*" . . . "Follow suit!" '

After the amateurs have exhausted their repertories somebody remembers that the *Kapellmeister* had left some music in the cloakroom, with his hat. He is therefore compelled to send for it and to begin to play Bach's *Goldberg Variations*, but his audience begins to drift away at Variation 3; after Variation 5, even his two pupils, the Misses Röderlein, find their

---

[5] Spohr: *op. cit.* Vol. 1. p. 10.

loyalty exhausted, and he has one listener left. After Variation 30, Kreisler is left alone to play Bach to himself.[6]

Kreisler's sorrows are all, in a sense, social comedy, but the Röderlein *Hausmusik* introduces a new note into writing about music; this is the bourgeoisie aping the manners of a decaying aristocracy, rejecting great music but insisting on popular works to show off their culture. Middle-class amateurs whose standards of taste are complacently third-rate, like a nobility which accepts great music played by its domestic musicians so long as their efforts are painlessly unobtrusive, are the signs of musical deterioration. It is obvious that the Misses Röderlein would not have missed the opera and the meetings of the local concert society, applauding and condemning enthusiastically for the wrong reasons.

Hoffmann's fictitious account of middle-class standards is borne out factually by Weber, who was concerned with the problems of the travelling virtuoso and decided that musicians needed a guide book to the conditions they were likely to find in the various towns through which they passed. He began the compilation of a *Musikalische Topographie* in the completion of which, he hoped, other musicians would join. Because he intended only to provide necessary information for touring instrumentalists, whose work would be largely with the amateur orchestral societies, he did not deal with the theatres in any of the cities whose musical facilities he described. His aims were purely practical, not critical; he notes the authorities who should be approached for permission to give a concert, the capacity and cost of the available hall or halls, the facilities for advertisement, the unavoidable expenses, such as the fees to be paid to any professional players needed in the orchestra (naturally, he expected the concert orchestras to be predominantly amateur), the advisability of arranging a subscription before his arrival, the season, day of the week and time of day when a concert would be most profitable, the days of the week when the hall would be unavailable, the price that could be asked for tickets and the profits that could be expected. The quality of performance, he writes in his notes on Basel, compiled in 1811, is something that he does not care to judge on the basis of his limited experience of music in the city. 'But as dedication and real love of music are generally lacking, little is done about standards.'[7]

Two years earlier he had dismissed Stuttgart fairly cursorily. 'As there are neither amateur theatres nor concerts in existence, it does not pay artists to come here.' The King's *Kapellmeister*, Franz Danzi (the son of the celebrated composer who had migrated with the Elector Theodor from Mannheim to Munich), had written excellent German opera. Its *Konzertmeister*, Abeille, composed charming music, and its second *Konzertmeister*, Sutor,

[6] E. T. A. Hoffman: *Johannes Kreislers, des Kapellmeisters, Musikalische Leider. Sämtliche Werke, Band* 1. pp. 24–6.

[7] C. M. von Weber: *Ausgewählte Schriften*, edited by G. Altmann. p. 119.

had composed an opera of which the critics had approved. For the rest, two amateurs were the only musicians in the city worthy of note.[8] It was equally impossible, Weber decided, to write enthusiastically about Darmstadt. The Archduke Ludwig I, he wrote in 1811, had done much to improve the playing of his own orchestra; he attended its rehearsals, following the music from the score, correcting errors or slipshod performance. But the townspeople depressed Weber. The Archduke allowed local amateur musicians to meet in the palace for rehearsal three times a week, but they looked on this privilege as an unwelcome court duty and never touched their instruments on any other day. Only a tiny handful of townfolk attended these rehearsals as listeners, and neither they nor the players had any interest in the private music-making which 'must always be the foundation of genuine musical achievement and real musical appetites'.[9]

Unfortunately, Weber's *Musikalische Topographie*, potentially a source book of the greatest possible historical value, remains incomplete, but it shows how, while concert music remained in most places the concern of amateur musicians, with professional players only for the less popular and less domesticated instruments, standards could hardly be high enough to achieve successful performances, or even a clear impression, of works as difficult as the Beethoven symphonies; Beethoven's music, nevertheless, was played all over Europe. It is worth while to remember that the Ninth Symphony was far too much for the Philharmonic Orchestra of London, the completely professional, international and highly regarded organisation for which it was written. Many Beethoven performances must have been little short of appalling. Weber himself conducted the concerts of the Prague Conservatoire Orchestra, a body of students, in 1814 when he was Director of the Conservatory; with it, he introduced Beethoven's Seventh Symphony to Prague; the experienced professional orchestra of the Opera had too full a schedule to undertake concert work.

The public concert had been the invention of middle-class amateur musicians in towns where there was no opera or where, as in Leipzig, opera had never developed the social pre-eminence it gained from its status as an entertainment designed primarily for the nobility. As the nineteenth century made opera increasingly dependent, even in Vienna, Dresden, Berlin and Munich, and the other great courts, on the support of a paying audience, brilliancies of singing, stagecraft and orchestral sound became more important to the success of a work than they had been in earlier days. From this point of view, the great opera houses maintained standards apparently far higher than those of almost every regular concert orchestra.

The determination to popularise opera, however, led managements into remarkable acts of disloyalty to any composer whose work might outstrip the conventions with which the audience was familiar. In London, where all

[8] *Ibid.* p. 124.   [9] *Ibid.* p. 137.

public music-making depended on success at the box office or on the support of wealthy subscribers, Sir Henry Bishop became director of music and house composer to Covent Garden in 1810; his success led to the offer of the directorship of music at the King's Theatre in the Haymarket in 1816, and for two seasons he held both posts. In 1825 he moved to Drury Lane Theatre. Bishop wrote a large number of operas and semi-operas designed to suit the taste of London audiences, but in addition he made other men's music as immediately palatable as he could to early nineteenth-century prejudices. In 1812 he added music to Arne's *Comus*; in later years, Boeildieu's *Jean de Paris*, *Fidelio*, *Don Giovanni* (renamed '*The Libertine*'), *The Marriage of Figaro*, *The Barber of Seville*, *Der Freischütz* and *William Tell* (first known as *Ninette* at its première in 1830 but transformed into *Hofer, The Tell of the Tyrol*, for a revival in 1838) were all presented to English audiences after they had been filtered through Bishop's style and usually interfering hand. Juggling with opera texts was a familiar occupation in censor-ridden Europe, but although the interpolation of new arias in any work—to suit the voices of the available singers for example— was a commonplace—Haydn, Mozart and many others were responsible for such interpolations—in the opera houses in London and Paris, the 'adaptation' of successful works to suit new conditions was almost a major industry. Bishop's version of *William Tell*, for example, turned the *ranz de vaches* which follows the storm in the Overture into a contralto aria in the body of the work. So much was altered, added and changed in Bishop's versions that it would be easy to believe that the adapter regarded other men's music as little more than a suitable context for his own.

Bishop was more objectionable than his French counterpart—François Henri Joseph Castil-Blaze—simply because Castil-Blaze's activities were far more restricted. As a translator of German libretti into French, Castil-Blaze was unusually gifted, but Auber, Boeildieu and Hérold all wrote operas which he to some extent travestied. His greatest distinction, however, was to draw the fire of Berlioz—Bishop was lucky in that he seems to have had no critic with either Berlioz's passion for authenticity or his knowledge of the originals which Bishop spoiled—over the first French production of *Der Freischütz*, which was produced at the Odeon Theatre as *Robin des Bois*, which, to Berlioz, was 'a great travesty, hacked and mutilated in the most wanton fashion'.[10] Berlioz, who had previously savaged Castil-Blaze for his treatment of Gluck's *Alceste*, was outraged to find that 'the plunderer of the masterpiece was richer to 100,000 francs'. Nevertheless, *Robin des Bois* was published before *Der Freischütz*. Castil-Blaze reorganised the order of the numbers, rescored whatever did not please him, rewrote the vocal line in various places, cut passages from Weber's score and inserted a duet from *Euryanthe* with his own accompaniment to Weber's vocal parts. 'And a

[10] Berlioz: *op. cit.* p. 86.

wretched sailor,' wrote Berlioz, 'gets fifty lashes for a minor act of insubordination!'

Castil-Blaze answered Berlioz with the classic apology of the arranger. He explained in the *Journal des Débats* that it was 'common knowledge that foreign operas cannot succeed on the French stage unless they conform to our dramatic standards. . . . The object of my endeavours has been to make this splendid masterpiece known in France.'[11] Berlioz, of course, was not appeased and likened *Robin des Bois* to a travesty of Mozart's *Die Zauberflöte*, which had been played in Paris as *Les Mystères d'Isis*, arranged by a German, Lachnith, who more or less rewrote Mozart's work and added to it snippets from other operas, turned the music of a chorus into an aria, converted arias into ensembles and generally spoiled a masterpiece. It was the reworking, adaptation and reinstrumentation of works he revered which led Berlioz to appoint himself leader of an unofficial *claque* applauding and booing on behalf of the composers of desecrated masterpieces.

Whilst the major opera houses provided performances effective in their own terms when they distorted or totally falsified a composer's style and purposes, the smaller theatres simply did their best. Wagner, in charge of the chorus at the tiny opera in Würzburg in his first musical post as a young man of twenty, had fifteen singers with whom to manage the vast choral effects of Meyerbeer's *Robert le Diable*. Eighteen years later, in 1841, Henry F. Chorley heard a performance of *Les Huguenots* with a chorus almost as weak and an orchestra with too few strings to balance Meyerbeer's scoring.[12] The triumph of French grand opera in the 1830s, which converted it into the fashionable international style, added to the repertoires of the small German and Austrian theatres a number of works which they could not fail to produce, although *Les Huguenots*, for instance, demands five solo singers of the highest quality, a huge orchestra and a choir which can effectively represent huge, opposed groups of catholics and protestants; whatever its demands, it was seen for fashion's sake wherever an opera management was determined to maintain the loyalty of its patrons. Naturally, managements with little money regarded the chorus as the most easily expendable element in a production, and as late as 1882 Mahler conducted a performance of Gounod's *Faust* at Laibach in which the 'Soldiers' Chorus' was replaced by a single bass who marched across the back of the stage singing Luther's Chorale *Ein feste Burg ist unser Gott*.[13]

The habit of reorchestration continued into the mid-century. In many theatres it was simply a matter of adjusting the score to replace instruments which the orchestra of smaller theatres did not contain, but Berlioz, in London for the Great Exhibition of 1851 as one of the international jury of the

[11] *Ibid.* p. 89. Editor's footnote.
[12] Chorley: *op. cit.* Vol. 2. p. 94.
[13] Henry-Louis de la Grange: *Mahler*. London, 1974. p. 84.

Musical Instruments section, wrote about London music for the *Journal des Débats*:

> That composers are great masters, armed with great authority, that they are called Mozart, Beethoven, Weber or Rossini, matters little. Mr. Costa has for a long time thought fit to give them lessons in instrumentation, and, I say it with regret, Balfe has followed his example. The two orchestras [of Covent Garden and Drury Lane theatres] include three trombones, an ophicleide, a piccolo, a big drum and cymbals; in their opinion, such things are there for use. In Mozart's masterpiece, while Don Juan's private band is playing the naive music of the *Cosa Rara*, an incredible solo on the ophicleide has been introduced.[14]

Berlioz noted the use of trombones and ophicleide in the accompaniment to Marcellina's aria in *The Barber of Seville*, their appearance at large in *The Marriage of Figaro* and their general indispensability. When he saw *Die Zauberflöte* at Covent Garden he noted with sarcastic amazement that Costa had been satisfied with Mozart's orchestration; all he had done was to add four bars to the Priests' Chorus in Act Two.

The concept of opera as 'Drama in music' meant little to the nineteenth century until the example of Wagner's Bayreuth Festival performances began to be felt in the 1870s and 1880s. House lights blazed throughout the performance on stages that remained open through the intervals and the scene changes. Mahler, in 1897, demanded the dimming of the house lights in the Vienna Opera during the action, and had the curtain closed at the end of each act; Toscanini, appointed to La Scala, Milan, in the following year, introduced the same custom there.

To consider the state of opera throughout the first sixty years of the nineteenth century is to understand the fanatical zeal which Wagner, Mahler and Toscanini brought to the task of reforming it. In most opera houses the orchestra sat behind the conductor as he faced the stage from immediately in front of the proscenium with no direct control of the orchestra. Even Hans Richter, accepted in Bayreuth as the most loyal of Wagner's disciples, accepted this situation in Vienna; it was Mahler who moved the conductor's desk back to the front of the orchestra to give the conductor complete control of every element of the performance, especially necessary in such works as *Fidelio* and the operas of Mozart, where the orchestra's contribution to the work is no less important than that of the singers.

The concert, until later in the century, had little of the prestige which the opera claimed, but the concert had one major virtue which opera lacked. The concert behaved with almost exemplary loyalty towards the composers whose works were played. The concert orchestras did not deal in adaptations of standard works meant to add to their popularity with audiences unfamiliar with their style or purposes.

[14] A. W. Ganz: *Berlioz in London*. London, 1950. p. 108.

The most celebrated concerts in Germany were those of the Gewandhaus Orchestra in Leipzig, organised by the city's wealthy music-lovers. In the late eighteenth century the largely amateur concert orchestra had been amalgamated with the orchestra of Leipzig Opera, which meant that it had become predominantly professional, though when Mendelssohn became its conductor in 1834 it still had amateur members; Mendelssohn's timpanist, for example, was a theology student at the university. In 1827, when the fourteen-year-old Richard Wagner returned from Dresden to his birthplace, he had already fallen in love with *Der Freischütz* and heard, among other music, the overture to *Fidelio*. In Leipzig, Mozart's *Requiem* converted him to a composer he had previously rejected because he rejected everything, like Mozart's operas, which had an Italian text. A performance of Beethoven's *Egmont Overture*, in Leipzig, sent him to Beethoven's piano sonatas, and in January 1828 he heard his first Beethoven symphony, the Seventh.

The Gewandhaus Orchestra at that time was still directed by its leader; a conductor only appeared when the orchestra was joined by a choir, and the conductor was, by appointment, director of the choir, not of the orchestra. On Good Friday, 1830, Wagner was present for the first time at a performance of the Ninth Symphony (a work which had been played in Leipzig several times before). The leader made his way as best he could for the first three movements; *tempi* were extremely slow because the orchestra could not play the work at the speeds Beethoven had marked; a good deal of the playing was extremely ugly and incoherent. The arrival of a conductor for the last movement did little to improve matters. Christian August Pohlenz, the conductor in question, was well known in Leipzig, a teacher of singing, organist of the Thomaskirche and conductor of the *Singakademie* and various other choral societies. His intervention in the Ninth Symphony when young Wagner heard it did not improve matters. The youth knew the work well from the score, but for one of the few times in his life he almost began to doubt himself; the music which on the page had appeared to him to be beautiful, miraculously logical and monumentally powerful emerged to his ears as a chaos of uncoordinated sound. Wagner's self-doubts did not last for long—it was beyond Wagner's nature to doubt himself for long—but the performance was possibly the most valuable music lesson he ever received.

For all that, in the context of its time, the Gewandhaus Orchestra deserved its high reputation. It represented, wrote Henry Chorley about ten years later, 'the most perfect expression of the musical spirit of Germany'.[15] It had always been adventurous: Beethoven's name had first appeared in its programmes in 1799, when the aria *Ah! Perfido* was sung at one of its concerts, and his works had come to Leipzig almost as quickly as they had become available. Mendelssohn, its first great conductor, ardent and

[15] Chorley: *op. cit*. Vol. 2. p. 99.

high-minded, was the ideal musician for serious-minded Saxon music lovers, and though both Berlioz and Wagner had reservations about his quality as a conductor, the orchestra which Chorley heard was considerably better than that which Wagner remembered with dismay.

'The concerts,' Chorley continued, 'are but indifferently provided. The Gewandhaus, a moderately sized room, is infinitely too small for the audience who crowd it and pay their sixteen groschen for entrance (think of such a concert for two shillings!)' But not even Mendelssohn, it seems, could achieve all that should have been possible. Berlioz went to Germany in 1841 believing that German *tempi* were invariably slower than those set by French conductors, but he found that Mendelssohn used faster *tempi*— Wagner regarded them as excessively fast—than those heard in France. Mendelssohn admitted that he erred on the side of speed to prevent the instrumentalists getting bogged down in music too difficult for them.

Berlioz's account of musical conditions in Germany during his concert tour of 1841–2 follows some quarter of a century after Weber's *Musikalische Topographie*, and Berlioz set out not to study the musical life of the amateur concert societies but to describe his work as a virtuoso conductor, a passionate leader of modern music, with the best available opera and court orchestras. His quality as a conductor—the clarity of his beat, his painstaking patience and the decisiveness of his intentions, together with the charm, wit and dignity of his personality—won the devotion of the orchestras he met as he made his way from musical centre to musical centre where, with the exception of Leipzig, the orchestras were primarily concerned with opera and where professional concerts were rarities. But the orchestras could rarely satisfy all Berlioz's demands: 'We tried in vain,' he wrote of his concert in Leipzig, 'to procure three additional instruments, cor anglais, ophicleide and harp.'[16] Six months earlier, he discovered, Mendelssohn had been compelled to send to Berlin for the harps he needed in his incidental music to *Antigone*. But Berlioz found the Gewandhaus itself 'admirable' and the orchestra to consist of 'capital musicians', and so well disciplined that a programme which included the *King Lear* and *Francs Juges* overtures, the Rondo and Caprice for Violin and Orchestra and the *Fantastic Symphony*—all works new to Leipzig—could be prepared in two rehearsals; at the concert the orchestra played 'faultlessly'.

'Almost everywhere I went in Germany,' he wrote, 'I found discipline and alertness combined with real respect for the *maestro*.'[17] The administrators whom he met and the orchestras which he conducted were dedicated and enthusiastic, determined to give him every ounce of their skill and co-operation. His only general dissatisfaction was with chorus masters, too many of whom were bad pianists and too few of whom were thorough enough to arrange sectional rehearsals even when the music proved difficult.

[16] Berlioz: *Memoirs*. p. 295.   [17] *Ibid*. p. 264.

In Frankfurt, where the orchestra served both the Opera and the regular concerts of the *Museum Gesellschaft* (in which, until 1861, it was joined by amateur players, Berlioz found that the orchestra consisted of eight first and eight second violins, four violas, five cellos, four double basses, two each of the woodwind, four horns, two trumpets, three trombones and timpani. 'The identical force of forty-seven players is, with minor variations, found in every German town of the second rank,' he wrote.[18] When he heard it in the Opera House—for his Frankfurt concerts, planned to open its German tour, had to be postponed till its end—he judged it to be first-rate. 'Not a nuance escapes it, the various timbres blend into a harmonious body of sound free from all trace of harshness, it never falters, its ensemble is precise; it plays like one instrument.' He found a similar orchestra at Stuttgart, 'full of energy and fire, and fearless sight-readers'.[19] It too managed a concert which included the *Fantastic Symphony* after only two rehearsals. But on the road to Stuttgart he had called at Hechingen, where he found only eight violins, three violas, two cellos and two double-basses in the strings. The Weimar Orchestra, in preparation for Berlioz's visit, had assembled all the extra string players that could be found to provide him with twenty-two violins and seven of each of the lower strings.

At Dresden he found 'the richest combination of musical resources that I had encountered since coming to Germany'. He had the services of the orchestra and chorus of the Opera, a military band, a famous tenor (Tichatscek, a great Rienzi and Tannhäuser), Wächter (the first Dutchman in Wagner's *The Flying Dutchman*) and Wilhelmine Schröder-Devrient, whose combination of a fine voice and great dramatic sense made her a great Leonore in *Fidelio*. Unfortunately he found, too, in the orchestra an oboist whose tone was remarkably good but whose sense of style was antiquated and who had a passion for adding ornaments to everything he played. Berlioz protested against this at the second of the four rehearsals, but the oboist returned to his customary tricks at the concert. The leader of the double-basses moved him not to anger but to pity, for he was so old that he could hardly 'support the weight of his instrument' and was no longer able to reach some of his notes.[20]

In Berlin, Berlioz found an orchestra of fourteen first and fourteen second violins, eight violas, ten cellos, eight double-basses, four each of the woodwind instruments, four each of the brass, timpani, bass drum, cymbals and two harps. Everything in Berlin's musical life appealed to him. In Hanover, on the other hand, there were only thirteen violins and three double-basses, with the rest of the orchestra built in proportion. The players were competent but lacking in warmth and feeling; while the Dresden players had been eager to rehearse Berlioz's programme until they knew the music

[18] *Ibid.* p. 270.   [19] *Ibid.* p. 275.
[20] *Ibid.* p. 305.

(after four rehearsals they were ready for a fifth if the composer considered it necessary), some of the Hanover players resented his demand for two rehearsals.[21]

Berlioz's concert tour of 1841–2 took in Mannheim, Hamburg, Brunswick and Munich, important cities with celebrated orchestras and proud musical traditions; players seem to have regarded the visit of so dangerous a musical revolutionary as a challenge to their ability even before Berlioz's personality and ability began to impress them. It may be that the temporary escape from Paris, where his music had impassioned supporters but was opposed by the critics and the academic establishment as well as by the Opéra management, may have influenced the composer's judgement of musical standards, because in Germany his music was accepted and he was offered the wholehearted co-operation and sincere admiration of those musicians with whom he came into contact.

In Brunswick and Dresden, for example, there was no professional concert organisation and no satisfactory concert hall, so that Berlioz gave his concerts in the theatre. An amateur *Konzert Gesellschaft* existed in Dresden, and soon after its creation, in 1821, it had invited Weber to become its director. Weber accepted the invitation but soon found that his official duties and his unsatisfactory health left him no time to train the orchestra of the *Konzert Gesellschaft*; he told the members that he had flattered his powers when he had accepted their invitation.[22]

Concerts in cities like Dresden, where court institutions had been or were in the process of being transformed into public organisations, were rare and special events in the lives of the professional musicians whose real preoccupation was the opera. In the 1840s, when Wagner was *Kapellmeister* at Dresden, the orchestra gave a concert every Palm Sunday for its Pension Fund. Occasional concerts had been given since Weber's successor, Karl Gottlieb Reissiger, had introduced concert music as a spare-time activity for the already overloaded orchestra, but the traditional Palm Sunday concert was a major event of the official musical year, and the standard of symphonic playing in Dresden can be judged from the fact that Wagner's performance of Beethoven's Ninth Symphony, on Palm Sunday 1846 (not the first performance of the work in Dresden or by the *Staatskapelle*), was the first to establish the work in the minds of the Dresden audience as a necessary masterpiece rather than as a piece of remarkable eccentricity by a composer whose sufferings had driven him out of touch with reality. More than that, Wagner's performance impressed visitors like Mendelssohn's assistant in Leipzig, the Danish composer-conductor Niels Gade, although the Ninth Symphony had been played in the Gewandhaus programmes since

[21] *Ibid.* pp. 346–7.
[22] Karl Laux: *The Dresden Staatskapelle*, translated by Lena Jaeck. London, 1964. p. 39.

the 1820s. It was Berlioz and Wagner in Germany and England, as it was Habeneck in France, who removed the impression that Beethoven's last symphony was simply a work of wild incoherence occasionally played out of devotion to its great composer.

In Vienna, in 1845, Berlioz heard one of the charity concerts of the *Gesellschaft der Musikfreunde*, with more than a thousand performers. He was more concerned about the Viennese habit, common both to musicians and to audiences, of closing the ears to all music later than Beethoven's than by anything he heard at the concert, but he was full of enthusiasm for the huge orchestra, which played with fire and accuracy, each of its amateur members arriving note-perfect for the first rehearsal. The orchestra at the Theater an der Wien, where newcomers like to make their Viennese débuts, was not, he noted, as good as that at the Kärntnerthor Theater, where the Court Opera functioned with Otto Nicolai as *Kapellmeister*. The Opera Orchestra began to give public concerts under Nicolai, in 1842, beginning its transformation into its dual personality as orchestra of the State Opera and Philharmonic Orchestra, eventually expanding to the size at which it is virtually a double orchestra capable of serving both the opera and the concert hall. It was this orchestra that Berlioz conducted in his concert in the Redoutensaal, not in the hall of the Conservatoire, where the Opera Orchestra's concerts were normally played.

In 1847, recouping his fortunes after the disaster of *The Damnation of Faust*, he found a 'large and well-rehearsed orchestra and chorus, and a military band to boot' in St. Petersburg. With these he gave two hugely successful concerts of his own music before setting off to Moscow. His first concert had brought him 18,000 francs and the second was equally successful. In Moscow he found 'third-rate musicians, incredible choristers and some bizarre obstacles' but an enthusiastic audience; he made a profit of 8000 francs.[23] In both cities all the musicians he needed were put at his disposal for as many rehearsals as he thought necessary.

With Berlioz's declaration that he could secure fine performances with existing European orchestras so long as he was given adequate rehearsal time, it seems that it was the organisation of European music rather than the accomplishment of musicians which was responsible for the deficiences about which he, like Wagner, Schumann and many others, inveighed. Some of these deficiencies were due to the slowness of orchestras and their organisers in realising how the novel, enlarged scale of music since Beethoven had created the need for new methods of performance and the presence at any concert of a capable conductor. Conducting, in the modern style, remained more or less a mystery even to most of the people who practised the art until in 1856 Berlioz wrote his essay *Le Chef*

23 *Op. cit.* pp. 422–4.

d'Orchestre, Théorie et son art and Wagner his essay *Über die Dirigieren* in 1869.

Since the nineteenth century addressed music to the general public gathered in large concert halls, the conductor had become necessary. He needed to be a skilled performer with a specific technique and skills which he did not necessarily share with other musicians. The small orchestras which had been responsible for court concerts and court opera in the eighteenth century could be adequately controlled by a player at the keyboard or by their leader or *Konzertmeister* from his desk at the head of the violins. In 1821 Paganini conducted the first performance of Rossini's *Matilde di Shabran* from the leader's desk when the conductor fell ill after a series of troublesome rehearsals. Mendelssohn was expected to conduct his music for the Philharmonic Society when he first visited London in 1829 from the keyboard of a piano which had already become redundant when Haydn directed his symphonies in the Hanover Square Rooms in the 1790s. Spohr claimed to have been the first musician to conduct the Philharmonic Society concerts with a baton in London during his first visit to England in 1820. In the theatre, with a greater number of players to direct over a greater area, conducting was accepted as necessary; Weber conducted *Oberon* at Covent Garden with a rolled-up paper instead of a baton.

Musically, too, a *Konzertmeister* at the first violinist's desk or a *Kapellmeister* at a keyboard could do justice to a well-rehearsed performance of a pre-Beethoven symphony; his activities could do no harm and possibly a great deal of good even though he had no special qualifications as a conductor. The idea of a time-beater was not new, but the special techniques required by the conductor of a large orchestra were not understood by, for example, Beethoven, who conducted until 1812, although by this time he could not clearly hear most of what was done by the orchestra; apparently he had no clear ideas about the indication of *tempi* and was almost, according to Spohr's account, exclusively interested in expression. Berlioz suggested that orchestras adopted the benevolently dishonest practice of paying no attention to his excessive gesticulations.

Both Wagner and Berlioz wrote with great respect of François Antoine Habeneck and the orchestra of the Société des Concerts du Conservatoire, which Habeneck founded, and conducted for the first twenty years of its life. The Ninth Symphony in Leipzig had, according to Wagner, been a chaotic disappointment in 1830. In Paris, about ten years later, he heard Habeneck conduct a performance which seemed to him to be superb in spite of his inborn conviction that French musicians were temperamentally incapable of understanding the introspection and *Innigkeit* of German music.

The orchestra of the Society was founded in 1828; it had fifteen first and sixteen second violins, eight violas, twelve cellos, eight double-basses, four flutes, three oboes, four clarinets, four bassons, two trumpets, four horns, four trombones, a timpanist and a harpist. To it was attached a professional choir of seventy-nine voices. It gave, according to its constitution, seven concerts in a season that began every January, giving an opportunity to prize-winning students of the Conservatoire to appear in its concerts as soloists or as composers. As well as the seven concerts of its official season, it played a programme every year for the players' concert fund.[24] The hall of the Conservatoire originally, at the foundation of the orchestra, accommodated a thousand and seventy-eight listeners.

Habeneck's pre-eminence as a conductor of the symphonic repertoire was based on thorough and painstaking rehearsal. The Ninth Symphony, when Wagner heard it in Paris, was a performance which had been rehearsed for several months until every member of the orchestra knew and understood his part. 'The orchestra,' said Wagner, 'has learnt to look for Beethoven's *melody* in every bar.' Habeneck was a stern disciplinarian and a fine orchestral trainer, and though Berlioz lists him among the 'barbarians' who, like the musicologist Fétis, presumed to 'correct' Beethoven's music, he made no complaint against the concert in 1832 when Habeneck conducted his *Fantastic Symphony* and its sequel *Lélio*. Habeneck silenced the double-basses at the beginning of the scherzo of Beethoven's Fifth Symphony and was condemned by Berlioz for this, saying that the cellos sounded better alone—a decision which probably owed more to the poor quality of the Paris double-basses than to Habeneck's philistinism.

Habeneck lived before the days when conducting became a skill which combined technique with mystique in more or less equal proportions; once a tempo had been firmly established, he would stop and treat himself to a pinch of snuff while the orchestra carried on. Berlioz, at the first performance of his *Requiem*, noted that he ceased to conduct and took snuff just at the point in the *Dies Irae* where the tempo broadens out for the entry of the four far-flung brass groups of the *Tuba mirum*, leapt to his feet and gave the beat himself; writing many years later, he saw the incident as an indication that Habeneck had joined in the determined persecution of everything that he did.

Habeneck's masterly conducting of the Beethoven symphonies was achieved by conducting with a violin bow from a first violin part in which essential cues had been noted; he conducted at the Opéra not from a full score but from a double-stave version which contained only the vocal line and the most essential strand of accompaniment. In modern terms, Habeneck was barely a conductor at all, for the proper technique, its invention and codification, was largely the work of Berlioz and Wagner. Berlioz's essay

---

[24] A. Dandelot: *La Société des Concerts du Conservatoire, 1828–1897.* Paris, 1923. pp. 29–30.

of 1856, which was added to the 1844 *Traité d'Instrumentation* as an epilogue, remains a fine textbook. It starts from the fact that a bad singer or solo instrumentalist ruins his own part, but a bad conductor ruins an entire work. He wrote:

> A conductor should *see* and *understand*; he should be *agile* and *vigorous*; he should know the composition he conducts and the nature of the instruments; he should be able to read a score.[25]

If it seems remarkable that Berlioz should need to point out facts so blindingly obvious, he does so because he wrote when conducting was a new technique not properly studied but left to what Wagner called 'professional routine'. Berlioz admits that as well as 'a special talent' the conductor needs other abilities which are

> almost indefinable and without which an impalpable barrier rises between him and those who he directs, the faculty of transmitting his feelings is denied him, and therefore power and authority, the directive action, completely escape him.

But he still has to point out that

> the making of any noise whatsoever, either by the conductor's baton on the desk or by his foot on the platform, is to be universally condemned. It is worse than a bad habit—it is a barbarism.

Obviously in 1856 the basic facts needed to be stated firmly.

Berlioz's essay deals precisely with matters of fundamental technique, with methods of beating time clearly yet in a way which prevents monotony of rhythm. He considers the control of scattered forces in the opera house or concert hall, the use of the metronome, the control of sub-conductors. He does not attempt to teach the indefinables of musical sensitivity but restricts himself firmly to knowledge of the kind that can be imparted.

Wagner's essay is as different from Berlioz's as Berlioz was from Wagner. What can be imparted by a textbook seems to have little interest for Wagner, because anybody could teach it. He set out to show how musical understanding and sensitivity can be transmitted by the conductor through an analysis of what he regarded as the common faults of German conductors; he considers not only the almost sacred German classical symphonies and the problems they pose but also the failings of German performances of the operas of Rossini and Bellini. The faults he discovers he attributes to two main causes—the incapacity and insensitivity of conductors who cannot sense the true *tempo* of a work; everything depends on this. The Paris performances of Beethoven's symphonies under Habeneck had been great because the orchestra, knowing and understanding the music, could

---

[25] Berlioz: *On Conducting*, translated by John Broadhouse, London, 1917. p. 3.

project its melodic line from bar to bar throughout whatever complexities of harmony and orchestration a long movement offers. German conductors who could neither sing nor understand real singing were incapable of bringing out a complex, varying melodic line; they did not understand such things as melodic phrasing and left a work like the Ninth Symphony to exist without any clear melodic continuity, regarding the music as sacred because they did not understand it. The tradition of Mendelssohn, the elegance and polish of which had got rid of 'a good deal of rawness and loutishness' preserved an academic rather than a living tradition of performance, though Mendelssohn's penchant for over-fast *tempi* suggested a dangerous lack of sensitivity. The essential Wagnerian teaching is conveyed through his analysis of standard performances of music by Haydn, Mozart and Beethoven; the essay is about musical sensitivity, not about the technique of conducting.

Berlioz's beat was clear and immediately legible, Wagner's more elaborate, designed to convey unusual subtleties of rhythm and *rubato*. London orchestras, trained for years by the bandmaster methods of Costa, who dominated both opera and concert hall in London for almost forty years, never understood Wagner's requirements, and his season as conductor of the Philharmonic Society was disastrous. Those who managed to grasp his style, however, were enthusiatic about it :

> The old flautist, Furstenau, of Dresden, told me that often, when Wagner conducted, the players had no sense of being led. Each believed himself to be following freely his own feeling, yet they all worked together wonderfully. It was Wagner's mighty will that powerfully but unperceived had overborne their single wills, so that each thought himself free while each followed the leader, whose artistic force lived and worked in him.[26]

The Wagnerian doctrines spread through Europe as his career achieved the apotheosis of Bayreuth and his disciples took more or less complete control of European music. But mere familiarity with the nineteenth-century orchestra created a real understanding of the problems of balance, control and interpretation involved in the conductor's work.

But in all fields of music-making the same faults were observable in the earlier years of the symphony. The permanently based string quartet hardly existed before the violinist Joseph Joachim founded his string quartet in 1869 and established real standards of chamber-music performance. Spohr played a vast amount of chamber music wherever he went, but he found the later string quartets of Beethoven to be completely baffling. To his mind, a quartet was a work in which he, as first violinist, was accompanied by the most satisfactory musicians who could be found to fill up the other desks. Even Berlioz was worried when, as a young man,

[26] Felix Weingartner: *On Conducting*, translated by Ernest Newman. Leipzig, 1925. p. 11.

he discovered that he could not make sense of the posthumous Beethoven quartets simply by studying their first-violin parts. The habits of the eighteenth century prevailed for fifty years into the nineteenth century, although music had long outgrown them.

4

The Virtuoso

Possibly the difficulties of eighteenth-century travel were all that restricted the activities of the great eighteenth-century virtuoso players. Eighteenth-century singers travelled widely, but tended to contract themselves for a season to whatever theatre offered them the most profitable terms. Instrumentalists moved on more quickly from their concerts but tended not to devote too much of their time to touring. Mozart's colleagues from Salzburg, Ignaz Leutgeb, the horn player and Anton Stadler, the clarinettist, for example, discovered that they could live well enough in Vienna without committing themselves to the rigours of long, extensive tours; Leutgeb helped to finance his freelance career in Vienna by running a cheesemonger's shop. Johann Simon Hermstedt, who played Spohr's clarinet music, toured with his composer, as did Weber's clarinettist, Heinrich Bärmann. But their tours were less frequent and less extensive than those of Spohr, and Weber travelled further in his early years as a concert pianist. Maria Theresia von Paradis, the blind pianist whose father, an Imperial Counsellor, was a nobleman, played in Paris in 1784, travelled on to London, staying there for five months and meeting all the best people before she returned to Vienna through Brussels and the major German courts. A single tour could establish a reputation, after that, further travelling seemed pointless.

The traveller made his way over appalling roads—the only record of a concert from which Paganini's audience went away disappointed refers to his appearance at Stuttgart on 3 December 1828; he had arrived in the city in the early hours of the morning after his coach had overturned. The touring musician was rarely able to plan a concert more than a week ahead, and his first advance publicity came from the gossip of travellers making their way over his route a day or two before him. He would send his business manager ahead, if, like Paganini, he could afford to employ one, to book a hall or rent a theatre, come to terms with the local orchestra and arrange as much publicity as time allowed.

Major cities stood outside this haphazard progress as fixed points by which his intermediate activities could be governed. In them, dates of arrival would be fixed in advance, other performers booked and possibly even a rehearsal arranged. But the traveller making his way, say, from a long-fixed performance at Nuremberg to another at Munich would pass through Eichstätt, giving himself time there to play to the Prince-Bishop's court if his offer to do so were accepted, and possibly to arrange a concert with the amateur orchestra of the city. His chances of planning any of this ahead were very limited; he was not, however, completely governed by the repertoire familiar to local musicians in small towns, for nobody would worry if the local orchestra sat down to play at sight the accompaniment to a concerto they had never seen before. He could, of course, maintain some sort of contact with the musicians of cities where he had already given a successful concert and, through them, plan ahead in spite of the difficulties of travel in the pre-railway age, which in Germany continued into the 1840s. The need for such a book as Weber's planned *Musical Topography* becomes obvious as we realise that the musician was hoping to play in places where had had no musical contacts whatever and where the facilities for concert performance were not known to him.

But just as Beethoven appeared to the early nineteenth century as a type of composer without precedent, above and outside all precedents by virtue of his genius, subject to no law but that of his own inspiration, so the super-virtuoso appeared a being as remote from normal considerations as was Beethoven. Paganini reached Vienna in 1828, the year after Beethoven's death. He was a physical wreck; in addition to acute and sometimes crippling digestive troubles and a nervously over-intense temperament, he suffered from tuberculosis. He did not even look like other men; he was emaciated to the point at which that it seemed as though he wore clothes to keep his skeleton from falling apart; black eyes glittered from a yellow-skinned, cadaverous face on each side of which hung long, lank black hair. His platform manner added to his strangeness; he bowed stiffly, like a marionette whose strings had suddenly been released, and he walked in a peculiarly stiff, wide-legged way. Of course, he played the violin as it had never been played before; his G string had an effective range of three octaves, and he produced harmonics the like of which were unheard of. His varieties of bowing and his left-hand pizzicato were equally new.

Legends accumulated round him. Imprisoned for murdering his wife or his mistress—nobody was quite sure which—men said that he had spent his years of imprisonment perfecting his playing because he could neither read nor write, so that less strenuous ways of killing time were not open to him. His peculiar walk was due to the years in which he had paced his tiny cell with a criminal's iron crossbar chained between his legs. The G string on which he performed incredible solos, including an entire sonata he had dedicated to Napoleon I, was made from the intestines of his wife or mistress, whichever of the two had been his murder victim. The more observant, or the more imaginative, saw the devil standing beside him on the platform, guiding his bowing arm or his left hand or both. He had won his mastery at the price of a Faustian bargain with the Evil One.

The terrifying, Mephistophelian Paganini—who seems to have been a man of great charm and considerable culture as well as lively intelligence—was forty-six before he began to travel outside Italy. The publicity stories, wherever they came from (and he himself protested that he disliked them), did nothing to decrease the size of his audiences; they turned him from a mere musician into a sensation appealing to crowds who would never have dreamed of attending a concert by a mere celebrity, like Spohr. When he started to move outside Italy he began to declare that the legends were an affront to his dignity as an artist, but they seem to have worried him not at all while he was establishing his reputation as a wonder man, and, ridiculous as they are, they stamp him with the seal of the romantic age; one can imagine the young Berlioz, if he had thought of the story first, composing another symphony of 'Episodes in the life of an artist' (the subtitle of the *Fantastic Symphony*) in which the artist sells his soul to the devil for the sake of superhuman skill, murders his beloved and makes a miraculous G string from her intestines. Even the streak of morbidity in the early romantic movement and its typical works is paralleled by the morbidity which is one of the elements of Paganini's life.

From the age of thirteen, when he played at a concert in Genoa to finance his further training, he had been almost continuously active, though for some three years (the years of mystery which prompted the story of his imprisonment for murder) he had apparently retired into the house of an aristocratic mistress, and from the age of nineteen until he was twenty-two had given the world nothing but compositions. He had been *Maestro-di-capella* in the court at Lucca while Napoleon's elder sister, Marianne Elise Bacchiochi, and her husband were Prince and Princess there. In 1809 he gave up court service, playing wherever he could earn money, never completely healthy, driven sometimes into retirement to recoup his health, gambling and wenching inexhaustibly. An action for abduction against him—though the girl he supposedly abducted seems to have been a prostitute who recognised that an abduction charge would be an easy way to make money from him—caused him some trouble and cost him a great deal of money but has nothing to do with the legend of his imprisonment. In 1814 he bought an annuity for his parents at a cost of 20,000 lire, and for the rest of his life his brothers and sisters depended upon him for frequent financial help.

He had not made so much money by exercising the highest musical taste. He had a genuine love for the music of Beethoven, whose chamber works he loved to play in private, but his public concerts contained no music of this sort, but only the almost impossible works he composed for himself, one or two popular virtuoso concertos by his contemporaries and, at times, farmyard imitations; he imitated the braying of an ass so effectively in Ferrara that his audience suspected that he was making a comment

on them, and drove him from the city; they had refused to take the singing
of his current mistress seriously. In Leghorn he arranged a concert without
asking the co-operation of the Orchestral Society, so that the concert
started belatedly, with only four of the orchestra present. In such a situation Paganini was at his best; he could spend the evening proving that he
needed no orchestra. He was always happy to dazzle his public by carrying
through a programme almost unaccompanied.

He made use of the most astounding gimmicks; in Lucca, as leader of
the orchestra, he directed an entire opera with only the two lower strings
in place on his violin; he fascinated audiences by his willingness to carry
on a work after a string had broken on his instrument rather than inter-
rupt the music and fit a new string, and though both his compositions and
his playing were genuinely creative, he seems to have enjoyed the breaking
of strings for the opportunities they gave him to stupefy an audience by his
ability to play without them. His G string solos may have begun as
gimmicks, but they became a vehicle for the melancholy poetry which
haunts his slow movements.

Spohr, the conservative purist, wrote:

> Connoisseurs say that it cannot be denied that he certainly possesses a
> great dexterity with the left hand, in double chords and in passages of
> every kind, but the very thing by which he fascinates the crowd debases
> him to a mere charlatan. . . . That by which he captivates the Italian
> public consists, on a nearer enquiry, in a succession of feats . . . viz: in
> flageolet tones; in variations upon one string, in which, for the purpose
> of imposing more upon the audience, he takes off the other three strings
> of the violin; in a peculiar kind of *pizzicato*, produced with the left hand
> without the help of the right hand or the bow; and many tones unnatural
> to the violin, such as the bassoon tone, the voice of an old woman, etc.,
> etc.[1]

This was the result of hearsay, Spohr defending traditional values against
an opponent whom he had never heard. When, later, Paganini played in
Cassel, Spohr was present at the concert and gave the famous traveller a
dinner without becoming a wholehearted admirer. 'His compositions,'
wrote Spohr, 'and his execution I found a strange mixture of the highly
genial and childishly tasteless.'[2] The Victorian translation of Spohr's
Autobiography is not without its eccentricities; it seems that both Paganini's
compositions and his playing seemed to the German virtuoso to be brilliant
and to have genius, but at the same time to be disfigured with circus tricks
of the sort that could only appeal to a child. To Spohr, revolutions in violin
technique were irrelevant to real musical considerations because the violin
as it had reached his generation could already do everything which it

---

[1] Spohr: *op. cit*. Vol. 1. p. 280.
[2] *Ibid*. Vol. 2. p. 168.

needed to do, its limitations having been laid down in the works of the classical masters.

To understand Paganini's influence on the course of music, it is not only necessary to note the expansion of technique which, notwithstanding the doubts of old-fashioned musicians, provided the entire string orchestra, as well as the violin, with a vast expansion of their vocabulary; it is also essential to consider the personality which gave rise to the highly coloured legends and made him a figure of wonder and terror; the sense of the dangerous, the uncanny and the superhuman which he imposed on his audiences was not only a valid part of the romantic atmosphere of the period; it was also a potent influence on new audiences and on a vast number of his successors. Meyerbeer and Rossini both admired and liked Paganini; Schubert wrote to his friend Anselm Huttenbrenner about a concert of Paganini's in Vienna: 'In the *adagio* I heard an angel sing.' The adagio was that of Paganini's D minor Concerto.[3]

This was Paganini away from home, where he disciplined himself to express his personality through music and not through the sort of frivolous cleverness which had often appealed to Italian audiences and where his influence was greatest. In central Europe. France and Britain he seems to have been no longer content simply to amaze huge audiences by his ability to do what had never been done before even when it was hardly worth doing. Wherever there was an audience he played to it, so that even in England he travelled to concerts in provincial towns where Spohr and Mendelssohn had never troubled to make themselves heard. All over Europe he doubled admission fees to his concerts and still packed the hall for every appearance; only the English resisted his demands after pointing out that admission prices in London were already nearly twice as high as those in theatres and concert halls even in the continental capitals. He made 20,000 florins out of his concerts in Vienna and averaged £1000 a night for his appearances in London; even in provincial cities like Norwich he packed halls in spite of prices as high as fifteen shillings a seat. His demands brought him a reputation for extreme avarice; in London in 1831 he refused to play at the benefit concert for the famous bass Lablache unless he were given one-third of the gross takings. He never became, or wished to become, a popular or beloved figure; he preferred his audiences to regard him with some dread. Occasionally, unaccountably but in a way which did no harm to his strange reputation, he would give concerts for charity so long as he was not importuned to do so; he could, apparently on impulse, attend a performance of Berlioz's *Harold in Italy* and at its close kneel at Berlioz's feet and two days later send him a cheque for 20,000 francs. The story has been denied, first by Paganini's adored son and then by others who wished him to be consistent in his miserliness, but it has not been disproved.

[3] Deutsch: *op. cit.* p. 737.

Between the man Niccolo Paganini and the diabolical public enchanter was a great, and apparently calculated, gulf. Canon John Edmund Cox of Norwich was his host and apparently his English secretary while he stayed in the city, and Cox noted the difference between the private musician and the public showman:

> In private—*for he had the violin constantly in his hand*—he would sit down and dash off by the hour snatches from the compositions of the best masters and give readings of such originality to passages that had been heard again and again, such as they have never been supposed to possess by any other player. As an instance of this, he, one morning while I was writing several notes for him, commenced the first motivo of Beethoven's Violin Concerto. To write then was impossible, and he, seeing how entranced I was, asked me whether I knew what it was. On my replying in the negative, he promised, if it could be managed, I should hear the whole movement. . . . On the last night . . . one gentleman . . . at a signal from the 'Master' sat down at the pianoforte and drawing a crumpled piece of paper from the inner pocket of his long black dress coat, began to play. Instantly I was on the alert, for I remembered the notes and his promise rushed back upon me.[4]

Paganini's activities in Britain alone were more exhaustive than those of any other international celebrity. He played in Great Yarmouth, went from there to Dublin, stayed in Ireland to visit Carlow, Clonmel, Kilkenny, Waterford, Cork, Limerick and Belfast. From there he crossed to Scotland and appeared in Edinburgh, Glasgow, Ayr, Kilmarnock, Perth and Dundee. In England he gave concerts in Brighton, Clifton, Cheltenham, Bristol, Bath, Liverpool, Manchester, Leeds, Sheffield, Chester, York, Birmingham, Winchester and Southampton before returning to France and, for a time, commuting between Paris and London to satisfy his admirers in both capitals. His aim, he said, was to leave his natural son, Achillino (who was later legitimatised), 2,000,000 lire, and after he returned to Italy in 1835 he was almost burnt out, incapable of any extended effort. He died in 1840, leaving Achillino all the money a son could require and the world a legend.

The influence of Paganini extended itself through his personality as well as his genius as a violinist; in future there was to be an inescapable equation between powerful, eccentric personality and supreme virtuosity. 'The grand manner' on the concert platform is part of Paganini's legend. But the influence of Paganini's compositions, though they seem to need his own personality to give them their full effect, went equally deep; they underlie much of the string writing of Berlioz and Wagner. He is one of the Personalities re-created by Schumann in *Carnival,* and Schumann used six of the solo violin *Caprices* of Paganini as bases for his Concert Studies *op.* 10. Liszt's *Études d'exécution transcendante,* the *Grandes Études de*

[4] J. E. Cox: *Musical Reminiscences.* London, 1872. pp. 196ff.

Paganini and his *Grande Fantaisie sur la Clochette* are works in which the master pianist set out to do for his instrument what Paganini had done for the violin. Brahms's *Paganini Variations* and Rachmaninov's *Rhapsody on a Theme by Paganini* are only two of the memorable acts of homage paid to his genius by later composers.

Not even Liszt travelled so extensively. After Paganini, the old virtuoso route round the courts of Central Europe, with visits to Paris and London, was no longer the most profitable route an instrumentalist could follow. Of course, any musician with a great reputation could collect audiences in Winchester, Bath or Norwich: the question was whether he needed to drive himself so hard as Paganini had done. Until Paris, London, Vienna and Berlin were tired of him, why should he endure the miseries of travel to smaller towns and less profitable concerts? Paganini's labours went beyond what was necessary; a couple of extra concerts in London—and there was never a time when he could not command a capacity audience paying more than the usual cost of admission to listen to him with bated breath in any capital in Europe—would have made him as much money as his exhausting journeys through the provinces, and this was a fact which he was quite shrewd enough to realise; his determination to leave every beaten track seems to have arisen from an inner compulsion to conquer every audience he could reach, no matter at what cost in exhaustion and what danger to his health came from reaching it. His determination to make his son rich— the rationalisation with which he explained his endless labours—could as easily have been served in the relative comfort of half a dozen great cities. Paganini was apparently under some compulsion to conquer wherever roads could lead him; not for him the establishment of a reputation among connoisseurs in a few historic, politically important cities.

It was Liszt who followed most closely in Paganini's footsteps. A beautiful and fantastically gifted child, he had played in Vienna in 1822, when he was eleven years old, and had, perhaps, been kissed by Beethoven (more probably in private than, as the legend insists, at a public concert). At twelve he reached Paris, at thirteen he appeared for the first time in London and at fourteen his opera *Don Sanche* was produced in Paris. He continued to tour until his father died, in 1827, and then he seemed to lose any sense of the direction in which he might develop. The arrival of Paganini in Paris in 1833 gave his art and personality the target they needed, the possibility of leading a revolution in keyboard technique as startling as Paganini's revolution in violin playing.

The pianistic revolution could not have taken place had it not been for developments in pianoforte design and building notably by the Parisian manufacturer Sebastian Érard. Iron-framed pianos gave the player a new range of dynamics and a wider range of colours; Érard's double-escapement action made possible the effects of speed and glitter through which

Liszt and his contemporaries transferred to the piano the effects and figurations inspired by Paganini in genuinely pianistic equivalents. The arrival in Paris of Chopin, in 1832, and the emergence of Berlioz's music, joined with the style Liszt had already developed, combined together to create the superman-virtuoso of the piano.

But while it is Liszt who is remembered as the supreme pianist, he was one of a remarkable generation of piano virtuosi. Mendelssohn, a splendid pianist, was born two years before Liszt; Chopin was a year Liszt's senior. The aristocratic Sigismund Thalberg, illegitimate son of Count Moritz von Dietricstein and Baroness von Wetzlar, was a year Liszt's junior. Adolf Henselt, in the eyes of some Liszt's superior but the victim of a shyness which would not let him play in public, was born a year later, in 1813, and Ferdinand Heller in 1814. It is almost as though the now perfected piano—for only Steinway's increase in the instrument's sustaining power and volume, an innovation of the 1850s, remained to be developed when the Liszt generation took command—created the possibility of the masters it needed. Their popularity, and the awe in which they were held, was increased by the rapidity with which the piano became the universal, all-purpose domestic instrument. It was the piano which young ladies automatically learned as a social duty, and it was the piano which enabled the serious amateur to come to terms with the orchestral repertory through transcriptions. The general fascination with the piano and its masters encouraged the pianist to take the risk of giving solo performances.

It is difficult accurately to chart the rise of the piano as the essential amateur all-purpose instrument. Shudi, the London instrument-maker, was producing about nineteen harpsichords and twenty pianos a year in the 1770s. Stein, of Augsburg, whose pianos pleased Mozart, produced a similar number. Broadwood, the London maker who learned his trade from Shudi, created about seven thousand square pianos and one thousand grands between 1782 and 1815. By the end of the nineteenth century there were about thirty piano-makers in London, and Broadwood, the most successful of them, had begun to use steam power and methods of mass production at a time when there were, according to a Scottish author, John Russell, in his *A Tour in Germany and some of the Southern Provinces of the Austrian Empire* (published in 1828), about sixty-five piano-makers in Vienna, none, however, using Broadwood's mass production techniques.

By the middle of the nineteenth century, Broadwood was making about two thousand three hundred instruments a year and Collard, the firm originally established by Muzio Clementi, about one thousand five hundred. France produced about a third of the entire English total, but the largest and most successful of Vienna's one hundred and eight piano-makers were producing some two hundred pianos a year. The piano was so firmly entrenched in amateur musical life that chamber music had drifted out of the home and was becoming the preserve of ensembles of professional players like the Joachim Quartet. As early as the 1830s, Mendelssohn had written to Zelter that there were 10,000 pianos in Vienna. A few days before he had been irritated in Munich by 'young ladies quite able to perform some adequate pieces very nicely' but who 'tried to break their fingers with juggler's tricks and rope dancer's feats of Herz'. Herz's music was flashy, empty showman's work, and Mendelssohn, the handsome, elegant darling of the salons, tried to convert the Munich girls to Beethoven's sonatas.[5]

Ignaz Moscheles, born in 1794, claimed to be the first pianist to have played in public without an orchestra, but when he did so, in 1837, he shared the programme with singers to avoid the danger of the monotony which his friends thought likely to afflict a solo performance. In 1839 Liszt began a series of solo performances, which he called 'Musical Soliloquies', in Rome. In a letter to Princess Belgiojoso he discussed his innovation: 'My impudence is so limitless that I am quite capable of importing my Musical Soliloquies (I cannot think of another name for these inventions of mine) to Paris.' He sent the Princess a note of his programme—his own transcription of the *William Tell* Overture, his Fantasy on *I Puritani,* some of his pieces which were billed as 'Studies and Fragments' and an improvisation on a given theme. All the music was by Liszt or arranged by him, probably for the reason that other men's music might not give him sufficient opportunities for display. When Liszt gave his first solo performance in London, the concert, in the Hanover Square Rooms, was announced as a 'Recital', apparently the first use of the term in publicity, though Dunneley's *Dictionary of Music,* published in 1825, had used the name 'recital' for a solo vocal performance.

Liszt's recitals were as much social events as they were concerts. It was possible to eat, drink and smoke between the items and the seats were arranged so that the audience could move at ease about the auditorium. Liszt would go to the piano and play for a time; then he would descend into the auditorium and talk to friends or to those lucky enough to be presented to him. Then he would play a little more, interspersing the entire programme with socialising descents into the auditorium. The programme invariably ended, of course, in London as in Paris or Vienna, with an outburst of the sort of hysteria associated in the eighteenth century with the singing of *castrato* opera stars and in the twentieth by the performances of 'pop' idols. It was a half-smoked cigar by Liszt that was retrieved by an aristocratic lady in his audience and carried round in her corsage until the day she died. Much of his appeal, apparently, was sexual, and nobody who wrote of his performances found it possible to isolate his musicianship from his personality; at the piano the paradoxes, inconsistencies, severities, in-

[5] Mendelssohn: *Letters,* edited by G. Selden-Goth. Elek, London, 1947.

dulgences and the charlatanism which went cheek by jowl with his devoted musicianship were all displayed.

The display was unusually lucrative. Wagner, when he was the merest acquaintance of the man who was to be his first and most devoted champion, was in Paris earning his living by the dreariest musical hack-work when he heard a Liszt recital and discussed it in an article for the *Abendzeitung* of Dresden:

> Liszt recently gave a concert here. He appeared alone; nobody else played or sang. The tickets cost twenty francs each, and he earned a total of ten thousand francs, with no expenses. He is soon to give another concert. What assurance! What infallibility! I am speaking of the speculative aspect; his playing is so assured and infallible that it is not worth wasting a single word on that.[6]

Liszt's programme of show pieces and transcriptions was not of the sort that could appeal to Wagner at his sunniest, and the penniless composer with a sense of his destiny and the sanctity of great art could not, perhaps, avoid the note of rancour when he found Liszt making great sums of money by cheapening and making a sensation out of the art he served.

Though Liszt's contemporaries had fervent supporters—some of them were popular enough to appear as his rivals—it was the hysterical sensationalism that accompanied Liszt, rather than his importance as a composer whose considerable creative power overflowed into performance, which made Liszt a legend while his rivals, apart from Chopin and Mendelssohn, are simply names in the history books. Chopin's originality—a quality which the twentieth century often finds it hard to appreciate—and the long, self-propagating melodic lines he developed from Italian *bel canto* opera were as startling as the unorthodox beauty and expressiveness of his harmony. Mendelssohn's letters, for example, dwell with delight not only on the beauty and appeal of Chopin's music but also on the remarkable keyboard style which Chopin had developed—he could not have learned it from any of his teachers—in order to embody his own music. Chopin used the sustaining pedal, for example, to secure *pianissimo legato* passages. Chopin himself gave few public concerts but lived on his earnings as a teacher with an extensive practice among the wealthy, by his performances at the private concerts of the rich and by the money made by his publications. When he played to an audience he avoided the startling, eye-catching mannerisms of Liszt.

Thalberg, too, whose speciality was so to surround a melody in the middle of the keyboard with fantastically elaborate arpeggios that listeners could not understand how two hands could achieve his effects, deliberately

---

[6] Richard Wagner: 'Farewell Performances'. In *Wagner Writes from Paris* . . . , edited and translated by Robert L. Jacob and Geoffrey Skelton. London, 1973. p. 124.

adopted a very restrained manner. Liszt's playing tended to be a dramatic struggle in which he was pitted against mighty forces which only a super-man could defeat; Thalberg made virtuosity sound easy, but Liszt, perhaps more shrewdly for the effect he had upon audiences, acted out both the technical problems he surmounted and the emotional responses the music demanded from him. Neither Liszt nor Thalberg played much apart from their own bravura works in public; Thalberg seems hardly ever to have gone beyond them, though those who heard him play Beethoven sonatas in private ranked him above Liszt because he never added his own embellishments to the music.

The works through which Liszt conquered the musical world in the 1830s were his own, and they extended piano technique in every direction beyond anything that had been thought possible before his appearance. Other men could do one or other of the things he did superlatively well, but he alone could manage them all. The works which he wrote to demonstrate his abilities are more than a meretricious exploitation of a phenomenal technique, and even at their most spectacular they express something deep in Liszt's personality—the virtuoso's delight in his mastery. Even the operatic fantasies—a type of composition extremely popular in the days when he was the lion of the keyboard with the longest mane and most musically intimidating roar—become re-creations by Liszt of other men's thoughts. The later Liszt blazed strange harmonic trails, was an orchestral innovator and pioneered techniques of symphonic narrative, but the early Liszt was essentially an interpretative artist; where he was not interpreting the music of other composers, he was interpreting the nature of the piano itself, and other people's music, when it became the basis of a Liszt work, reappeared as his own view of the notes with which he had been provided. When he played music by Beethoven he used the notes set down on paper for him with a freedom which many of his contemporaries condemned and which would be unforgivable to twentieth-century ears. It was from Liszt more than from anyone else that the idea grew of the interpretative artist's right to freedom of expression through other men's music.

Until 1840, when Liszt played music by other composers he was more likely to play his own transcription of one of their orchestral works than to embark on a piano piece. His piano versions of the Beethoven symphonies appeared far more frequently than any of Beethoven's pianoforte works in his programmes. There is no record of Liszt's attempting any of Beethoven's concertos except the G major and the E flat (the *Emperor*), and the sonatas he chose to play, apart from the *Hammerklavier op.* 106, were the extremely popular works with titles, like the so-called 'Moonlight'; he seems to have played only five Beethoven sonatas in public. He acknowledged a debt to Chopin, but played little of Chopin's music. When, at a Beethoven concert, the audience demanded his transcription of the Skating

Scene in Meyerbeer's *The Prophet,* he obeyed the public; he was, he said, its servant.

The *Hammerklavier Sonata,* regarded as an impossible and incoherent work, was the work with which he chose to declare his superiority over Thalberg, when Thalberg challenged his mastery of the Paris audience. According to Berlioz, who followed the performance from the score, the performance made a previously unintelligible work appear for the first time as great music. A sight-reader of almost incredible swiftness, he was capable of fine performances at sight from manuscript orchestral scores; he achieved such performances at sight of the Mendelssohn Concerto in G minor and Grieg's Piano Concerto as well as with Grieg's Violin and Piano Sonata, in each case to the amazed delight of the composer. Joachim, the great violinist of the nineteenth century, enjoyed first performances with Liszt but said that at every later performance the piano part would become subject to more and more elaborate embellishments until in the end it was as much a Liszt paraphrase as a performance of another man's music.

The legend which Liszt alone, of the great generation of virtuoso pianists, left behind him has done as much as his enormous body of compositions to keep our interest alive; there is no doubt that, like Paganini, Liszt was conscious of the need to dominate his audience by dazzling it and playing upon its emotions, but the audiences which feared Paganini loved Liszt. We do not know the extent to which the excitement of contact with an almost hysterical audience affected him so much that he stretched interpretative liberty into licence; Berlioz wrote that an intense responsiveness of temperament was responsible for inducing Liszt to play magnificently whilst distorting Beethoven, whom he as well as Berlioz worshipped. In private, Berlioz noticed, Liszt played Beethoven's music as powerfully as he would play it to an audience, but with the discipline that Berlioz found natural in approaching the works of a great master.

Charles Hallé was already a fine pianist when, in 1836, at the age of seventeen, he settled in Paris and became a friend of Liszt, Berlioz and Chopin. In the late 1880s Bernard Shaw wrote of him with the admiration he refused to mere showmen pianists:

> Sir Charles is not a sensational player, but nobody who heard him play the *largo* of this sonata [Beethoven's op. 10 no. 3] has ever accepted the notion that his playing is 'icy and mechanical'. Is there any audience in the world that would come to hear [Anton] Rubenstein play a Beethoven sonata for the twentieth time? Yet Hallé is always sure of his audience. . . . The reason is that he gives you as little as possible of Hallé and as much as possible of Beethoven.[7]

[7] G. Bernard Shaw: *London Music in 1888–89 as heard by Corno di Bassetto.* London, 1937. p. 41.

For a time, Hallé had been swept off his feet by Liszt's example. He first heard the great magician at the concert in which Berlioz first conducted the *Marche au Supplice* from the *Fantastic Symphony* in its orchestral dress and then Liszt played his transcription of the same movement. The example could not be resisted, and Hallé found himself in hot water with the Paris critics in 1844 when he played Beethoven's E flat Concerto at a Conservatoire concert and copied Liszt, by playing in octaves passages written in single notes; but Hallé was never really a showman and learnt to judge Liszt accurately. He wrote:

> If before his marvellous execution one had only to bow in adoration, there were some peculiarities of style, or rather of musicianship, which could not be approved. I was very young and most impressionable, but still his tacking on the finale of the C sharp minor Sonata [the '*Moonlight*'] to the variations of the one in A flat *op*. 26 gave me a shock in spite of the perfection with which both movements were played. Another example: he was fond of playing in public his arrangement for piano of the scherzo, 'The Storm', and the finale from Beethoven's *Pastoral Symphony*. 'The Storm' was simply magnificent, and no orchestra could produce a more thrilling tempest. The peculiarity, the oddity, of the performance consisted of his playing the first eight bars of the scherzo, rather more quickly than they are usually taken, then the following eight bars, the B major phrase, in a slow *andante* time.[8]

This was written by Hallé later in life, when he was a devoted classical pianist almost crowded out of concert life by his work as a conductor. On the unveiling of Beethoven's statue, in Bonn, a year after his infection by Lisztian excess, Hallé heard Liszt play the E flat Concerto again. 'I think he must have felt equal scruples,' wrote Hallé, 'for . . . he adhered most scrupulously to the text, and a finer and grander reading of the work cannot be imagined.'[9]

The virtuoso introduced a new element into instrumental performance. He won a new audience through his mastery of showmanship, transferring to the concert hall from the opera house the element of danger and physical excitement. By doing so he not only captivated new audiences but enlarged the orchestral vocabulary and extended the composer's range of colour. They led the way not only to more and more startling individual feats but to the virtuoso orchestra and the dazzling effects of such movements as the 'Queen Mab' scherzo in Berlioz's *Romeo and Juliet* Symphony. In an age of public music, they were their own, and music's, most effective publicity agents.

[8] C. E. & M. Hallé: *op. cit*. p. 38.   [9] *Ibid*. p. 85.

5

The Commercialisation of Opera

Once, when opera was an entertainment designed for monarchs and their courtiers, public taste mattered little to the providers of opera except in the Italian theatres where the public's support was financially necessary. In most German and Austrian court theatres the general public was originally admitted free of charge so long as it conformed to accepted standards of dress and behaviour. It was only when the public's contributions were demanded that they were in a position to call the tune and influence the repertoire.

As early as 1768, the Royal and Imperial Opera in Vienna had been put under the care of a commercial manager who, in 1768, turned down an opera by the twelve-year-old Mozart. Leopold Mozart, in Vienna with his children for the first time since the beginning of the concert tour which had taken them across Germany and France to London, wrote to the Chancellor of his Archbishop in Salzburg about the new situation at the Vienna Opera:[1]

> The theatre is farmed out, or rather entrusted to a certain Affligio, who has to pay some 1,000 [florins] a year to certain people whom the court would otherwise have to pay. The Emperor and the Imperial family pay nothing for their boxes. Consequently the court cannot say a word to this Affligio, for everything is undertaken at his risk.

Mozart, with his son's work turned down, seems to have found the new system objectionable, but it took much of the cost out of the hands of the court and left businessmen to undertake the administration.

The rising cost of opera after the Napoleonic Wars produced a new type of opera management in Italy and Germany, the type which was already familiar in the Italian theatres. In 1821 the Imperial Court in Vienna leased the management of the Kärntnerthor Theater, the home at that time of the Opera, and the Theater an der Wien, to an Italian, Domenico Barbaja, who had started life as a waiter, had managed a circus and had taken charge of the gambling rooms attached to the Scala Theatre in Milan. With the profits he made from the gaming rooms, he bought control first of the San Carlo Opera in Naples and then of La Scala itself, and he ran

[1] Anderson: *The Letters of Mozart and his Family*. Letter of 27 July 1768. Vol. 1. p. 190.

both these Italian theatres in conjunction with his two Italian companies. In Vienna he had almost complete freedom of action under the supervision of the Court Chamberlain; artists and repertory were solely his concerns unless and until for any reason he became subject to some official complaint; such a complaint, in the terms of his management, could only be a fall in the public's esteem for the opera.

Barbaja was commonly regarded by the Viennese to be an illiterate barbarian concerned not with music but with money, but his record in Vienna is not discreditable. He exploited German operatic successes and took *Die Zauberflöte* on to the stage of the Kärntnerthor for the first time, invited Weber to conduct *Der Freischütz* there and commissioned *Euryanthe* from him. Josef Weigl, *Kapellmeister* of the Opera, who had won a great success in 1809 with *Die Schweizerfamilie,* was commissioned to write *Die eiserne Pforte* in quite a different vein to a libretto adapted from a tale by E. T. A. Hoffmann. Barbaja commissioned the ill-fated *Alfonso und Estrella* from Schubert.

But five years before Barbaja had accepted office in Vienna, Rossini's music had already created a sensation there, and Rossini had worked under contract to Barbaja, as manager of the San Carlo Opera, expected to compose two operas a year and assist in the management of the theatre; Barbaja had been rewarded in 1816 by the incredibly popular *Otello.* It was therefore natural that Barbaja, whose primary duty was to fill the theatre, should take Rossini to Vienna in 1822, and the visit was a triumph; it entirely vindicated Barbaja's policy of holding on to the support of popular German composers while encouraging the taste for Italian works. At the same time, he kept the company under firm discipline and dismissed its less efficient members. In spite of his reputed lack of education and culture, Barbaja was a gifted judge both of singing and of theatrical effectiveness; and he understood the taste of the public. Apart from his functions as a new broom in a dusty opera house, he introduced the Italian system of regular subscription throughout the season and brought to Vienna the best available Italian singers. He did not only ensure that the theatres under his control did not run at a loss; he permanently influenced Viennese taste. Although his rule lasted for only nine years, he established a system and a policy for his successors to follow.

In Paris the situation of the Académie Royale de Musique, by this time familiarly known as the Opéra, demanded more radical changes. The traditional battle of French opera against Italian styles had led to the opening of a theatre for Italian opera, established in 1829 in the Théâtre Italien after functioning in several other Paris theatres, while the Opéra Comique, already a venerable institution founded in 1715, occupied a variety of theatres in succession; its speciality was not comic opera but opera with spoken dialogue in place of recitative. Serious opera, with sung dialogue, elaborate ballet and a high degree of scenic grandeur, belonged to the Opéra itself. It had survived the revolution and the Empire, first as the Théâtre des Arts and then as the Académie Impériale de Musique. Napoleon had reimposed the tax on all other entertainments which had provided a major part of its subsidy, drawn up regulations to control its personnel and compelled its staff to make good any deficit on their yearly accounts. Productions at the three state theatres—the Opéra, the Opéra Comique and the Comédie Française—were controlled by the Ministry of the Interior. Since 1807, the Opéra management was in the hands of a Director, a Treasurer, and Inspector and a Secretary-General, all members of the Opéra staff, but a government Inspector of Theatres had supreme power over all the theatres of Paris. The restoration of Louis XVIII had changed but the name of the institution, which again became 'Royale' instead of 'Impériale', and it remained under the nominal control of a puppet director under the authority of an all-powerful Superintendent.

The Opéra, its management after the Restoration hamstrung by a Superintendent, the Vicomte de la Rochefoucauld, whose chief preoccupation was the respectability of the *corps de ballet* (he ordered that the skirts of the ballerinas be lengthened), ran more and more heavily into debt in spite of a lavish subsidy. The tax on other entertainments brought in some. 300,000 francs a year to add to the annual state subsidy of 750,000 francs, but in 1827 it had to apply to the King for another 996,000 francs (almost as much as its official income) to make good its debts. The July Revolution of 1830, with the enthronement of the Orléanist dynasty and its 'Citizen King by a triumphant bourgeoisie, put the reins of power into the hands of the financially experienced business men of the middle class. The new regime had no wish to diminish the prestige of the Opéra—indeed, the new government wished the Opéra to shine as the great showplace of French culture—but it saw no point in a management which was incapable of organising a year's work within an extremely generous budget. In 1831 the government announced that: 'The administration of the Académie Royale de la Musique, known as the Opéra, shall be entrusted to a manager–entrepreneur, who shall manage it for six years at his own risk and fortune.' The subsidy would continue, decreasing during the Director's reign from 810,000 francs in his first year to 760,000 for the next two years and finally to 710,000 for the rest of his period in office.[2] What the government wanted was primarily a business man as director to manage the theatre within the limits of the subsidy; if the new Director happened also to be a musician, so much the better. If he ran the theatre at a profit, so much the better for him; if he ran it at a loss, the loss was his own. At the same time, the conditions of the appointment insisted that: 'The entrepreneur shall be able to

[2] William L. Crosten: *French Grand Opera; an art and a Business.* New York, 1948. p. 18.

maintain the house in that state of splendour suitable to this national theatre.'[3]

The appointment of a commercial manager to provide the necessary financial expertise and business experience was in itself an indication of the way in which the audiences in all European theatres were changing as the middle classes began to share power with the aristocracy if not entirely to supersede the traditional arbiters of taste. Benjamin Lumley, the London solicitor who became manager of the King's Theatre in the Haymarket, the traditional London opera house since the days of Handel, noted the change in his *Reminiscences of the Opera*:

> The Opera House—once the resort and the 'rendezvous' of the *élite* of rank and fashion, where applause received its direction from a body of cultivated, discriminating 'cognoscienti', and the treasury of which was furnished beforehand by ample subscriptions in reliance upon the provisions made by the manager—now mainly depends for support upon miscellaneous and fluctuating audiences. . . . Boxes, which of yore were lent to friends if not occupied by the possessor, are now, it is well known, sold for the evening to any stranger who wishes to attend the performance.[4]

Lumley's unsubsidised theatre was, of course, more completely at the mercy of its audience than any continental theatre which backed its manager's presentation of opera with reasonable financial support, but the symptoms of social change which made Lumley's work in London especially hazardous were present in all the major European opera houses. It was in Paris that a new operatic style was evolved to exploit them.

The first director appointed in Paris under the system worked out in 1831 was Dr Louis Véron, born in 1798, the son of a stationer who had qualified in medicine, written a book about children's diseases and made a fortune out of a chest ointment bequeathed to him by an apothecary friend. Abandoning medicine for journalism, Véron had founded the *Revue de Paris*. Totally ignorant of music, a small, fat, scrofulous dandy, Véron put himself forward for the Directorship of the Opéra by explaining 'how a brilliant and skillful direction of the Opéra might be politically valuable at the beginning of a new reign'. The Opéra could attract foreigners by its musical quality and, by 'displaying crowded audiences in a sumptuous theatre, could demonstrate the order and tranquillity brought to France by the new order.'[5]

With the support of a corruptible press which he recognised as well worth

---

[3] *Ibid.*

[4] Benjamin Lumley: *Reminiscences of the Opera*. London, 1864. Introduction, p. viii.

[5] Auguste Véron: *Memoires d'un Bourgeois de Paris*. Quoted in Crosten: *op. cit.* p. 19.

the money it cost, with a cool sense of efficiency which economised by reducing the size of orchestra, chorus and *corps de ballet* while paying astronomical salaries to star singers, and with the aid of a *claque* as efficiently organised as everything else in his theatre—its leader was granted tickets to key points in the theatre for distribution to his subordinates and allowed to attend rehearsals to judge those points at which applause could be most effective—Véron set out to make the Opéra pay its way and earn him a fortune. In his attempt, he was instrumental in the development of a form of opera calculated to exploit the taste of the well-to-do bourgeoisie, who had nothing of the strict conservatism of the old aristocratic audience with their long exposure to the French operatic tradition. The new audience consisted of self-made business men and members of the professions who found themselves at last with time for amusement and the money to pay for it. Many of them lacked any extensive education; they wanted their eyes pleased and their ears tickled. Véron, in his *Mémoirés*, declared:

> The Revolution of July is the triumph of the Bourgeoisie. This victorious middle class will be anxious to reign and to amuse itself. The Opéra will become its Versailles, and it [the middle class] will rush there to take the place of the great lords of the exiled court. The plan to make the Opéra at once brilliant and popular appeared to me to have a fine chance of success.[6]

The fact that the first Director of the new dispensation was a man who could easily have stood as a symbol of the conquering middle class and its standards naturally meant a change of orientation not only in the works produced at the Opéra but in the standards of manners and conduct prevailing there. French opera since its foundations had been formal and dignified; it had made little effort to exploit or express deep emotions; its triumph was the expression of society, not the investigation of personal joy or tragedy. The place for intimate emotional expression was the Opéra Comique or the Théâtre Italien. What was performed at the Opéra under Véron extended the French tradition in accordance with the ideas of the July Revolution. The German poet, Heine, writing from Paris as a journalist, noticed the new attitude when he set out the reasons for Meyerbeer's domination of the Opéra after the triumphs of *Robert le Diable* and *Les Huguenots*. He wrote:

> Meyerbeer's music is more social than individual; the grateful present, that sees its own inner and outer discoveries, its own dissensions of the spirit, its own needs, its own hopes, reflected in his work, celebrates its own passions and enthusiasms when it applauds the master.[7]

[6] *Ibid.* quoted in Crosten: *op. cit.* p. 20.
[7] Heinrich Heine: *Uber die französische Bühne. Sämtliche Werke, Band.* xi. Quoted in Ernest Newman: *The Life of Richard Wagner.* London, 1933. Vol. i. p. 259.

Traditionally, whatever was performed in the Opéra was transformed to suit French taste, and the groundwork for Véron's revolution had been laid in the 1820s. In 1825 Rossini had composed *Il Viaggio a Reims* for the Théâtre Italien; it had not been successful. A year later he turned his *Maometto II*, written for the San Carlo Opera in 1820, into *Le Siège de Corinthe* for the Paris Opéra itself, emphasising these elements of the libretto which could make the work appear to be a story of national, public action. The tale of the Greek girl who refuses to marry the Sultan of Turkey because he ill-treats her people was reorganised to achieve a French emphasis on a national, political struggle instead of on the love story which is its Italian *raison d'être*; emotions were simplified and large-scale scenes were introduced to exploit the French love of spectacle and dramatic choruses. *Le Siège de Corinthe* was so complete a transformation of its Italian original that, retranslated into Italian, audiences in Italy accepted it as a new work. In 1827 *Moise in Egitto*, also written for Naples, was transformed into *Moïse et Pharaon*, taking over the ballet from *Armide* (Rossini's only Italian work with a ballet) to bring it into line with French demands. *Le Comte Ory*, with a libretto by Eugène Scribe, the father of the nineteenth-century French libretto who found the correct literary forms for the operatic prejudices of his fellow countrymen, gave Rossini his first French text in 1828, exploiting his genius for frivolously effervescent gaiety. In 1829 *Guillaume Tell*, an unwontedly clumsy adaptation of Schiller's drama by Etienne de Jouy, improved by Hippolyte Bis and polished up by Armand Marrast, never really won the heart of the French audience, though its six hours' length contains a wealth of splendid music. Rossini adapted himself to French taste but never ceased to be Rossini the inexhaustibly fertile and unmistakably personal.

The critic and musicologist Joseph d'Ortigue, a friend of Berlioz, whom he succeeded as music critic of the *Journal des Débats,* wrote a study of the controversy which arose in France over Rossini's music, *La Guerre des Dilettanti*; it provided an explanation for Rossini's failure completely to subjugate the Paris Opéra after annexing every other opera house in Europe:

> Rossini's music is far from being universal in its appeal. One must already be something of a dilettante and have reached some degree of musical civilisation to appreciate it. The people, as well as the genuine music-lovers, can remember an air by Mozart, by Mehul or by Gretry. Rossini, like Voltaire, writes for semi-scholars, for the people who can remember a cavatina. . . . His music is too refined, too far removed from simplicity; it is too artificial. It can perhaps become popular among a certain type of clever people, but I doubt if it can ever appeal universally.[8]

Ortigue, writing of Rossini as a disturbing newcomer to French music,

[8] Joseph d'Ortigue: *Le Balcon de l'Opéra*. Paris, 1833. p. 23.

offers an unusual angle of approach to a composer whom the twentieth century is rarely prepared to consider intellectually, but it seems to have been the naturally Italianate exuberance of Rossini's melody, its use of florid decoration at points where a French composer would write an eloquently simple vocal line, which disturbed the French critic in spite of the inventiveness and brilliant panache of the music. Such a style, at the Théâtre Italien, could be adorable, but the Opéra, the home of the French tradition, saw it as a brilliant disturbance.

The real pointer to the future of French opera was Auber's *La Muette de Portici*, known to English and Italian audiences as *Masaniello*, taking its name from the heroic peasant, who, avenging his dumb sister for the cruelty and betrayal of a lecherous aristocrat, saves his people from the tyranny of an alien monarchy. *La Muette de Portici* was produced a year before *Guillaume Tell*; Auber, normally a composer of graceful, stylish, light operas, manages in it to cope with big choral masses confronting each other in conflict in the way that French audiences demanded and at the same time to capture the emotions of all those European audiences who were permitted to see so inflammatory a work. It was *La Muette de Portici* which in 1830 precipitated the riot which turned into Belgium's struggle for independence. Auber's music is not a matter of powerful, large-scale structures. The grandeur and the passion were basically scenic rather than musical, and its plot takes a story of personal suffering and makes a national, political work from it; if Auber had been capable of deeply passionate, introspective music, such music would have been out of place, so that the excitement of the work came from its big, fundamentally simple, choral confrontations and the opportunities it gave to designers to create impressive stage pictures. It was closer to the French tradition than *Guillaume Tell*, which determinedly personalises great political issues, making Tell a hero and Gessler flamboyantly a villain while throwing in a pair of lovers whose personal story is caught up in great political events.

This style, rather than any individual work, was the foundation on which Véron built, knowing that the audience he had to win was not musically sophisticated. The English critic Henry F. Chorley visited Paris for the first time in the Véron period and immediately became an ardent francophile. He described the Opéra orchestra in glowing terms; after discussing each section individually—the tone of the wind instruments, he notes, 'partakes somewhat of that thin shrill which seems generic to all wind tones (the human voice included) in France'—but concludes,

> there is a uniform and well-proportioned care in finish, and consent of execution—an understanding with the chorus—an understanding with the singers—a sensitiveness as to every nice gradation of tone, slackened or hastened, never displayed by our most sensitive orchestras.

The Opéra orchestra is 'a machine in perfect order', because of the quality of Habeneck's conducting.[9]

In other words, Véron's economising on numbers did not detract from high standards because he maintained the best men he could find in the essential posts. Habeneck was worth his hire whatever Habeneck cost. The best available singers were kept under contracts which satisfied them (and incidentally seem to have been responsible for a considerable inflation of the fees paid to leading singers all over Europe); the leading dancers were Maria Taglioni and Fanny Elssler. The old prohibition on admission back stage was relaxed so that members of the fashionable audience—optimistic young men and their seniors who ought to have known better—could delight themselves with glimpses, if no more, of the young ladies of the ballet at close quarters. The Opéra balls, previously occasions of great formality, became functions marked by a delicious freedom in manners. The theatre itself was gorgeously redecorated.

Véron did not pander to the tastes of a rich, philistine public; he shared them. Véron's audience did not want formalised or simplified stage settings but looked for a high degree of accurate representation. The stage was darkened and the curtain was lowered (important innovations) while scenes were changed. Gas lighting, introduced in 1822, already allowed the designer a new range of effects including dawns, sunsets and twilights. Under Véron, flat backcloths were replaced by concave representations of the world behind the stage, with scenes continued on them in careful perspective. Edmond Duponchel, an architect and archaeologist who eventually succeeded Véron as Director, and Pierre Ciceri revolutionised the art of stage setting; for the first act of La Muette de Portici they created a Mediterranean beach leading by a flight of huge stone steps to the palace of the Spanish viceroy and with a view of Vesuvius in the distance; in the last act, at the summit of Vesuvius, the dumb girl Fenella casts herself into the crater of the erupting volcano. Guillaume Tell presented splendid Swiss landscapes and the lake across which Tell rowed to safety, but nothing so breathtaking as the eruption of Vesuvius.

The opera libretto, with its insistence on political, social or religious themes, naturally dealt with its materials from the point of view of the new middle class and its monarchy: kings and aristocrats are corrupt and cruel —it was to escape from a detested aristocratic seducer that Fenella chose to die so spectacularly. Eugène Scribe was the most prolific writer in the French theatre of the time. Auber (in La Muette de Portici), Suppé, Rossini (in Le Comte Ory and Guillaume Tell), Halévy (in La Juive), Meyerbeer (in Robert le Diable, Les Huguenots, Le Prophète and L'Étoile du Nord), Donizetti (in Les Martyrs, La Favorite and Don Sebastien) and Verdi (in Les Vêpres Siciliennes) all wrote successful operas to his texts,

[9] L. Chorley: op. cit. pp. 17ff.

as did many others, including the Polish Moniusko, and he found time to write plays and vaudevilles. He had an infallible sense of what was theatrically effective in terms that Véron's audience could accept. Not only did his texts demonstrate the wickedness of the aristocracy and the stalwart, virtuous independence of their opponents; Scribe's libretti also integrated ballet into the dramatic action and built each to a climax which involved a scene of pageantry, huge dramatic choruses and the participation of several principal singers with fine voices. The weakness of Scribe's libretti is that their excitements tended to work to a formula, that his great scenes of procession and pageant were often peripheral to the action and could, with little sense of strain but with some adaptation of costume, be transferred from one work to another. Even the social orientations of his plots created similarities both of character and incident.

For all that, Scribe was the architect of 'Grand Opera', for it was the text of *La Muette de Portici*, *Robert le Diable*, *Les Huguenots* and Halévy's *La Juive* which created the form and demanded the style of treatment which dominated Europe until Wagner's early operas began to replace it. If the dignity, formality and pageantry of Scribe's libretti is as old as French opera itself, his delight in visual effects won the half-educated, as Ortigue called them, to delight in the opera.

Véron ruled the Opéra until 1835, less than the period originally offered to him but long enough to enable him to retire with a fortune of 900,000 francs. When he took over the theatre the average receipts for each performance had been between 1100 and 2000 francs. *Robert le Diable*, in 1832, raised the average evening's takings to between 9000 and 10,000 francs. He maintained this standard of financial success without winning much gratitude from the musically educated. 'The name of Véron will live for ever in musical history,' wrote Heine. 'He has beautified the temple of the Goddess, but he has turned her out of it.'[10] His successors could not rival his financial success; they shared Véron's ignorance of music but not his genius for publicity or his immediate identification with the tastes of the 'common man'. Duponchel, the architect–archaelogist–stage designer who followed him, achieved only one success on the scale of Véron's—that of Meyerbeer's *Les Huguenots* in 1836, and in his days the decline began. He was succeeded by Léon Pillet, whose mistress, the *prima donna* Rosina Stoltz, was, according to Berlioz, the directrice of the Director, and Pillet failed to revive the suffering theatre. Louis-Victor-Nestor Roqueplan shared the directorship with Duponchel from 1847 to 1849, after which Roqueplan reigned alone for five years. Berlioz, whose relationship with successive directors is described in his *Memoirs* in a special tone of amused scorn, dismissed them all with contempt:

[10] Heine: *op. cit.*

> Musically speaking, they are all heathen Chinese who happen to believe
> themselves gifted with unusual taste and discernment, thus embodying
> the fatal combination of unshakable confidence in themselves with
> profound ignorance and barbarism.[11]

Only an angel of forgiveness could have written of the successive directors
without bitterness after the treatment Berlioz received from them, but in a
theatre which had been designed to depend upon smash hits the departure of
Véron began a period in which the smashes became far more notable than
the hits and Berlioz, intermittently, became the chronicler of the decline.

> The Opéra, that large theatre with its large orchestra, with its large
> choruses, its large government subsidy, its numerous staff, its huge sets,
> imitates the sorry bird of the fable on more than one score. Sometimes it
> is to be seen motionless, sleeping on one leg; at others it goes on some
> vague, flustered trek, looking for food in the merest trickles. . . . However
> urgently it strides, it will never reach its journey's end, the more so as
> it does not know itself in which direction it should go.[12]

The Ninth 'Evening' of Berlioz's *Evenings in the Orchestra* is devoted
to a comparison between opera in Paris and opera in London, where
Berlioz had recently endured some startling experiences as conductor of
the company created by the conductor Jullien at Drury Lane Theatre.
Opera in London, dominated by an eccentric with a streak of charlatanism
and a genius for publicity, is simply a joke which, try as he will, Berlioz
cannot take seriously, but the Opéra in Paris is a national disgrace, to be
scarified and scourged with all the scornful rhetoric Berlioz could command.
Cardinal Mazarin, at the birth of French opera, had declared, 'The Opéra
sings, it does not pay', but Berlioz inverted the cardinal's dictum: 'The
Opéra pays, but it does not sing.' It is in love with mediocrity, passionate
in its adoration of the trite, bludgeoning its broken-spirited audience into
submission. He declared:

> The heavy guns were brought out to shake its [the audience's] drowsi-
> ness, it was given chest Cs of every sort, bass drums, organs, military
> bands, antique trumpets, tubas the size of engine funnels, bells, cannon,
> horses, canopied cardinals, gold-spangled emperors, diademed queens,
> funerals, weddings, banquets and everywhere the famous canopy, the
> magnificent canopy, the plumed and feathered canopy, borne like Marl-
> borough by four officers, then jugglers, skaters, choir-boys, censers,
> monstrances, crosses, banners, processions, orgies of priests and naked
> women, the bull Apis, an army of calves, screech owls, bats, Hell's five
> hundred devils, all there for the asking, the final earthquake, the end of
> the world . . . the whole interspersed with a few colourless cavatinas and
> a lot of claquers.[13]

[11] Berlioz: *op. cit.* p. 446.
[12] Berlioz: *Evenings in the Orchestra*, translated by C. R. Fortescue.
London, 1963. p. 118.
[13] *Ibid.* p. 120.

Music had become a pointless decoration for an uncoordinated stage spectacle, and stage spectacle, with no dramatic motivation, had lost its power to excite because it had worn out every spectacular trick of which it was capable. So long as the money flowed in, the directors did not care, but Véron's successors, unable to find more exciting tricks than those already worn threadbare, had nothing on which to pin their faith but expensive star singers. The Meyerbeer style had exhausted itself.

Meyerbeer had arrived in Paris with the score of *Robert le Diable* in 1830. He was forty years old and had for a time been one of Weber's comrades at Darmstadt in the attempt to rejuvenate German music and establish German romantic opera. He had written three German operas in his twenties, then the Rossini craze had swept him off his feet and he had gone to Italy to study the Italian style, which meant to write operas as Rossinian as he could make them, but, alas, without Rossini's stylish and elegant excitement. His six Rossinian operas had some success and the last of them, *Il Crociato in Egitto*, had been played in Paris in 1826. He met Scribe, who gave him the libretto of *Robert le Diable*; in 1830 he returned with the score complete. In spite of some doubts, the Opéra accepted it.

The July Revolution and Meyerbeer's demands for more and more rehearsals—it took five months of preparation to get the opera on to the stage —held up the production until November 1831. In *Robert le Diable*, Scribe had managed to find a place for every ingredient which Véron's audience —'business men, professional men and politicians, all looking for distraction and eager to prove that money could replace nobility of birth' was Véron's own description of them—could enjoy; the synthesis of thrills and sensations provided by the libretto had never been attempted before. The first act offers a gambling scene; then the heroine is tormented, sadistically enough to titillate but not to distress; then comes a ballet of the ghosts of debauched nuns; there follows a scene in which the entire court is put into an enchanted sleep, and the opera ends with a magnificent cathedral wedding and a brilliantly designed transformation scene.

Meyerbeer's music dresses all this brilliantly. According to Ortigue, it is 'a marriage of unusual happiness between Weber and Rossini, Italy and Germany'.[14] Although the only really original feature of *Robert* is its splendid orchestration, his successfully eclectic style enabled him to match everything in a libretto with the appropriate musical expression. His German training helped him to build up big scenes into convincing musical forms, so that in respect of sheer theatricality *Robert le Diable* eclipsed *Guillaume Tell* and *Le Muette de Portici*. Even the orchestration (which so impressed Berlioz that his *Traité de l'instrumentation et d'orchestration modernes*, published in 1843, before Meyerbeer's final operas had been produced, can cite no scores but Meyerbeer's for a large number of

[14] Ortigue: *op. cit.* p. 183.

orchestral effects which later became common practice) is simply an inventive response to the demands of the dramatic moment which such effects accompany. If the music's cleverly calculated effectiveness is close to being meretricious it delighted the public, proving that, like Véron, Meyerbeer was immediately capable of feeling exactly as his audience felt. The total effect of *Robert le Diable* was to give the public what *La Muette de Portici* and *Guillaume Tell* (really a far greater though sometimes flawed work) had been struggling to find for it.

Having found the necessary formula, Meyerbeer's later operas followed a similar plan. *Les Huguenots* begins with an orgy of catholic noblemen; Act Two includes a ballet of bathing beauties; Act Three sets a protestant chorus in direct opposition to a catholic chorus, has a gipsy ballet, a duel and a wedding procession. Act Four provides the solemn blessing of the daggers to be used in the St. Bartholomew's Day massacre and a spectacular love duet. By Act Five, the real drama has ended, but we are still allowed to watch the massacre itself. *Le Prophète* has a skaters' ballet, a coronation scene, an exorcism and a final explosion to settle the fate of most of the characters: in a sense, Meyerbeerian opera is never very far in spirit from the Hollywood screen epic of the great days, but it includes a good deal of spectacular incident written into the libretto because each act must achieve a great climax involving crowds of people and a huge orchestra.

Meyerbeer set out to please his public, and to do so used every trick available for the intensification of atmosphere and every style which could be judged appropriate. He was not, hovever without artistic conscience; he worked slowly, preparing each of his Paris operas with painstaking historical research to establish the right atmosphere, but the limits of his imagination made it possible for him to accept Scribe's formulae, just as his sincere though limited artistry made it possible for him to apply those formulae with complete sincerity. In his own day, his music was deemed irresistible both in power of expression and grandeur of design. Chorley, a devout traditionalist who loved Beethoven's symphonies and the operas of Rossini, Bellini and Donizetti, was overwhelmed by Meyerbeerian opera as soon as he encountered it, but he did not pretend to overlook its weaknesses. He wrote:

> I can content myself with studying, for their own intrinsic dramatic force or melodic sweetness, the *Fidelio*, or the *Euryanthe* of Weber, even when cut down to the meagre shadow of a pianoforte arrangement; but I must see Meyerbeer's operas as well as hear them, and at the Académie Royale. . . . There are only about three separate items—Isabelle's two cavatinas in *Robert* and the couplets of the Page in *Les Huguenots*, which are effective in a concert room.[15]

[15] Chorley: *op. cit.* Vol. I. p. 45.

Manner, he explains, is 'all predominant'; musical substance takes second place.

The Italian composers who accepted commissions from the Opéra—all those who had won a great reputation at home and whose works had begun to travel—were expected to compose a grand opera on Meyerbeerian lines and scale. Donizetti was at work on *Polliuto*, for the San Carlo Opera, when Duponchel asked him for two new operas. Donizetti asked for a libretto by Scribe but rejected the first that he was offered in terms which sound like a total rejection of the principles of grand opera. 'I want a characteristic drama with two or three interesting and moving situations that will be outside the ordinary [things] done a thousand times in Italy',[16] but not suggesting any interest in the scenes of spectacular pageantry and disaster which were essential in Duponchel's theatre. *Polliuto*, for which Corneille's drama *Polyeucte* had been Italianised by the librettist Salvatore Cammarano, telling the story of a Christian martyr, might offend the authorities in Naples and could, perhaps, in that case be adapted to the needs of Paris. As he feared, it did not suit Neapolitan restrictions and was therefore transformed into *Les Martyrs* and given the full Parisian treatment; its choreography was designed by Corati, and six designers worked on the sets, the second of which was based on a painting by Delacroix of a great square in Mytilene. *Les Martyrs*, produced in 1840, was followed in the same year by *La Favorite*, a conversion into grand opera of an unproduced work *L'Ange de Nisida*; to reach the stage of the Opéra, it jettisoned a character and divided its first act into two so that it could reach the four acts which were the smallest acceptable size for grand opera. Its ballet employed both Carlotta Grisi and Petipa in a *pas de deux*.

Donizetti seems to have coped with professional aplomb in the task of adapting his works and style for the Opéra. Verdi, in 1854, found it difficult to assume a French accent and objected to Scribe's libretto for *Les Vêpres Siciliennes* as a travesty of history, its inaccuracies dishonouring to Italy.[17] At the end of a year's struggle with an unsympathetic libretto, the style of grand opera which he felt to be undramatic, and the musical standards of the Opéra, which disappointed him, he tried unsuccessfully to have his contract cancelled. For all that, *Les Vêpres Siciliennes* was a great success, achieving, according to one critic, French operatic form without losing Italian ardour. Each act has its grand spectacular scene and the work ends with the Italian massacre of their French overlords signalled by the ringing of the bell for Vespers. The complete work lasts six hours, but they are six hours of middle-period Verdi, authoritative in their energy, melodic power and superb vitality. Translated into Italian and reshaped to Verdi's requirements, the work scored a success in Italy.

[16] Quoted in H. Weinstock, *Donizetti*. London, 1964. p. 136.
[17] Geoffrey Toye: *Giuseppe Verdi*. London, 1931. p. 93.

In the twelve years between *Les Vêpres Siciliennes* and *Don Carlos*, the death of Scribe had made room for librettists who, if less infallible than Scribe in their presentation of theatrical high points, were disposed to use their materials more freely and with less regard for a basic formula. The Italian revision of *Don Carlos*, however, is tauter and swifter than the original French form of the opera; in both versions, Verdi's instinctive command of dramatic reality was at war with the preconceptions of grand opera as dramatic pageant, and in each Verdi won his victory though at some cost to the incidentals of his work. By the time that Verdi was called to Paris, the Meyerbeerian form was international; before 1840 Chorley had found that the audience in the Leipzig Theatre—and Leipzig is, in one sense, the centre of the German musical tradition—was 'as devoted to French opera as the other towns I visited', though Chorley remained convinced that only the Paris Opéra could cope with the vast scenic, choral and orchestral demands of Meyerbeer's French works. Chorley's account of the small-scale production of *Les Huguenots* in Leipzig[18] must have compared very favourably with the performance of *Robert le Diable* in Würzburg in 1833, when the young Richard Wagner, in his first post as chorus repetiteur of the Würzburg Theatre, drilled a chorus of fifteen singers through Meyerbeer's gigantic score.

In one form or another, often shorn of the visual excitements which French audiences found indispensable to a production, grand opera became the only effective alternative to the *bel canto* opera of Bellini, Donizetti and early Verdi. The German opera of the 1830s and 1840s was so essentially German in outlook, attitude and atmosphere that, after Weber, there was nothing to win international popularity until, in the 1850s, the early works of Wagner began to win acceptance. As Heine had clearly seen, grand opera in general, its Meyerbeerian form in particular, was essentially 'contemporary', its social preoccupations and its subject matter reflecting, though often in strange disguises, the preoccupations of the nineteenth century, together with a certain vulgarity of style endemic in the period itself but expressed at its most highly developed in Paris after the 1830 Revolution. To put the point in its simplest terms, nothing by Rossini, and not even the ardour, vehemence, vitality and beauty of Weber's operas, instigated a revolution; it was the musically light-weight *Le Muette de Portici* which helped Belgium to win independence from Holland, and it did so because it dressed up the preconceptions and the social ideals of the nineteenth century in attractive historical clothes.

At the same time, there are few masterpieces of nineteenth-century opera across which the shadow of Meyerbeer does not fall. Berlioz's Troy is destroyed to music infinitely more subtle and indisputably more original than anything by Meyerbeer, but the idea, like that of the ballet of the Car-

[18] Above, p. 42.

thaginians celebrating the glorious reign of Dido, is a Meyerbeerian conception, and there is a sense in which *Aïda,* and not *Les Huguenots,* is the greatest Meyerbeerian opera. Meyerbeer did not consciously aim at a *Gesamtkunstwerk,* a Wagnerian union of all the arts through music, but his operas are the unconscious move of a clever, clear-minded composer towards a future that he could not foresee through mere intelligence.

Wagner, whom Meyerbeer tried ineffectually to help, in 1855 wrote *Opera and Drama* to work out his own finished, personal stylistic aims. He attacked Meyerbeer as an opportunist composer who had no aims beyond exploiting his audience, but he could not dismiss his apparently unprincipled predecessor. 'Only the most perfect works of art,' he wrote, 'are worthy to be set beside the love duet in *Les Huguenots',* and at the end of his life, when Meyerbeer's failure to help him had grown in Wagner's mind to a deliberate attempt to hold him back, and Meyerbeer's Jewish birth had put him beyond the Wagnerian pale, Wagner still shamefacedly admitted the power of the fourth act of *Les Huguenots;* most of Wagner's set pieces, from the conception of the grand operatic *Rienzi* to the Grail scenes of *Parsifal,* owe a great debt to Meyerbeer. The style which was developed in Paris as a means painlessly to hold the attention of the relatively unmusical was the last important stage on the road to Wagnerian music drama.

Commercial managements, however, faced the future only by accident. They existed to keep theatres solvent and therefore crowded. As they did so, they accidentally replaced royal control with a complex system of internal politics based on the dynamic stresses, attractions and repulsions of a number of powerful, possibly indispensable, subordinates. A musical director, a stage designer, a choreographer, *prime ballerine* and, above all, star singers with great popularity and natural gifts, were the powers whom every director had to placate: the singers often exercised an authority out of all proportion to their musical understanding and were able to exert direct control over everything a company did. A composer's success in those opera houses where great reputations were made depended on the skill with which he could manoeuvre these various, antagonistic powers into working in his favour; the mere quality of a score was rarely enough to decide its future; the support of a powerful coalition of the theatrical powers counted more than quality in the composer's search for success. It was natural that the nineteenth-century opera house should become known as a centre of intrigue, conspiracy and double-dealing.

The story of the failure of Berlioz's *Benvenuto Cellini* and its apparently deliberate sabotage by the Paris Opéra after the work had been accepted is perhaps the best known of the many stories of skulduggery which surround the opera, and Berlioz's subsequent dealings with the Opéra's successive directorates reinforces its effect. Duponchel accepted Berlioz's opera simply because Berlioz was the critic of an influential newspaper, the *Journal des*

Débats, and a close friend of its proprietors, Armand and Édouard Bertin. Apart from Berlioz's own uncompromising criticism, no director could afford to have an influential newspaper among his enemies, so *Benvenuto* was to be produced and to fail, so that the Bertins and Berlioz would be convinced of Duponchel's right-mindedness. When rehearsals started, Habeneck, fine conductor though he was, could not catch the lightness and élan of the 'Roman Carnival' scene, but, according to Berlioz, the music itself won over the orchestra when he had taken the players through it. By this time, however, it was clear that Duponchel wanted the work to fail and professed to find the orchestra's change of front simply comical. When the chorus discovered that the Carnival scene gave ample opportunity for horse-play with the dancers, Duponchel was never in the theatre to enforce discipline, and Berlioz, merely the composer with no authority over the production, had no right to do so himself; he was forbidden, like every other composer, to take an active part in the rehearsal of his work. Berlioz knew, of course, that the rehearsal time allotted to *Benvenuto* was insufficient for a really polished performance.

None of the impediments, however, would have long stood in Berlioz's way had he taken the trouble to ingratiate himself with a director painfully aware of the rough side of Berlioz's tongue and the point of his pen. At the first performance some of the audience professed to find the line 'In the early morning, roosters crowed' too unpoetic and banal to be heard without laughter, and that was the end. *Benvenuto* was murdered after three performances; after a riotous first night there was no reason why the director should keep it on the stage until it made friends among the audience, although most of the critics wrote favourably of it. Berlioz, realising this, withdrew his opera.

The débâcle of *La Nonne Sanglante*, a Scribe libretto handed over to Berlioz in 1847 by the new directorate of Duponchel and Roqueplan, shows how powerless a great composer could be made by a management determined to control him. Berlioz had used his influence, and that of the Bertin brothers, to establish the new directorship, which in gratitude offered not only Scribe's libretto but also the assistant conductorship. But the statutes of the Opéra forbade the performace of works by members of its staff, so that the libretto was withdrawn from Berlioz and handed over to Gounod; then they manoeuvred Berlioz into refusing the assistant conductorship; they circulated the story that he had demanded the musical directorship of the theatre and attempted to oust its exciting musical director, actually a close friend on whose behalf Berlioz had refused any post more exalted than that of assistant conductor when, at the beginning of their negotiations, Duponchel and Roqueplan had offered it to him. Their final discovery was that the only post available for them to offer to Berlioz was that of chief coach, a post so junior that they knew he could do nothing but reject it. Thus a dangerously inflammatory conductor and composer was kept out of a theatre which sorely needed him.

A commercial manager whose position owes itself to his abilities as a business man cannot be expected to encourage works which lose money. If Duponchel had persisted in keeping *Benvenuto Cellini* in the repertoire, and given audiences a chance to come to terms with its originality, the whole course of Berlioz's future life might have followed a different pattern. But commercial managements exist to see that all possible seats are filled on all possible occasions, and they themselves were subject to a harsher dictatorship than their own. Opera in the nineteenth century existed first for its audience and then for the singers who drew the public. Just as the ballet of the period existed to show the grace, lightness and essential pathos of a *prima ballerina*, the purpose of opera was to give the greatly gifted tenor and soprano a chance to shine and to thrill the audience by doing so; from *Norma* to *Le Prophète*, through all the operas of Donizetti, it was the soprano and tenor—the former with an almost obligatory mad scene—who filled the house, and they had to be pleased. It had been possible for Handel, rehearsing Cuzzoni, to threaten to throw her out of a first-floor window, but Cuzzoni was a great soprano who was paid £2000 for her singing. The aggressive Handel was merely a paid musical director, not responsible for any financial loss if she hurt herself on the pavement or simply, following the age-old, infallible method of the great singer, felt too ill too sing; fortuitous ill-health is the singer's most powerful weapon when circumstances seem adverse. However dearly a director loved an opera, he was forced to love his audience still more dearly, and the audience came to hear a great voice doing something brilliant more often than it came to hear an opera. So long as the singer was preferred to the work, the singer had his way.

The singer's temperament, like that of the virtuoso instrumentalist, was always a fact to be reckoned with because of the nervous intensity of a singer's work and the potentially disastrous effect of nervous strain on a fine voice. A singer was not expected to be calm and untempestuous, for a placid singer suggests that he or she lacks the histrionic attitude to life which wins an audience's devotion.

Benjamin Lumley, the solicitor-manager of Her Majesty's Theatre, arrived in the Haymarket as legal adviser to his predecessor, Laporte, who, learning that his conduct of the opera was likely to be subject to interference by Queen Victoria, suggested the drafting of a courteous letter to justify his management. 'I have been at war all my life with the Semiramides, Anna Bolenas and such queens,' he said, 'but I did not expect to have the honour to oppose a real queen.'[19] 'War' was not a serious exaggeration of the relationship between managers and singers who could always feel ill or plead

[19] Lumley: *op. cit.* p. 8.

a cold to evade obligations which displeased them. Laporte managed the London opera at a time when all real decisions were made by his leading singers, whom Lumley called a 'cabal', because they found themselves able through their popularity to dictate the repertoire and the casting of operas. Lumley's own struggle against their arbitrary rule and usurped authority finally led to the foundation of a second Italian Opera at Covent Garden in 1846; the new company was one in which the real power lay with the singers, who worked through a management appointed to express their intentions.

The power of the singers can be seen in the case of Sir Michael Costa, an Italian who had settled in England and imposed discipline if no high degree of interpretive skill on the opera orchestra. In 1842 he composed an opera, *Alma*, for Her Majesty's, and it won some success; another opera, *Don Carlos*, had failed two years later. In 1846 the Philharmonic Society, belatedly recognising its orchestra's need for a skilled permanent conductor, offered the post to Costa, who accepted it in spite of his heavy commitments at Her Majesty's; Lumley promptly offered him an increase in salary commensurate with the fees he would earn from the Philharmonic Society, but refused Costa's demand that his new contract should include his right to compose an opera and a ballet in alternative years for Her Majesty's. The opera owed Costa a great deal, probably not less than it owed to any of the stars of a golden age of singing, but Lumley accepted his resignation without a qualm when Costa found that his terms were refused; his secession was not in any way comparable to the catastrophe which followed the resignation of any leading singer whose tyranny led Lumley to desperate measures. Almost inevitably, Lumley's sixteen years in control of the opera at Her Majesty's, where he had brought all Europe's leading singers and established Verdi as a popular composer while maintaining all the old favourites of the repertoire, ended with the manager heavily in debt.

The composer accepted and endured the power of the star singer. Rossini was musical director of the Théâtre Italien in Paris when, in 1832, the manager, Severini, decided to stand up to the demands of the legendary Malibran. The *diva*, convinced that her departure would empty the theatre, offered to cancel her contract, convinced that her offer would not be accepted. To her surprise, she was replaced by the young Julia Grisi, new to France and not yet adored. 'Monsieur,' said Rossini to Severini, 'you have just thrown away 100,000 francs a year.' He knew that he was the most admired and successful composer of the day, but he also knew that any popular singer had powers that he would be a fool to attempt to resist.

Berlioz follows the absurdity of singer worship to its logical conclusion. The tenor Duprez, at the height of his fame, was paid 100,000 francs a year. Berlioz elucidates:

this means that he sings perhaps seven times a month, which means that he appears in eighty-four performances a year, and earns something like 1,100 an evening. Now, supposing his role is made up of eleven hundred notes or syllables, this represents one franc a syllable. Thus, in *William Tell*.

'My' (one franc) 'presence' (two francs) 'perhaps will seem to you an outrage' (nine francs).

'Matilda,' (three francs) 'my indiscreet steps' (five francs) 'have boldly dared to make my way into your presence!' (thirteen francs).

Total, thirty-four francs. Your words are golden, my Lord!

Given a wretched *prima donna* whose miserable pittance is only 40,000 francs, Mathilda's reply naturally comes cheaper (in commercial parlance), each one of her syllables only reaching the eight sous price bracket.[20]

In the *Journal de Débats*, where this financial analysis originally appeared, Berlioz contrasted the rewards of the singer with those of the composer who has given the singer a reasonably attractive role:

> At the time of Louis XIV, who created the Académie Royale, the principal artists had a revenue of 4,000 francs, the author's share, for a grand composition, was 100 francs. At present, this same share, for the first forty representations, has amounted to 250 francs; and if it had kept pace with the monstrous increase of which we have had a specimen in the salary of 100,000 francs recently received by Duprez (for instance), it should have reached 2,500 francs.[21]

Commercial opera was, in the last resort, singers' opera; the composer remained, in the eyes of both management and public, the necessary functionary who provided singers with the means of delighting their audience. That he could do so most effectively by observing routines and conventions while providing the stars with opportunities for their most effective vocal tricks went entirely against the attitude of the nineteenth-century composer, who had learned that in all other musical fields the primary necessity was to work with the utmost originality and emotional intensity. Opera needed the heroic determination of Wagner to break the moulds which delighted semi-musical audiences attending performances for the sake of fashion, and the effect of Wagner's work was not only to establish new forms for musical drama but to revivify opera in general.

[20] Berlioz: *Evening in the Orchestra*. pp. 81–92.
[21] Berlioz: in the *Journal des Débats*. Translated by Henry Chorley: *op. cit.* Vol. 1. p. 163.

6

Choral Music
in Germany and England

As the nineteenth century transformed the orchestra into a predominantly professional body and as composers gave it duties which amateur instrumentalists found increasingly difficult, building the orchestra as they did so up to a size that except in large cities precluded amateur performance, the hitherto professional choir was transformed into an amateur body. Amateur choirs were linked to professional music-making through their performances of oratorios and liturgical works which needed the participation of an orchestra. While oratorio belonged to the concert hall, the choirs gradually took liturgical music out of church, breaking its links with public worship.

It is possible to link the rise of the German choral societies with the political situation on the Metternichian reaction as well as in the greater social freedom which followed the French Revolution. The Handel revival which spread across Europe in the closing years of the eighteenth century and the Bach revival of the 1830s both influenced the growth of the choral movement, as did 'colossal' works for massed voices and orchestra encouraged by the early music festivals. The researches of such historically minded scholar-connoisseurs as Baron van Swieten, patron of Haydn and Mozart, and of Raphael Kiesewetter, civil servant and amateur musician in Vienna, who after 1817 helped to found the Vienna Conservatoire and whose private concerts explored a wide range of choral music from Lassus and Palestrina to Bach's *Magnificat*.

The earliest of the great German choral societies was the Berlin *Singakademie*, which grew from the singing class held in Berlin by Carl Friedrich Fasch from 1787 onwards; the class, originally of wealthy bourgeois ladies, was one of Fasch's ways of augmenting the exiguous salary he received as a Berlin court musician when he found that, after the Seven Years War, it had lost a great deal of its value. In 1791 Fasch's class began to meet in the garden of an official in the Prussian War Ministry and to accept men into its membership; four months later, in October 1791, it was heard in public for the first time, singing in the Marienkirche. In 1796, when Beethoven visited Fasch in Berlin, its original membership of twenty-seven had expanded to ninety; when Fasch died in 1800 it had grown to a hundred and forty-seven singers.

Carl Friedrich Zelter, friend of Goethe and of the Mendelssohn family, succeeded Fasch. Like his predecessor, Zelter had a more than scholarly interest in the music of the past; Fasch had composed a great deal of music in the style of the early baroque composers, while it was Zelter who fired Felix Mendelssohn's enthusiasm for the choral works of Bach and was instrumental in initiating the 1829 revival of the *St. Matthew Passion*, which Mendelssohn conducted. He broadened the base of his work in Berlin by forming the *Liedertafel*, a men's singing club which met once a month for supper and the singing of its members' compositions. As the repertoire of the *Singakademie* expanded beyond unaccompanied choral works to embrace oratorios, Zelter organised an orchestra to take part in its performances. When he died, in 1832, the *Singakademie* had three hundred and fifty-nine members.

A similar organisation was created in Erlangen in 1806, and in 1807 J. F. Reichardt formed a choir in Weimar—he based it on the family of friends with whom he stayed in the city—to sing Handel's *Messiah*, and the choir remained in being after this inaugural performance. *A Singanstalt* came into being in Dresden. A Leipzig *Singakademie* was formed in 1802, and another in 1805; in 1817 the two began to work together, creating a choir of about a hundred and fifty voices. In Cassel the *Baldweinische Singinstitut* began operations as a choral society for 'young people of good family'; it took its name from its founder, a Cassel cantor active in the concert life as well as the church music of the city. A choral society was formed in Mannheim for the *Singende höhere Töchter* and the *Musikalische Bürgersöhne* of the citizens. A *Singakademie* founded among the students of Halle University numbered three hundred and seventy-one members by 1829. A Lübeck choral society formed to take part in oratorio performances was founded in 1816, and in Frankfurt the *Cecilienverein* was founded in 1818 and soon began to co-operate in oratorio performances with the already established orchestra of the Museum Concert Society. In 1823, when he had been *Kapellmeister* in Cassel for only a year, Spohr founded a *Cecilienverein* 'after the example of the majority of the larger towns in Germany, to strive towards the same noble aim, to awaken and cultivate a pure and correct taste for music of an exalted and earnest character'.[1] Similar amateur choral societies came a little later in Austria; the *Singschule* of the *Musikverein* in Carinthia began operations in 1849, and the *Singverein* of the *Gesellschaft für Musikfreunde* in Vienna was founded in 1858. The Vienna *Singakademie* was founded in 1863; until these organisations began their work, choral music in the Austrian cities was the duty of the theatre choruses.

The work of Hans Georg Nägeli in Switzerland was contemporaneous with that of Fasch and Zelter in Berlin. Nägeli, born in 1773, was a colleague and disciple of the educationalist and social reformer Pestalozzi, and his work ran parallel to that of Fasch and Zelter in a different social con-

[1] Spohr: *op. cit.* Vol. 2. p. 147.

text and with precise social aims as important to him as its musical purposes. Nägeli's organisation of singing classes began in the schools of Switzerland because singing together, he believed, should produce a sense of social unity and purpose while awakening the taste for good music and a sense of spiritual values. Among adults, it seemed to Nägeli, a problem of leisure was beginning to make itself felt; what was the adult to do with leisure hours his limited education could not immediately employ? How could that leisure be used both to enrich a working man's life, add to his enjoyment and be socially advantageous?

In a country where there was no organised musical life outside a handful of large towns—Zürich, Basel and Berne in particular—and where the musical traditions of the people consisted of folk songs and the psalm tunes permitted in Calvinist worship, and where there were three native languages and a variety of local traditions, Nägeli wished to use choral music as a means of social enjoyment sugaring the pill of spiritual uplift and social improvement. In 1805 he formed the Zürich *Singinstitut*, which included a mixed choir and a children's choir, and its public performances were designed to show what could be done by the sort of organisation he had created as a musical and social amenity for the general public.

Since 1792 Nägeli had been publishing music as a necessary educational service (it was he who roused Beethoven's fury by adding four bars to the first movement of Beethoven's Piano Sonata *op.* 31 No. 1) and composing keyboard pieces and songs for use in schools. His primary interest in his *Singinstitut* was pedagogical, and what he learned from the *Singinstitut* became the foundation of his *Gesangbildunglehrer*, the textbook of the choral societies formed all over Switzerland and affiliated to the *Singinstitut* in Zürich; from the individual choral societies came the *Allgemeine Schweizersiche Musikgesellschaft* with its headquarters in Lucerne. From Nägeli's work developed a number of music festivals which were held by large choirs founded to copy his original *Singinstitut*, assembling singers from all over their locality. Oratorio performances on a choral scale almost as massive as that of the Handel Festivals in London (though Haydn's *The Creation* was the favourite work of the Swiss choirs) were heard in Zürich, Winterthur, Aaraus, Schaffhausen and St. Gallen. Between 1808 and 1867 the *Musikgesellschaft* was responsible for festivals not only in the large cities, Zürich, Basel, Berne and Lucerne, but in any centre where a large number of members and member choirs could gather.

Nägeli's work, like the whole of the Pestalozzi movement, coincided with and expressed the spirit of the new political organisation of Switzerland which gave the state its modern structure. These changes were hotly debated and the creation of a democratic state, paradoxically, divided a country which had before seemed reasonably united in spite of differences of language, religion and culture. Nägeli's belief in the unifying influence of music was prompted by political conditions of the sort which require social rather than political cure, and the growth of the Swiss festival movement had precisely the social influence for which he had designed it.

Music festivals in Germany, too, encouraged the growth of choralism, though they had no clearly stated aims outside the desire to make music. In 1810 Spohr was invited to direct the first festival at Frankenhausen; the twenty-six-year-old conductor–violinist–composer was, apparently, asked to take charge because of his position as leader of the court orchestra at Gotha nearby. Spohr's efficiency and style had impressed the Frankenhausen cantor, Bischoff, who in 1804 had raised a choir of eighty to sing *The Creation* with the court orchestra from Gotha; the festival was simply designed to involve a still larger number of participants in two great musical events. The festival choir which Bischoff collected came from Weimar, Rudolstadt, Gotha and Erfurt as well as from Frankenhausen and several other nearby towns. The orchestra, with twenty players from Spohr's orchestra in Gotha as its foundation, numbered one hundred and six. A hundred singers were present at the rehearsal of *The Creation*; ninety-nine of them took part in the actual performance on the second day of the festival. An orchestral concert included an overture by Spohr and his Clarinet Concerto in E flat, played by his friend Hermstedt, with Beethoven's Fifth Symphony as its climax.[2]

In 1814 the French military governor of Erfurt ordered a festival to celebrate the birthday of Napoleon and commissioned Spohr's oratorio *The Last Judgement* as its main feature; Spohr, as the festival's musical director, made his own orchestra the nucleus of a large festival orchestra and co-opted Bischoff to create a properly numerous choir. The fact that an oratorio on a very large scale was to be the main feature of the festival itself presupposed the availability of large amateur choirs.

Spohr was in Vienna during the second Frankenhausen festival; the third, in 1815, celebrated the defeat of Napoleon with his cantata *Das befreite Deutschland* and Gottfried Weber's *Te Deum*. In 1818 Spohr was involved in the first Lower Rhine Festival; most of his soloists were musicians who had taken part in his two Frankenhausen festivals, with a large orchestra and a huge choir recruited throughout the festival area. In 1820 he directed a festival at Quedlinburg, where the big choral work was *The Last Judgement* by J. C. Friedrich Schneider, himself in later years director of Festivals at Magdeburg, Nuremberg, Strasbourg, Halle, Wittenberg, Halberstadt, Dessau, Köthen, Koblenz, Hamburg, Zerbst, Meissen and Lübeck. Such festivals were organised for the people of the area in the centre of which they took place and depended upon the performance of one or more big choral works; many festivals were isolated events, not repeated year after year, but they were all rooted in the activities of choral societies

---

[2] Spohr: *op. cit.* pp. 140ff.

which could band together for spectacular events. In 1826 the indispensable Spohr was in Düsseldorf for the year's Lower Rhine Festival, and though none of his later oratorios was written as a German festival commission, he continued to be involved in the festival movement until 1848, when he was in his middle sixties; festivals of Nordhausen, Hesse, Brunswick, Daderborn, Cassel itself and Lucerne all claimed his attention at one time or another.

Mendelssohn, a greater composer, as efficient, dedicated and charming as Spohr, became no less indispensable to the major German festivals and an enthusiastic supporter of all their activities. In Frankfurt, in 1832, he wrote to Zelter in Berlin about the excellence of the St. Cecilia Society, which, he said:

> would alone make it worth while to be in Frankfurt. The singers work with such enthusiasm and precision that it is a sheer delight to listen to them. It meets once a week and has two hundred members. Besides that Schelble [the choirmaster] has a small group of about thirty voices who meet at his place every Friday and he works with them at the piano; little by little they prepare his favourite compositions which he dare not give directly to his big chorus. I have heard a great deal of lovely music there, several of Bach's 'Sunday Services', his *Magnificat* and the great Mass. Just as in your own Academy, the female singers are always the more eager; the males sometimes leave something to be desired; their heads are full of their business affairs. . . . In the big society, I heard, among other music, the motet [*sic*] *Gottes Zeit ist die allerbeste Zeit,* which we used to sing at your Friday nights.[3]

Both the choirs and the proliferating festivals were self-propagating. A combination of local patriotism, local pride and the determination to keep up with whatever musical Joneses had recently distinguished themselves, ensured that they spread. Apart from their bringing new audiences into contact with orchestral as well as with choral music, they were directly educational, creating in their members and would-be members not only the ambition to join effectively in exciting performances of great music but also the incentive to undergo the training their ambition demanded.

Possibly too the appeal of choral music in German-speaking, Metternichian Europe was that it allowed each individual member, man or woman, to become involved in the thoroughly democratic processes that were denied to him in political life. In the choral societies all decisions, democratically arrived at, were the results of general votes of all the members; in a sense this gave the choral societies political implications unwelcome to the authorities. The fact that large and efficient organisations could function successfully by democratic methods suggested a criticism of the authoritarianism by which Central European states were controlled. At the same time, the regular meet-

---

[3] Mendelssohn: *Letters*, edited by G. Selden-Goth. Elek, London, 1947. Letter of 15 February 1832. p. 189.

ings of large bodies of men and women could very easily, in the eyes of governments and police, cloak other and less innocuous purposes, so that the German and Austrian choral societies were hemmed in by police regulations.

In 1816, at a time when individual decisions were completely circumscribed by political control, Zelter published the principles and rules of the Berlin *Singakademie* in a pamphlet, *Grundriss der Verfassung der Sing-Akademie zu Berlin*. Whoever wished to join the Society had to apply to its Director and give an audition. Then he would be subject to election by the existing members of the Society. The business administration was in the hands of three members, one of whom should be Treasurer, and all three were elected by their colleagues, so that the Society offered an opportunity to members to exercise possibly unused talents in carrying out not the wishes of a Director (though he himself was elected by the members from whatever professionally qualified choral conductors were available) but the decisions of their fellow members.[4]

The Lübeck *Gesangverein* formally organised itself in 1819. It began its public career in November 1820 with a performance of the vocal sections of Johann A. P. Schulz's incidental music to Racine's *Athaliah* and a Mass by Haydn. The latter work was repeated a month later, sharing the programme with Mozart's *Requiem*. The *Gesangverein*'s original statutes apparently dealt only with the timing of rehearsals and concerts, but later statutes, drawn up in 1832 under the influence of a new Director, Gottfried Meyer, decided that eight members—four women and four men—were to be elected as a committee of management; they examined the new statutes and offered them for the approval of all the members. Matters of finance were to be decided by a general vote.[5]

The Carinthian *Musikverein*, with its headquarters in Klagenfurt, was a much larger organisation, responsible for orchestral and chamber concerts as well as the organisation and staffing of a conservatoire. Its choir was an outlet for many of the would-be members who were not instrumentalists. Its statutes, drawn up in 1827, show the attractively democratic principles on which such societies worked. The entire *Musikverein* was to be controlled by an elected president and a committee of five, all of whom were to hold office for three years and could then, if they wished, offer themselves for re-election. The various officials, too, held their posts as the results of election, and new members were elected to the Society. The process of voting was carried out with exaggerated punctiliousness; voting papers, correctly filled in and endorsed by the member's signature, were kept under

---

[4] Werner Bollert (editor): *Singakademie zu Berlin*. Berlin, 1966. pp. 61ff.

[5] Johann Hennings and Wilhelm Stahl: *Musikgesichte Lübecks*. Cassel, 1951. *Band* 1 (*Weltliche Musik*). pp. 211ff.

lock and key (in a case with two locks and two key-holders) until the time had come for the count. Incorrectly used voting papers were not counted, and votes received after the closing date were not scrutinised but added to the majority.[6] In so far as the Carinthian *Musikverein* and the other societies prospered during the Metternichian repression, they provided a valuable lesson in practical democracy.

Possibly the democratic methods adopted by amateur choirs and musical organisations in general seemed all the more deplorable to the rulers because they drew their membership largely from the educated middle classes who were, perhaps subconsciously, troubled by the problem of leisure which Nägeli had set out to solve for his poorer fellow countrymen. The register of Fasch's original singing class in Berlin survives, and, writes Friedrich Herzefeld:

> The names are less interesting than the titles that accompany them. We find a Mrs. Medical Councillor, a Mrs. Legation Councillor, a widowed Mrs. Court Councillor, a Mrs. City Councillor, a Mrs. Ministry of Justice Councillor, a Mrs. Privy Councillor, a Mrs. Court of Appeal Councillor, a Mrs. Education Councillor, a Mrs. Privy Council Secretary, a Mrs. Doctor and a Mrs. Rector's Widow as well as a member who is simply described as 'Madam'.[7]

The German Karl Halle, in the throes of his transformation into the English Charles Hallé, settled in Manchester in 1848, and in 1850, eight years before the foundation of the orchestra for which he is remembered with veneration, he had found

> So many amateurs with fair voices and an ear for music that I was able to found the 'St. Cecilia Society', in imitation of the German *Gesangverein*, which dwelt in my memories since the days of my childhood. It consisted of ladies and gentlemen of the best society, at first about fifty in number.[8]

Hallé's St. Cecilia Society grew, he writes, from year to year and after 1858 was an adjunct to the performances of his orchestra.

The Hallé Orchestra, however, rooted itself in a city where music was traditionally lively. Hallé had established himself in Manchester as a teacher and recitalist and had then taken over the conductorship of the semi-professional orchestra of the Gentlemen's Concerts there; the Gentlemen's Concerts was an organisation which could trace its history, perhaps a little deviously, to the earlier Music Club of the eighteenth century.

---

[6] Gotbert Moro and Ambros Wilhelmer: *Zur Musikgesichte Kärntens*. Klagenfurt, 1956. pp. 52ff.

[7] Friedrich Herzefeld: *Sing-Akademischer Alltag*, in Bollert: *op. cit.* p. 11.

[8] C. E. and Marie Hallé: *The Life and Letters of Sir Charles Hallé*. London, 1896. p. 116.

Music in Liverpool, on the other hand, grew almost entirely out of the impetus provided by amateur choral societies. Liverpool was both large enough and prosperous enough to be visited by famous singers and the great touring instrumentalists; intermittently it enjoyed performances of opera. Its home-grown music, however, was choral, and orchestral work existed to support choirs in their performances of oratorio. Music festivals held in 1784 and 1790 were concerned with choral music, and from them grew the Apollo Glee Club, which continued to meet for close on a century. The later Festivals of 1830 and 1833 rested primarily on the work of two societies, the Liverpool Musical Society, a semi-professional orchestra, and the Cecilian Society, a choir, both active from the early 1800s and both directed by local organists, meeting in Liverpool churches. For the 1836 Festival, at which Mendelssohn's *St. Paul* was heard for the first time in England, the Festival Choral Society was founded. In 1831, when it was heard in public for the first time, singing Handel's *Jephtha*, it numbered twenty-six sopranos, fifteen (male) altos, twenty-three tenors and thirty-five basses. The necessity for an orchestra to join in its activities meant the expansion of the Music Society's orchestra with whatever musicians were available, many of them normally active in orchestrally-minded Manchester. The orchestra existed to provide the necessary accompaniment to choral music.

While choral music in London depended on the professional choirs of the theatres and the opera (so that the finale of Beethoven's Ninth Symphony had to be translated into Italian for the work's first performance in England in 1825) and it was not until 1881, in a performance of Berlioz's *Romeo and Juliet*, that an amateur choir was heard in a concert of the Royal Philharmonic Society, the music of massed voices had been an English passion at least since the later eighteenth century and the early Handel Festivals. Haydn in the 1790s and Berlioz in the 1840s had been overwhelmed by the effect of several thousand children's voices singing in unison in St. Paul's Cathedral simply because the musical effect was one with which they were entirely unfamiliar. Outside London, Manchester and Liverpool, the development of the amateur choirs in England was a matter of carefully designed 'social engineering'. Hallé's middle-class singers and the Church of England choralists of Liverpool were not typical of the large choral societies of the industrial towns which provided probably the vast majority of the English people with their only real contact with music.

To say that English choral music in the nineteenth century was largely the result of a union between music and nonconformity as they acted together on a depressed and degraded working class is hardly an exaggeration. John Wesley, the founder of Methodism, was a member of an extremely musical family which in the next two generations was to produce two of the finest English composers of their day, his nephew Samuel and Samuel's son,

Samuel Sebastian. But whatever interest John Wesley felt in music was controlled by his vocation; he wanted hymns which the simplest and most illiterate people could remember and sing to simple, emotional or rousing tunes 'with the spirit and understanding'. Wherever Methodist congregations met, they sang lively or moving tunes while the Church of England, outside the cathedrals, provided little music except settings of the metrical psalms.

Methodists taught the children of their congregations to sing, and Wesley demanded that care be taken in their training, but anthems and any elaborate music were forbidden; the whole congregation was to sing and not to sit silently while others sang to it. Methodism, and nonconformity in general, were urban, industrial movements wherever there was a working class alienated by its conditions and its lack of either education or any place in the traditional society of the past from the Anglican religious tradition. Methodism conquered the new industrial working class in new towns, or in the old towns which industry swelled to bursting point. It was a relief from squalor and deprivation, and it is at least arguable that music attracted people to Methodism as much as Methodism attracted people to music. Music unites; singing together, Wesley knew, individual men and women become a community, a congregation. There was no Methodist activity, from vast open-air services to the small, intimate 'Class Meetings' for instruction and discussion, which did not demand hymn singing. In the minds of a vast number of English people, Methodism created a feeling that music, to be worth while, was inextricably tied to worship.

It was from Methodism, too, that the appetite for education developed. In the early nineteenth century the new working class came to be convinced that the way out of its misery was through education. By learning, the workers could win promotion, and from promotion better positions, better wages, better housing and a hope for the future. Those who were not totally dehumanised by their lot developed an enthusiasm for education which led to the foundation of a variety of institutions to provide the opportunities for 'Self Help' that they needed. In 1823 the London Mechanics' Institution opened to offer specialised practical knowledge to workers whose aim was to make themselves more useful to their employers and thus reach a position where they could earn higher wages. The example of London was rapidly followed in other towns and cities throughout industrial England. But the specialised, practical training which had been the first aim of the Mechanics' Institutes proved to be less than their members needed; classes in Latin and the classics, and in both music and mathematics, were rapidly formed, and music became a popular subject. Naturally, more often than not the music studied was vocal music.

The autobiography of Thomas Cooper, a Leicester cobbler, provides an example of the musical enthusiasm awakened by the Mechanics' Institutes.

Cooper was a Methodist and a Chartist, self-educated to the point at which he became a newspaper reporter. In 1834, while he was still in his twenties, he went to Lincoln to teach Latin in the Mechanics' Institure there; he had a gift for languages and rapidly found himself teaching French as well. He had not long been involved in his educational work when what he called 'a new attraction' demanded his attention:

> A few young men wished to form a choral society and asked me to allow them the use of my schoolroom for rehearsals. I consented readily, and became a member of the new society, taking my stand, weekly, as a tenor singer in the choruses. My heart and brains were soon on fire with the worship of Handel's grandeur, and with the love of his sweetness and tenderness. They made me their secretary; and my head went to work to make the music of the choral society worth hearing in old cathedralled Lincoln.[9]

Cooper became the moving spirit and the recruiting officer of the Society. He made the best sight-reader in the city, who was also the 'most experienced in the music of Handel', its conductor; found an alto and a bass capable of leading their sections of the choir and of singing solos; enlisted the cathedral organist as a viola player, and found the best cellist in Lincoln to lead the cellos. In the first year of the Society he raised £200 for its support and obtained permission for its performances in a church in the centre of the city. The Society sang *Messiah, Judas Maccabeus, Israel in Egypt, Solomon,* The Dettingen *Te Deum,* Haydn's *The Creation* and music by Mozart and Beethoven. Later, the Society bought drums, a slide trumpet and the nucleus of a library—Arnold's complete edition of the work's of Handel, Mozart's *Requiem, The Creation* and Beethoven's *The Mount of Olives.* There was a committee of performers, but it was content to leave the business of the Society in the hands of the enthusiastic, and better educated Cooper.

Other institutes were equally active. Music classes were available at Institutes in York and Newcastle, amongst many others. The Miles Platting Institute, in one of the most squalid parts of Manchester, founded in 1836, offered a class for instrumental music. The music teacher at the Manchester Mechanics' Institute formed a group of those who attended his class into a glee and psalm singing group. In Bradford a special committee of the music class, meeting with the general committee of the Mechanics' Institute, began to organise the weekly concerts for the working classes in 1845.

It would, no doubt, be cheap irony to suggest that working-class enthusiasm for music was fostered by employers because music was an inexpensive alternative to drunkenness, supported for this reason by nonconformist employers because sober, music-loving employees are more

[9] Thomas Cooper: *The Life of Thomas Cooper,* written by himself. London, 1872. p. 107.

efficient than the drunken and dissolute. Nevertheless, while music became an instrument in the hands of those who saw it as a way of enriching deprived lives, it was also a tool in the hands of 'do-gooders' whose interest was in its social effects and not in the art itself. The result was that some employers began to encourage musical activities among their employees. An American visitor to Robert Owen's community at New Lanark, where children under ten were sent to school instead of to work, noted that children were taught to sing there. Samuel Gregg, at Bollington, in Cheshire, opened a mill in 1832 and began to provide amenities for his workers, among them a singing class which rapidly became popular. From the singing class grew a weekly glee class and a much larger choir which met twice a week to sing sacred music. Before long, Gregg's workpeople had founded a brass band and, with their employer's support, taken up other instruments.[10]

The general educational level of the working-class singers was responsible for the various simplified methods of notation which evolved into the system of Tonic Sol-fa eventually worked out by John Curwen, a nonconformist minister and educationalist, in his book *Singing for Schools and Congregations*, published in 1843 to assist those who were intimidated by conventional musical notation. Parallel with the work of the choral societies, Joseph Mainzer, a German musician who had instituted large-scale singing classes for the poor in Paris, moved to England and continued his work in this country. His example was followed by John Hullah, who originally set out to train singing teachers for the schools but found himself with large, enthusiastic classes of members of the general public. With a choir formed from his London classes, Hullah gave a series of ambitious concerts, four of which, in 1847, were designed as a history of English choral music.

The alliance with nonconformity continued. When the Huddersfield Choral Society was formed in 1836 it refused membership to anyone who attended the secular, politically orientated Owenite 'Halls of Science'. The first of the great London choral societies, the Sacred Harmonic Society, began in 1832. The violinist-critic John Ella noted its origin in his *Musical Sketches*: 'The Sacred Harmonic Society first held its meetings for choral practice and prayer in a dissenting chapel.'[11] The chapel was that in Gate Street, Lincoln's Inn, but after two years the officers of the society secured the use of the smaller of the two halls in the Exeter Hall complex, in the Strand. Exeter Hall was the citadel of Methodism, and its statutes permitted it to be used only for religious purposes or the meetings of charitable societies. Apparently the activities of the Sacred Harmonic Society were religious enough to satisfy the authorities, who soon permitted it to use the

[10] E. D. Mackerness: *A Social History of English Music*. London, 1964. pp. 129–32.

[11] John Ella: *op. cit.* London, 1869. p. 428.

larger hall, which seated 3000 in its auditorium, for a charity performance of *Messiah*. It continued to use Exeter Hall until 1880, its performances of oratorios and of Haydn's *The Seasons* apparently being acceptable to the hall's management. By 1837, the Society's choir and orchestra numbered five hundred, and when Sir Michael Costa became its conductor ten years later it increased its membership to seven hundred. By this time, apparently, the members had began to feel that their first conductor, Joseph Surman, could not realise their musical ambitions.

The Sacred Harmonic Society was an extension to London of the main feature of northern industrial music, the huge amateur choir. Ella, writing in the 1860s, spoke of the change which such bodies had brought to the performance of the great choral works:

> During the early part of my professional employment in the orchestra of the King's Concert of Ancient Music [Ella played the violin in the Ancient Concerts from 1832 to 1848] the principal female choristers were brought from Lancashire. These ladies, who were supposed to have finer voices and a more intimate acquaintance with the *chefs d'œuvre* of the sacred composers than the theatrical choristers in London, were adequately remunerated to remain the whole season in town and sing exclusively in twelve concerts. . . . Choral societies are now increased to such an extent that if it were required to bring together in London a thousand good treble voices and choristers, I do not apprehend there would be the slightest difficulty.[12]

Wagner, during his unhappy tenure of office as conductor of the Philharmonic Society Concerts in 1855, heard several of the Sacred Harmonic Society's concerts and, despite his dislike of London and everything that happened there, could not bring himself totally to condemn the Society's activities; their atmosphere was, to him, strange and not altogether congenial:

> The oratorios given there [in Exeter Hall] nearly every week have, it must be admitted, the advantage of the great confidence to be gained from frequent repetition. Neither should I refuse to recognise the great precision of the chorus of seven hundred voices, which reached quite a respectable standard on a few occasions, particularly in Handel's *Messiah*. It was here that I came to recognise the true spirit of English musical culture, which is bound up with the spirit of English protestantism. This accounts for the fact that an oratorio attracts the public far more than an opera. A further advantage is secured by the feeling among the audience that an evening spent listening to an oratorio may be regarded as a sort of service and is almost as good as going to church.[13]

Among the few critics to show any sympathy to Wagner as a composer

[12] *Ibid.* p. 141.
[13] Richard Wagner: *My Life.* 'Authorised translation', London, 1963. pp. 634-5.

was George Hogarth, music critic of the *Daily News*, of which his son-in-law, Charles Dickens, was editor. Hogarth was Secretary of the Philharmonic Society at the time of Wagner's visit, and it is interesting to see that Wagner's diagnosis of the 'true spirit of English music' is stated very forthrightly, and with entire approval, at the end of Hogarth's *Musical History, Biography and Criticism*. Though he was deeply involved in English music-making, Hogarth's delight in the art seems to be for its ethical values, as he interprets them. He refers less to the musical standards of the opera or of London's concert life than to the process of moral reform through choral singing:

> The cultivation of a taste for music furnishes to the rich a refined and intellectual pursuit, which excludes the indulgence of frivolous and vicious amusements, and to the poor, a *laborem dulce lenimen*, a relaxation from toil, more attractive than the haunts of intemperance. . . . In the densely populated districts of Yorkshire, Lancashire and Derbyshire, music is cultivated among the working classes to an extent unparalleled in any other part of the kingdom. Every town has its choral society, supported by the amateurs of the place and its neighbourhood, where the works of Handel, and the more modern masters, are performed with precision and effect, by a vocal and instrumental orchestra consisting of mechanics and workpeople. . . . Their employers promote and encourage so salutary a recreation by countenancing, and contributing to defray the expenses, of their musical associations; and some provide regular musical instruction for such of their workpeople as show a disposition for it. . . . Wherever the working classes are taught to prefer the pleasures of the intellect, and even of taste, to the gratification of sense, a great and favourable change takes place in their character and manners. . . . Sentiments are awakened in them which makes them love their families and homes; their wages are not squandered in intemperance, and they become happier as well as better.[14]

Hogarth wrote in 1835, before the choral movement had grown to its greatest extent, and if it is difficult to estimate how many of the industrial working class were saved by singing from pauperdom, drink and degradation, the moral fervour behind English music in the nineteenth century is clear from the words of Hogarth, the activities of so many employers and the determination of the English people to associate good music with religion rather than with musical quality. The choral movement, with its insatiable appetite for works to religious words, together with the activities of a number of publishers, most effective of whom was Vincent Novello, who in 1811 made himself publisher in chief to the choral societies by producing the necessary supply of cheap vocal scores that the choirs needed, prove the movement's importance. It gave the English composer, out of touch with most continental developments, a reason for existing. The nineteenth cen-

[14] George Hogarth: *Musical History, Biography and Criticism*. London, 1835. pp 430–1.

tury is littered with the remains of well-meant if dull choral works, of the highest possible ethical and religious intentions, composed at an age when choral music flourished but England looked elsewhere for its operas and concert music.

7

Concerts and Orchestras

The orchestral music of Haydn and Mozart, and the power exerted by
Beethoven's symphonies wherever they were heard (as well as the curiosity
about Beethoven's music created by critics and commentators in places
where concert music was not regularly available) gave the concert a new
prestige equivalent to that of the opera. Cities where concerts had been
established in the eighteenth century found themselves regarded for the
first time as among the centres of musical life. Until Beethoven's contribution to musical expression was understood, listeners in the 1830s and
1840s found nothing in the other works available to them equal in importance to the symphonic world of the dead master for all its apparent obscurity of utterance and technical difficulty. The spread of European concert life was largely the result of the determination of early nineteenth-
century musicians and their audiences to understand Beethoven. The
musical necessity of performances of the concert works of Beethoven,
Haydn and Mozart virtually created the 'standard repertoire'.

Possibly, too, it would not be merely fanciful to regard the orchestra,
expanded by Beethoven and both enlarged and refined by Berlioz, Liszt
and Wagner, eventually transformed by Mahler and Richard Strauss into
a small army of musicians as an essential expression of the personality of
the nineteenth century. While artists in general looked away from the age
of industrialisation, the orchestra reflected the character of the age not so
much in what it did as in what was and still is. The age of great orchestral
forces designed to exploit new, compulsive powers of tone had begun in
the age of the Napoleonic armies, winning an empire not only by their
commander's unprecedented military genius but also by a new conception
of warfare which depended on the precise co-ordination of many disparate
specialist functions. The ensuing age was, increasingly and ever more ubi-
quitously, the age of industrial expansion which, in a sense, applied to peace-
time occupations the same employment of masses individually skilled but
all necessary to the complete achievement of more and more production
of more and more necessary materials. The co-ordination of diverse specialist functions in the orchestra could be regarded, in its manner of work but
not in the purposes for which the work was done, as the perfection of industrial method; the orchestra was a combination of sixty, eighty, ninety or
even more highly skilled workers offering contributions to a task even more

complex and difficult to co-ordinate than the diverse tasks of workers in any industrial process. There was a sense in which the symphony orchestra reflected the character of European industrial civilisation.

The creation of the Philharmonic Society in London in 1813 was, perhaps, natural in a city where the public concert dated back to the late seventeenth century. Regular London concerts with trained professional musicians suffered a prolonged interval after Salomon's third season of concerts had come to an end in 1796, after the glories of the seasons to which he had brought Haydn and killed off the rival organisation, the Professional Concerts which were the true forerunners of the Philharmonic Society. The Professional Concerts had been the creation of a group of professional musicians, most of them—like Clementi, Wilhelm Cramer and Salomon himself—who began to give public concerts after the Bach–Abel concerts had come to an end. The struggle of Salomon against the 'Professionals' during Haydn's first visit to London, each attempting to capture a numerically restricted audience, ended in the collapse of the 'Professionals', and after Salomon's 1796 season no organisation remained to provide regular concerts in London.

In 1813 thirty musicians, including J. B. Cramer, Clementi, J. A. Moralt, Ferdinand Cramer and Salomon, with a number of native musicians, among whom were the composers Attwood, Bishop, Dance, Horsely, Knyvett, Smart, Shield and the younger Samuel Webbe, set out to provide a new concert society. Among them were Charles Neate, who had met Beethoven and for a time became the new Society's intermediary with him, and Vincent Novello, whose determination to publish cheap editions of music for catholic choirs recovered large quantities of otherwise unobtainable music from the renaissance and Tudor periods.

The Philharmonic Society gave its first concert in March 1813, determined from the start to provide London audiences with the best modern music; this meant, before all else, the symphonies and overtures of Beethoven. Symphonies by Haydn and Mozart appeared frequently in the programmes, each of which at first included choral items and chamber music; solo vocal and instrumental pieces were not permitted until 1830, when Beethoven's concertos were allowed to take their place in the repertory. The Philharmonic Society was largely responsible for the introduction of Mendelssohn's music to England and commissioned his C minor Symphony as it had previously commissioned Beethoven's Ninth. Later composers who wrote for the Society included Spohr, who conducted his own works during his visits to London, and Dvořák. From time to time it did what it could to encourage native composers, but without finding much British work to set in its programmes.

The concerts, however, depended for their existence on subscriptions and on box-office receipts. The early concerts were given in the Argyle Rooms, which held audiences of eight hundred; these were burnt down in 1830, and after two years in the concert room of the King's Theatre the Philharmonic Society settled in the Hanover Square Rooms, which again accommodated audiences of only about eight hundred; this meant that subscriptions and admission charges had to be high and that the audiences were as a result socially exclusive. Though the concerts never had the social prestige of the opera or of the long-established Concert of Antient Musick, which had been in existence since 1776, continued until 1848, admitted no music which was less than twenty years old and numbered members of the royal family in its membership, attendance at the Philharmonic Society's concerts implied a degree of wealth and a social position. When, in 1869, the Society moved its concerts to the new St James's Hall, which could accommodate audiences of two thousand one hundred and twenty-seven, the Society could offer unreserved seats for five shillings or half a crown. The critic H. F. Chorley greeted this influx of new listeners with no enthusiasm; he wrote in the *Athenaeum* that, in losing their exclusiveness, 'the Philharmonic Concerts have lost their distinctive charm and the Society its only *raison d'être*'.

The Philharmonic Society created no orchestra for its own exclusive use but depended, so far as possible, on the orchestra of the opera, engaging its members not for a season but for individual concerts. From the start it was at the mercy of the deputy system, accepting the fact that members previously engaged would accept any more lucrative engagements that offered themselves, either for rehearsals or for the concert itself, sending a deputy to fill their places. At first the concerts were directed by members of the Society, sharing control of the performance from the leader's desk and from the keyboard of a piano on the desk of which lay the score; the piano, of course, was a redundant survival of the old days of the *basso continuo*. Spohr, visiting London for the first time in 1820, claimed to be the first musician to conduct the Philharmonic Society's orchestra with a baton, though Mendelssohn, in 1829, was 'conducted like a young lady to the piano' (so he wrote to his sister Fanny) to conduct his C minor Symphony. Although conducting in the modern style became customary in the 1830s, no specialist permanent conductor was appointed, and in 1843 the critic J. W. Davison suggested in *The Musical Examiner* that the decline in the Society's fortunes which had prevented the commissioning of new works and the open rehearsals of works submitted to it was in part at least due to the need of a permanent conductor who should be able to take full control of performances. In 1845 Sir Henry Bishop, not a specially auspicious choice, became conductor for a year; ill-health made it impossible for him to complete a single season, and in 1846 he was replaced by Michael Costa who, by virtue of technical competence and strict orchestral discipline, seemed to dominate English music through the mid-century.

The possibility of an audience less socially restricted than that served by the Philharmonic Society is proved by the success of Promenade Concerts, immediately acceptable to London audiences because they brought to England an idea already successful in Paris and made no exorbitant demands on the attention of a largely untutored body of listeners. In December 1839 a series of 'Promenade Concerts à la Musard' (Musard being the conductor of such concerts in Paris) began at the Drury Lane Theatre with an orchestra of sixty musicians. The capacity of the theatre— well over two thousand—permitted the attendance of a whole class of people who could not afford to attend the Philharmonic Society's concerts. The conductor of the series, Negri, offered programmes guaranteed not to alarm the most timorous: each concert normally consisted of four over-tures, four waltzes, four quadrilles and a piece for a solo wind instrument.

The natural consequence of their success in a musical world dominated by the need to make a profit at the box office was that a rival series of con-certs began, a month after Negri's, at the Crown and Anchor Tavern; the conductor was the violinist Eliason, who was almost indiscreetly ambitious— most of his programmes contained a complete symphony. The Crown and Anchor, however, could not accommodate audiences large enough to ensure success, and it may be that Eliason's audiences were not prepared for so much concentrated listening as was demanded of them, so that the series failed.

In the autumn of 1840, Eliason embarked upon another series, this time at the Lyceum Theatre, with the French Louis Antoine Jullien as his assis-tant conductor, while a smaller and less successful series occupied the Prince's Theatre, and in the winter Philippe Musard himself took over Drury Lane with a series of *Concerts d'hiver*. The informal, not too demanding concert was, it seems, sufficiently established at a time when the Philharmonic Society existed in permanent financial anxiety. In 1841 Jullien himself took over Drury Lane Theatre for his own Promenade Con-certs and achieved almost unparalleled success; during his ascendancy, other conductors tried to rival him with concerts based on a similar pattern of music-making, among them Balfe, with his National Concerts, but nothing disturbed Jullien's command of his huge, devoted audience; that command was won by a fine orchestra and choir, skilled programme build-ing and, above all, by his combination of brilliant showmanship, blatant sensationalism and genuine musicianship; whoever else appeared on his platform, he was always a star of sufficient luminosity to outdazzle any of his guests. Elegantly eccentric, with splendid moustaches and luxuriant black hair, he had a gilt armchair behind him on the podium, and into this he would sink exhausted after acknowledging the applause. At the climax of any work he would seize a violin, or perhaps a piccolo, and play with the orchestra.

Each concert included a quadrille, usually linked by its title to some great topical event, and in this a military band, or two, or three, or on special occasions even six, would join. There was a good deal of the charlatan about Jullien and his determination to become the focal point of the audience's attention by showing how great a man—a combination of Napoleon and Svengali—a real conductor must be. But he conducted music by Beethoven to audiences who would never have dared to set foot in the Hanover Square Rooms, proving that the music of Beethoven was special and precious by putting on a pair of white gloves, brought to him on a silver salver, and using a jewelled baton; the performances, however, were scrupulously rehearsed and accurate. Whilst Eliason had failed to win a popular audience for symphonic music, Jullien's unblushing showmanship succeeded to such effect that he plunged into the recklessly disastrous venture of the ill-prepared opera season at Drury Lane, to which he brought Berlioz as conductor for the first time in England, and later into even more grandiose catastrophically ill-founded schemes. But he created audiences for others to sustain, and in this way was responsible for developments in more normal musical fields.

The history of such organisations as the Philharmonic Society, not only in England, is normally one of enthusiasts determinedly creating a body of musicians dedicated to an up-to-date musical style; the style of its founders, however, becomes a norm and without anyone's realising it, the taste of the founders becomes an orthodoxy beyond which no particular expansion is acceptable. The Orchestra of the *Société des Concerts du Conservatoire* began operations in 1828 and gave authoritative performances of the Beethoven symphonies which delighted the hearts of both Berlioz and Wagner. Its association with the state-supported conservatoire and its use of a hall which seated more than a thousand listeners made its financial situation less precarious than that of the Philharmonic Society in London, but both these once almost revolutionary organisations had, within thirty years of their creation, begun to face criticism for their reactionary attitudes and their neglect of new music.

In London the New Philharmonic Society was founded in 1852; its prime mover was Henry Wylde, organist, Professor of Harmony at the Royal Academy of Music, and, in 1863, Gresham Professor of Music. The New Philharmonic Society, according to its prospectus, intended to provide 'more perfect performances of the works of the great masters than have hitherto been attained'. The prospectus continued:

> The growing taste for the arts, more especially for music, in this country, demands a new institution where the greatest works by the greatest masters of all the ages may be heard by the public at large. . . . Exclusiveness, the baneful hindrance of all progress in art, will not be tolerated in this society. . . .

> The New Philharmonic does not entertain the opinion, acted on by an older institution, that no schools but those which can be called classical are to be considered capable of affording pleasure, and that such schools can only be enjoyed by a select few amateurs and artistes.

The New Philharmonic Society was controlled by Wylde and a committee not of professional musicians but of socially eminent and wealthy concert-goers. It was, at first, able to use Exeter Hall, with an auditorium capable of holding more than three thousand, for its concerts. Thus, although its orchestra was built to the scale of twenty first violins and although it engaged a professional choir, its subscription for the six concerts of its inaugural season was only two guineas—one guinea for professional musicians—and single tickets for the cheaper parts of the auditorium were within the reach of working people.

Originally, the New Philharmonic Society was an outstanding success. The concerts of the first season were conducted by Berlioz, popular in England since Jullien had first brought him to London. The first concert included movements from his *Romeo and Juliet*, and the season contained two revelatory performances of Beethoven's Ninth Symphony which were the first in England to do justice to the work; the clarity, incisiveness and insight of Berlioz's conducting, added to the more humdrum fact that the work was, in Berlioz's manner, scrupulously rehearsed, secured a triumph. The cost of the sectional and choir rehearsals, and the seven full rehearsals, was not, however, something the New Philharmonic Society was inclined to repeat as a matter of course for difficult works.

In the second season the orchestra was matched to the scale of twenty-four first violins; Berlioz was replaced by Peter Joseph Lindpainter, who shared the conductorship with Wylde until his death in 1856. In 1858 Wylde became sole conductor. Already by 1854 the concerts moved from their insecure base in Exeter Hall, where the authorities of the Methodist Church had never been completely easy in their consciences at housing mere orchestral concerts—the hall was designed 'for religious meetings and the activities of charitable associations'—and in 1857 they were driven to the Hanover Square Rooms, where concerts on their original scale were out of proportion both to the orchestral accommodation it offered and to the hall's acoustic qualities; the move naturally impeded the idea of social inclusive-ness. Eventually, with the opening of the St. James's Hall in 1858, Wylde moved his organisation there, and continued as conductor and manager until his retirement in 1879. The German-born William Ganz, who had come to England as an orchestral violinist, opera rehearsal pianist, accom-panist and conductor before the New Philharmonic Society was born, took over the New Philharmonic Society's activities, converting it into 'Mr. Ganz's Orchestral Concerts' and continuing the New Philharmonic Society's traditional devotion to the works of Berlioz; it was, too, at Ganz's concerts that the *Dante* Symphony of Liszt had its first performance. By the 1880s, however, the New Philharmonic Society's pioneering functions had been taken over by the Crystal Palace Concerts, conducted by August Manns.

The Crystal Palace Concerts took place in an auditorium—originally a transept of the huge exhibition building—large enough to accommodate those who could not afford to pay even the lower prices charged at West End concerts, and the hall was even able to find room for the army of singers and instrumentalists assembled for the monster Handel Festivals of the late nineteenth century with as many as two thousand performers in choir and orchestra. Apart from the apparently considerable merits of Manns as a conductor—he was, it seems, clear and decisive and a sensitive interpreter of a wide range of music. His programmes included not only works by Schubert, Schumann, Raff, Liszt, Brahms and Smetana previously unknown in England in his programmes but also found room for works by Sullivan, Mackenzie, Parry and Stanford, the forerunners of 'the English musical renaissance' before such composers could hope for a hearing at any of the longer-established London concerts. To insist upon the importance to nineteenth-century concerts of the size of the auditoria they frequented is not, of course, to note a mere triviality; concerts which had to survive more or less entirely through takings at the box perforce depended either on high prices or on the availability of a hall large enough to allow the sale of tickets at prices within the financial reach of the more or less poor.

By the end of the nineteenth century, England was a land in which music was heard by audiences with a considerable social range; there was space for the *hoi polloi* at the various Promenade Concerts and the Crystal Palace; the New Philharmonic Society played to audiences socially inferior to those of the 'old' Philharmonic Society as well as to patrons of the older Society, and the opera catered for the wealthy. But at the same time England was '*das Land ohne Musik*'. In Wagner's season as conductor of the Philharmonic Concerts he conducted a single English work—a symphony by Cipriani Potter which he did not find as detestable as he found most new music. Berlioz conducted a symphony by Charles Lucas for the New Philharmonic Society, but perhaps tactfully wrote nothing about it. The rest of the music, some of it, in the Philharmonic Society's palmy days, commissioned from the famous, came from foreign composers. Conductors and soloists were mostly foreign.

England's dependence on foreign musicians was not restricted to the concert hall and the opera house. John Ella, founder of the Musical Union which gave chamber-music concerts from 1845 to 1880, was music critic of the *Morning Post* and from time to time wrote for other periodicals. He quotes the remark of a Venetian soprano in a story by Balzac that England and France robbed Italy of the best singers: *'Paris les juge et Londres les paye'*.[1] The English public, he declared, 'is often the victim of *charlatanerie*, and its patronage most shamefully abused by the importunities of the most inferior talents with letters of introduction'.[2] 'Most of the pianists, getting their guinea per lesson in London, would receive in Vienna not more than six shillings,' Ella declares. '. . . I have known a *maestro di canto* from Naples obtain a number of pupils on his arrival in London, at one guinea per lesson, who, to my knowledge, in his native city was glad to give seven lessons for the same amount.'[3]

Nevertheless, Ella, organising his own concerts in London, depended on foreign musicians, not necessarily for their superior accomplishments. He tells the story of an English lady who called on him one morning without an appointment: she had dreamed that she was playing the piano at a Musical Union concert and was determined to make her dream come true. She insisted upon playing a Hummel sonata to Ella, who was surprised by her performance but felt compelled to reject her offer. 'My expenses,' he said, 'are considerable, the subscription very low, and without attracting visitors by the engagement of new and eminent professors from the continent, I could not afford to pay my artists.'[4]

After thirty-two years of Musical Union concerts, Ella in 1877 provided some statistics: at his concerts seventy-four pianists, a hundred and two string players and twenty-seven wind players had appeared at his concerts:

> Analysis: Englishmen, forty-eight; French, thirty-one; Germans and Austrians, sixty-four; Italians, fifteen; Belgians, fourteen; Hungarians, eight; Poles, three; Russians, five; Dutch, eight; Swedes, one; Spanish and Portuguese, four.[5]

Ella's assemblage of foreign artists, however, included Mendelssohn, Dragonetti, Moscheles, Thalberg, Hallé, Ernst, Sivori, Piatti, Sainton, Joachim, Leopold Auer and Anton Rubinstein; in the nineteenth century it would have been hard to find any more illustrious collection of instrumentalists.

While foreign musicians increasingly dominated London music throughout the nineteenth century, provincial music-making followed the eighteenth-century pattern of semi-amateur performance in most towns and cities, with such events as the Three Choirs Festival of such cities as Norwich, Liverpool and Birmingham to diversify the fare and bring together local amateur choirs with professional orchestral musicians from London and solo singers of international reputation. The establishment of

---

[1] Ella: *op. cit. Italian Opera.* p. 350.
[2] *Ibid.* p. 105. *Composers and teachers of music at home and abroad.*
[3] *Ibid.* p. 104. *Foreign musicians in London.*
[4] *Ibid.* p. 332. *A Lady's Midsummer Night's Dream.*
[5] *Ibid.* p. 434. *The Musical Union (1877).*

'modern' concert societies in English towns and cities when and where it came, yielded English music into the hands of Central European musicians and the musical attitudes they brought with them.

Liverpool had a Festival Choral Society with a choir a hundred strong and its own semi-professional orchestra when, for reasons which have never been made really clear, the Liverpool Philharmonic Society was founded in 1840. The founders were Liverpool business men who controlled the organisation of their foundation in everything except its musical policy. In three years the Society had outgrown its first home, 'Mr Lassall's Saloon', a dancing academy, and moved to the hall of the Liverpool Collegiate Institute. Its first concert included overtures by Kalliwoda and Auber, the *Macbeth* music attributed to Matthew Locke and a sextet for flute, clarinet, horn, cello, double-bass and piano by Onslow; the rest of a long programme consisted of madrigals by Morley and Wilbye and choruses by Rossini and Bishop, but with no star singers to dazzle the audience with spectacular arias. The early conductors were local church organists.

With the move to the new hall in 1843, Jacob Zeugheer Hermann was appointed conductor. Born in Zürich in 1805, Hermann had studied in Munich, where he had founded a string quartet with which he had toured from 1824 to 1830, and had first reached Liverpool to give six concerts there on his way to Scotland and Ireland. In 1830 he had tired of a nomadic life and settled in the north of England, becoming conductor of the Gentlemen's Concerts in Manchester from 1831 to 1838. Hermann based his programmes on the familiar continental music of the day; from 1844 onwards, symphonies were regularly played in Liverpool programmes, but audiences continued to enjoy 'selections' from the popular operas—*Fidelio, Der Freischütz,* Balfe's *The Bohemian Girl,* Wallace's *Maritana,* Rossini's *Semiramide* and Spohr's *Jessonda.* Mendelssohn's choral works were as popular in Liverpool as they were everywhere else. Amateur players gradually disappeared from the orchestra, their places taken by professional players imported from London. A single year at the Collegiate Institute was enough to convince the Society that its concerts needed a larger hall with better acoustics, and in 1844 the foundation stone of the Original Philharmonic Hall was laid. In 1849 the Hall was opened; it accommodated audiences of 2100 and an orchestra and choir of 250.

The rules of the Society were, perhaps belatedly, published in 1845. A committee of not more than thirty-six members, including the Secretary and the Treasurer, would control the Society's business. There were to be four 'full-dress' and six 'undress' concerts a year; 'full-dress' concerts would be distinguished by performances of 'metropolitan talent' (usually singers of international reputation). The Society's insistence on dress was, apparently, part of a yearning for the social exclusiveness which at that time was beginning to worry London musicians, but it was the decision of

Liverpool business men who wanted their society to reflect their own social attitudes and ambitions. In their pursuit of social grandeur the Society's rules, and some later regulations, go to great and sometimes barely intelligible trouble. They declare:

> No gentleman within seven miles of Liverpool, not being a member, or a member in the family of a member, shall be admitted to any concert.

When the Philharmonic Hall was opened, those not wearing evening dress were banished to two side galleries; evening dress was obligatory in stalls and boxes: great care was taken to be sure that the right people were in the right places and that the wrong people did not obtrude on them. Until the original hall was burned down in 1933, a list of 'Gentlemen having the *entrée*' was displayed in its corridors, and, until 1909, when it was 'temporarily suspended', an intimidating notice was repeated from time to time in the programmes:

> The attention of proprietors and those who rent boxes and stalls is drawn to the following regulation, which will be strictly enforced:
>
> No gentleman above twenty-one years of age residing or carrying on business in Liverpool or within ten miles thereof, and not being an Officer of the Army or Navy, or Minister of Religion, is admissable to the Boxes or Stalls unless he be a Proprietor, or member of the family residing in the House of a Proprietor, or have his name upon the List of Gentlemen having the *Entrée* exhibited in the corridors.
>
> Resident Gentlemen who are not Proprietors can acquire the Right of Purchasing Tickets or of making use of Proprietor's Tickets during the season on the Payment of an Entrance Fee of 10s. 6d.
>
> N.B. Gentlemen above twenty-one, although members of the family residing in the house of those who *simply rent* Boxes and Stalls, are only admissable after payment of the Entrance Fee.[6]

Apparently, though earlier accounts do not mention the fact, it was possible for those who wished to do so to buy their own boxes or stalls rather than simply to subscribe to them; this was the system later to be used for the Royal Albert Hall in London. The members of the Liverpool Philharmonic Society seem to have been agitated by the possibility that 'proprietors' might pass on their rights to the socially unacceptable, and one suspects that a small audience of the acceptable would please the committee more than a hall thronged with the *hoi polloi*. It is possible to assume that the suspension of these regulations in 1909 may have been the result of diminishing audiences as the rights of original proprietors were inherited by children or grandchildren who did not wish to make use of them. Mere subscribers, who '*simply rented*' their seats, could not, however, claim any particular rights; their subscriptions could not be transferred to

---

[6] W. A. Argent: *The Philharmonic Jubilee: Half a Century of Music in Liverpool*. Liverpool, 1889.

members of their families without the payment of a new entrance fee by the recipient of the subscription.

When the twenty-nine-year-old Karl Halle (born at Hagen in Westphalia but a member of the Parisian *avant-garde* which included Berlioz, Liszt and Chopin) was driven from France by the revolution of 1848, he planned to settle in London and quickly established himself there as a concert pianist and teacher. Before long he left the Metropolis, invited to 'take Manchester in hand'. A year later, he was given the conductorship of the Gentlemen's Concerts in his new home. He had already established his chamber-music concerts, which, because of the large German colony in Manchester, rapidly drew a satisfactory audience; in 1849, their first season, Hallé (as he had become) won sixty-seven subscribers; after four years they filled a hall which held an audience of 450 and had a waiting list of over a hundred would-be subscribers. His first chamber-music concert in Liverpool, incidentally, was played to an audience of eleven, but by 1852 his Liverpool concerts were prospering.

The Manchester 'Gentlemen's Concerts' were, like the Liverpool Philharmonic Society's, administered by a committee of members; the conductor was a salaried official responsible for no more than musical policy and performance, limited in respect of both by the finances made available to him by the committee. It says much for Hallé's impact that in 1849 the committee accepted the almost ruthless conditions he advanced before accepting the conductorship; he was empowered to discharge inefficient members of the orchestra, recruit new ones, rehearse works until he was satisfied with the quality of performance before including them in a concert programme. When he had first attended a Manchester concert in 1848 to hear his friend Chopin play with the orchestra, he almost fled the city; he was fresh from the Conservatoire Orchestra's concerts in Paris and the conducting of Berlioz. In the September of 1848 he himself played with the orchestra; his performance in Beethoven's E flat Concerto was only part of a programme which included songs by the soprano Grisi (whom Hallé accompanied in Beethoven's *Adelaide*), Mario, the tenor, and Tagliaficio, the bass. Zeugheer Hermann returned from Liverpool to conduct, but the standard of orchestral playing was no better than when Hallé had first attended a Manchester concert. Hallé was, it seems, an unusually gentle man of great simplicity and kindness, but he would not accept the conductorship until his conditions were met.

In 1857 Manchester held an 'Art Treasures Exhibition', for which the authorities determined to create a first-class orchestra and empowered Hallé to engage the players capable of forming such an orchestra from London and from the continent to play with the best of his local musicians. Rather than disband an orchestra which had proved itself to be effective after the closing of the exhibition, Hallé planned a series of weekly concerts to keep the new ensemble together. He gave his first concert in January 1858, realising that he would have to create an entirely new public. He could, perhaps, depend upon the support and patronage of the members of the Gentlemen's Concert Society, but his success as concert promoter would depend upon the appeal of his new organisation to a much wider public. Those who had been fascinated by the quality of music heard at the exhibition had not attended specifically to listen to the orchestra, and the higher prices he would have to charge when his orchestra was no longer a subsidised feature of the exhibition would, perhaps, be a strong deterrent: thirty concerts, he decided, would be enough to decide on the success or failure of his scheme. He announced his programmes in advance, hoping for the patronage of many to whom orchestral music was unknown, depending in part on arousing the interest of a public which, he knew, had no notion what the words 'symphony' and 'concerto' implied, and pressed on with his plan in a manner which seemed foolhardy even to his well-wishers. His autobiography, with its naively direct account of the early struggles, is superior to any retelling of the tale:

> Beethoven's Symphony in C major headed the first programme and was vehemently applauded by the meagre audience. The loss upon the concert was a heavy one, and was followed by similar losses week after week, until my friends were debating whether for the sake of my family I ought not to be locked up, and I myself began to feel rather uneasy. It was not before nearly half the series of thirty concerts had been given that things took another aspect; the audience gradually became more numerous and more appreciative; at last full houses succeeded each other, and the day after the thirtieth concert my managers and dear friends, Messrs. Forsyth Brothers, brought me with the statement of my receipts and expenses ten brand-new threepenny bits, the profits of the whole series— a penny per concert! Perfectly satisfied with this result, which I considered most encouraging, I at once made arrangements for a second series to be given during the winter season of 1858–9.[7]

The Hallé Concerts were the personal responsibility of their founder-conductor. Until he reached his seventies Hallé had no committee of management sharing the financial burdens of the concerts and taking a share in their control. Hallé was not bound by the social preconceptions of well-to-do Mancunians as to the types of people who could enjoy orchestral music and those whose social status made them virtually untouchable. The advertisement of the first concert read:

> Reserved seats 2s. 6d., Gallery and body of the hall (unreserved) 1s., Subscription for a series of eight concerts 20s.[8]

[7] C. E. and Marie Hallé: *op. cit.* pp. 131–2.
[8] Michael Kennedy: *The Hallé Tradition*. Manchester University Press, 1966. p. 30.

It was Hallé's policy always to have some seats available for the lowest-paid members of the Manchester community, and these seats were never empty. The social exclusiveness of concert societies in London, copied by the Liverpool Philharmonic Committee, seem to have been imposed by their own members, not by limitations of public taste. Hagen, Hallé's birthplace in Westphalia, where his father was organist and director of the town's amateur orchestra and choral society, was not an industrial town and Hallé did not, therefore, grow up inside a rigid class system, so that the various boundaries which separated Englishmen seem to have meant nothing to him, and the idea of appealing to a concert audience on the basis of social class apparently never occurred to him. According to his son and daughter, who completed his *Autobiography* and edited the correspondence which is added to it, he specially treasured the appreciative letters he received from the occupants of the cheaper seats: one such letter was 'written on a narrow sheet of paper such as is found in most workshops'. It is signed 'An Operative' and was accompanied by a gift of 'two yards of fine white flannel', the gift of a workman who in November 1873 had attended his first concert and offered the conductor his tribute.[9]

Hallé's son and daughter meditated upon their father's achievement:

> How many a factory hand or office clerk in the busy towns of Manchester and the North of England may have owed his only knowledge of what was beautiful to the music he had an opportunity of hearing at my father's weekly concerts during the dreary winter months.
>
> It is impossible to believe that some element of refinement has not developed in the large audience of working men who, standing packed together in great discomfort, have yet listened for hours, and evidently with much appreciation, to much intricate and delicate music; or that the taste thus formed in one direction should not have its effect in others, and possibly have coloured their whole lives?[10]

The Hallé, as a permanent orchestra engaged by the season, set new musical standards which by the 1880s startled London audiences whom the orchestra regularly visited. London concerts were bedevilled by the 'deputy system' which elsewhere continued as something unavoidable until, in 1911, Henry Wood took a firm stand against it and created an orchestra which was bound by contract to play at all the concerts for which he booked it.

At the same time, Hallé was destroying the social pattern which in the past had restricted the availability of music in Manchester to gentlemen and ladies, just as the social pattern restricted the availability of concert music outside the traditional Promenade Concerts to those who could pay highly for a seat and dress well enough to occupy it without causing con-

[9] Hallé: *op. cit.* p. 144.   [10] *Ibid.* p. 143.

sternation to those sitting nearby. Hallé did not, as Henry Wood was to do after 1895, when he took charge of the Promenade Concerts, educate the musically illiterate in his audience by leading it through shoals of light music to easy classics and from them to the profundities of Bach, Haydn, Mozart and Beethoven. The Hallé policy was simply to play great music as well as his orchestra could play it, and his audience—'operatives', 'factory hands', Lancashire business men and exiled German textile merchants nostalgic for the life they had enjoyed in Germany—accepted his offerings enthusiastically.

The Hallé and the Liverpool Philharmonic Society naturally handed over provincial music-making to German domination, just as London opera had been ceded to the Italians and London concerts to Germans. The only alternative to foreign domination would have been a stultifying provincialism more harmful than indoctrination into the music of Beethoven, Mendelssohn, Brahms and Wagner. German domination of the concert hall brought up English musicians on the most adventurous and stimulating music available; all that was needed was a group of composers strong enough to resist domination while up-to-date enough to profit from its example. When at the end of the nineteenth century Elgar arrived to lead English music back into the world of musical adventure, English musicians and their audiences were able to take their place in the mainstream and not simply to fight their way out of a remote musical backwater.

In Paris the formation of the *Société des Concerts du Conservatoire*, in 1828, created the orchestra which was responsible for what seems to have been the best, most conscientiously prepared performances of Beethoven's symphonies to be heard at that time in Europe. Berlioz, however, after his first visit to London, spent 1850 and 1851 attempting to create a Philharmonic Society similar in organisation to that of London in order to bring Paris musicians and music lovers up to date with works which the Conservatoire concerts neglected. Though anything which Berlioz attempted was almost sure to be attacked by the heads of the French musical establishment, his plan to promote new music within the context of the great masterpieces of the past succeeded sufficiently for him rapidly to build up a first-rate orchestra and choir, to be paid from the profits of the concerts in which they took part. The first concert was an unprecedented success, making a profit of 2700 francs. This, however, was to be divided into equal shares for ninety orchestral players and a hundred and ten choralists; the chorus master took three shares and Berlioz four. In return for this, Berlioz had undertaken the administration and publicity, rehearsed the music, composed works to be played and arranged others; while the players and singers each received thirteen francs, his reward was fifty.

Even the most exemplary loyalty could not ensure the regular, industrious attendance of singers and players at rehearsals and performances for so low a fee, and the fact that, although his music invariably drew large, and mostly enthusiastic, audiences, his colleagues, notably Pierre Dietsch, the chorus master, had compositions of their own to include in the programmes, less appealing to the public than those of their flamboyant leader. Berlioz, unusually generous in such matters, was prepared to conduct such works, planned to give performances of any new works composed by Prix de Rome winners on their return to France and, in order to increase the profits, allowed room in one programme for a new and not specially gifted Italian *prima donna*; he even accepted payment for the inclusion of a new work by a wealthy amateur composer. But the public wanted to hear music by Berlioz and the great familiar classics, so that the Society survived only for about eighteen months. It had, however, proved the possibility of an alternative organisation to the Conservatoire Concerts if finance could be assembled to keep it alive; in this it led the way to the concert organisations of Pasdeloup, Colonne and Lamoureux.

The *Société des Jeunes Artistes*, the first concert of which was conducted by Jules Pasdeloup, the Society's founder, in 1851, was fortunate in having a conductor who could treat his musical duties as a hobby. Pasdeloup, who had collected notable prizes from the Conservatoire and was a completely equipped musician, had entered the Civil Service; in 1848 he became Governor of the Château of Saint-Cloud, a post which took him among the rich and influential while paying him generously both in money and in leisure. Like Berlioz, he had discovered the need for a new orchestral organisation to give a hearing to the works of new composers, himself included. In 1858 Berlioz described the concert situation in Paris in a letter to Henry Litolff which justified his and Pasdeloup's attitude:

> The *Société des Concerts du Conservatoire was* instituted under the best possible conditions. It has the right to an excellent concert hall; its instrumentalists are in general the most skillful musicians to be found in Paris. . . . But the Conservatoire Society has limited its aims to conserving a certain number of masterpieces by the famous dead; for the Society, the living do not exist. Its aims are splendid nevertheless; it does its duty with dignity, and the works which are heard in its concert hall, and the composers who make their way through the hall of Society of the Conservatoire concerts are treated with respect as they cross its threshold, just as French officials look at the Great Pyramid in which the Egyptians, through the ages have conserved the mummies of their Pharaohs.[11]

Pasdeloup, Berlioz continued, conducted the concerts of the *Société des Jeunes Artistes* 'with zeal and devotion', but the Society was handicapped by the limited number of rehearsals that was possible in preparation and by the fact that musicians of its orchestra had to earn their livings else-

[11] Berlioz: *Correspondance Générale*: edited by Pierre Citron. Flammarion, Paris, 1972. Vol. 1. p. 209.

where. He painted a touching picture of Pasdeloup's players crawling exhausted to a morning rehearsal after playing in a ballroom until the small hours.

The experience of conducting the concerts of the *Société des Jeunes Artistes* convinced Pasdeloup that his real vocation was not composition but conducting; he introduced Paris to the symphonies of French composers, gave the first performance of Mozart's *Die Entführung aus dem Serail* in a concert version, and brought Schumann's orchestral works into his programmes. The *'Jeunes Artistes'* of his orchestra were ex-students of the Conservatoire who had not yet found their way into regular orchestral employment and from 1861, rechristening his concerts *'Concerts Populaires'*, he challenged the Conservatoire Concerts by mounting his own programmes at the same time, on Sunday afternoons. After the Franco-Prussian War of 1870, his organisation was given a government subsidy of 25,000 francs per annum, and continued in Paris until 1884. The advent of stage performances at Sunday matinées in the Paris theatres had by that time seriously weakened his grip on his audience.

Édouard Colonne, his successor, was at first a violinist in the Opéra Orchestra and then a member of the Lamoureux Quartet; he had his first experience of conducting at Pasdeloup's concerts. In 1873, with Hartmann, a publisher, he founded the *Concert National*; in the two seasons for which these concerts continued, Gounod's *Redemption* and Massenet's *Marie Magdaleine* had their first performances, and in 1874 Colonne set out to create an organisation of musicians which would appeal to the public by its performances of works by younger composers. What began as the *Concerts du Châtelet* eventually became the *Concerts Colonne*, and although they were at first overshadowed by Pasdeloup's *Concerts Populaires*, their attention to the music of Franck, Massenet and Lalo, amongst the composers of a younger generation at a time when Pasdeloup was inevitably growing out of touch with the style and tastes of the young ensured him a following which remained dangerously limited until, in the 1880s, he revived the works of Berlioz, which had been suffering almost total neglect.

Charles Lamoureux, the violinist founder of the Quartet in which Colonne played second violin, opened his career as a conductor in 1873, with performances of oratorios previously unknown, or virtually unknown, in Paris—*Messiah* in the first year as well as *Judas Maccabeus*; Bach's *St. Matthew Passion* followed in 1874 and Massenet's *Eve* in 1875. The *Société de l'Harmonie Sacrée* which he founded for these performances was based on the model of the London Sacred Harmonic Society and performances which he heard at German festivals. From 1872 he was second conductor of the Conservatoire Concerts and from 1877 to 1879 conductor at the Opéra. Disputes about details of performances in large organisations made him determined to work independently, and in 1881 he founded the

Nouveaux Concerts, which became known as the *Concerts Lamoureux*. Like Pasdeloup, he was a fervent Wagnerian, but he advanced the repertoire beyond that of Colonne to the music of D'Indy, Royer, Chabrier and Debussy.

The establishment of a regular concert life in those German cities traditionally devoted to opera was, on the whole, a slow development. Occasional concerts, or even more frequent events arranged for the benefit of favourite performers, and concerts arranged to enable a touring virtuoso to make his presence felt were not a substitute for the sort of concert familiar in Leipzig, the hall of the Paris Conservatoire or the homes of the Philharmonic and New Philharmonic Societies in London. For one thing, the orchestras of the old German capital cities were heavily engaged in the opera houses, and the underpaid musicians had little, if any, time, after the teaching which made their livelihood possible, to undertake new musical activities. Nevertheless, to the musicians of the German and Austrian opera houses in the first half of the nineteenth century it was obvious that the most exciting and valuable new music—which in most places continued to be the works of Beethoven—belonged to the concert hall. Enthusiasts like the leaders of the Munich Court Orchestra, who added regular concert performances to their duties in 1810, and, like Spohr in Cassel, won audiences for their concerts. Wagner's career in Germany before his exile in 1849 is full of determined though fruitless efforts to enrich the music of the cities in which he served with regular series of concerts in a way which would benefit any underpaid orchestral musicians of the theatre orchestras which he conducted; but he was met either by lack of interest from players on whom he depended or by the obscurantism of political or municipal authorities. As conductor of the Opera in Riga in 1838, when he was twenty-five, he addressed a letter to the members of the orchestra proposing that they undertook regular annual concert series.

With the apparently unenthusiastic support of the theatre manager, Karl von Holtei, who was ready to release the orchestra on Tuesday evenings, when the stage was normally given over to spoken drama, Wagner proposed six subscription concerts in a first season. The subscription would be four silver roubles and admission an extra rouble. He himself would conduct the concerts but would take no remuneration; the entire profit would be divided among the players; leaders, who might appear as soloists, would receive a larger share than the rank and file. The Riga players, twenty-four men, were warned that an inaugural season might not be specially rewarding, but later seasons would probably work to the financial as well as the musical advantage of the players.

> The project should be in itself an advantage to an artist through its very concept of a perfectly organised body, as we may now call our orchestra, which may display its ability for independent development. For what

true musician would not be distressed to see such a fine ensemble used for nothing but routine and never of its own accord venture on what gives deep enjoyment and inspiration?[12]

Wagner's signature is followed by twenty-four others, apparently those of the entire orchestra, prepared unanimously to follow their conductor's lead. The plan, however, came to nothing, perhaps because of the lack of enthusiasm of Holtei, who dismissed Wagner six months later.

In a much stronger position as *Kapellmeister* in Dresden Wagner set out to add an active concert life to the traditional operatic life of the city. Maria Schmole, daughter of Ferdinand Heine, costume director of the Dresden Court Theatre during Wagner's *Kapellmeistership*, wrote in 1895 of Wagner's occasional concerts with the Opera orchestra as though they were events quite fresh in her memory and not recollections called up after half a century:

> By the consummate performance of musical works which he put on the programme of the so-called Palm Sunday Concerts, he probably laid the foundations of the subscription concerts of the Dresden Court Theatre Orchestra which in our time are enjoying a fame and attendance not surpassed by any town in Germany.[13]

Wagner's attempts to create a concert organisation in Dresden were frustrated by the power of opera in a city where it absorbed all the attention of a royal patron and of an audience familiar not only with the ever-growing Italian repertory but also with the German repertory which the Kings of Saxony had cultivated since the end of the Napoleonic Wars. The great virtuosi visited Dresden and played to the court and the public. Amateur orchestras of varying quality existed for their own pleasure rather than for the benefit of the public, but any orchestra attempting to pay its way without a regular scheme of subscriptions was hampered by the fact that in Dresden no concert hall existed capable of accommodating an audience large enough to make concerts financially viable. The theatre, rarely available for concerts, was the only auditorium large enough to support an orchestra except at excessively high prices.

In addition, the Court Orchestra was unwilling to encourage any rival ensemble; its single annual concert, played on Palm Sunday each year for the benefit of the widows and orphans of past players, was, to the orchestra's mind, sacrosanct. The musicians believed that any multiplication of public concerts would steal the audience of the all-important pension concert. Audiences, too, preferred the familiar music of Italian opera to the still unexplored music of the symphonic tradition.

[12] Wagner: *Letters—The Burrell Collection*, edited by John N. Burke. Gollancz, London, 1951. The letter to the Riga Orchestra is given on pp. 341–3.
[13] *Ibid*. p. 128.

Wagner reached Dresden in 1842, but before his abortive plans for regular concerts with the Court Orchestra had been worked out, Ferdinand Hiller, a thirty-three-year-old composer whose achievements at that time outshone Wagner's, came to Dresden in 1844 intending to make a position for himself in the city's music-making. He had won a great reputation as a pianist in Paris and as a conductor in Leipzig and Frankfurt. He arrived in Dresden after his lifelong friendship with Mendelssohn had broken down and brought his work in Leipzig to an end. With no official standing in Dresden despite his popularity, he began to establish himself by collecting as good an orchestra as he could from unattached musicians there. Although there was no suitable hall, he found an appetite for orchestral concerts which, despite high prices, were profitable enough to continue until Hiller had made his rough and ready ensemble into a satisfactory orchestra. In 1847 Hiller's organisation failed, partly because of the limitations of his audience and partly because of the hostility of the Court Orchestra and its *Kapellmeister*. Wagner had little faith in Hiller's interpretative powers and he was determined to bring concert music into the Court Orchestra's normal sphere of activities.

On Palm Sunday, 1846, Wagner conducted Beethoven's Ninth Symphony for the Pension Fund Concert after enormously painstaking rehearsal (the double-basses alone had twelve individual rehearsals). The work, which the Dresden authorities had expected to empty the theatre, was so successful that it took more money than had ever been gained from a Palm Sunday Concert in the past and its performance became almost a tradition for the Pension Fund Concert. Wagner's attitude had not changed since he had tried to find room for symphony concerts in the Riga orchestra's schedule: the symphonies of Beethoven, he believed, were a necessity for orchestras and for their audiences; to neglect them was to neglect the possibility of mastering modern orchestral style; to play them correctly it was necessary to understand them and to convey that understanding to every member of the orchestra; to understand them was to be musically enlightened and spiritually enriched. There were other works from the past of almost equal value. Modern opera, on the other hand, was usually meretricious, showy and still awaiting its Wagnerian redemption.

The hundred-page report, *Die Königliche Kapelle betreffend*, which Wagner sent to the authorities at the beginning of March 1846, is like all his musical thinking—exhaustive, precisely worked out and entirely practical. It lists the deficiencies of the orchestra and the additional instruments needed if it were to do justice to 'modern' works; it points out the shamefully low salaries of the players and the excessive overwork to which, partly as the result of bad planning, they were subjected, and provides a reasonable cure for this. He describes the inadequacy of the orchestra pit in the Opera House —neither the tone nor the ensemble could be satisfactory while the orchestra's depth was only a quarter of its length; and the music desks were an old-fashioned nuisance.

But these immediate practicalities are followed by Wagner's insistence that the orchestra, for the sake of its style and the cultural life of the city, should give regular concerts. At least six concerts should be given in the winter months so that the masterpieces of instrumental music which are the glory of the German school could be played to the Dresden public. Wagner believed that regular concerts would not decrease the takings of the Palm Sunday Concerts but that greater familiarity with the symphonic repertoire would make the Pension Fund Concert, which could be given a specially ambitious programme, more popular than it already was. The overworked orchestral players, after a rationalisation and reorganisation of their duties in the Opera House and the Royal Chapel, would support the proposed venture, which would cost the court authorities nothing, if the profits of the concerts were divided among them. As Wagner admitted, the King could not increase the orchestra salaries, the concerts would bring the players a much-needed increase in pay.[14]

Wagner's plea for reform was rejected, but at the beginning of 1848 he was able to conduct three concerts with the Opera Orchestra. Unlike Hiller, Wagner depended on the music of the past; choral works by Palestrina and Bach belonged, in 1848, to the special sphere of the 'Historical Concert', and the only modern composer represented in Wagner's 1848 programmes was Mendelssohn, who had died two months before the first of Wagner's programmes. After 1848, orchestral concerts in Dresden again depended on the initiative of two freelance musicians, Kunze and Hartung, who inherited the organisation which Hiller had abandoned, with the result that they were able to play the symphonies of Beethoven and other difficult 'modern' works without being forced into a financially ruinous multiplication of rehearsals. Their auditoria were public gardens and on Saturday afternoons the Brulschen Terrace; such auditoria were to their obvious financial advantage; they could count on a much larger subscription audience and fewer expenses. The profitability of symphony concerts was amply proven before the Court Orchestra undertook to provide them regularly.

It was natural that Wagner, exiled to Zürich after 1849 and with no other way of earning his living, should involve himself in the music of the Zürich opera and of the *Allgemeine Musik Gesellschaft* there. It was equally natural that he should attempt to put the affairs of both organisations on a more satisfactory musical footing while providing for improved pay and conditions for the players. Though he refused the vacant conductorship of the Zürich Opera in 1851, he secured the appointment of Karl Ritter, a devoted disciple who turned out to be hopelessly incompetent. Wagner, whose

[14] Ernest Newman: *The Life of Richard Wagner*. Vol. 1. Cassell, London, 1937. See pp. 464–9 for a summary of the entire memorandum.

sense of musical responsibility was as highly developed as his sense of responsibility to people was lacking, found himself morally bound to take over Ritter's duties until he was relieved by the arrival of Hans von Bülow, a born conductor still in his twenties. Wagner worked behind Bülow until the young man resigned and Wagner decided that he had discharged his responsibilities to the management.

From 1850 onwards he appeared at concerts of the *Allgemeine Musik Gesellschaft*; his first appearance was to conduct Beethoven's Seventh Symphony in a vastly distended programme of vocal and instrumental trivia. The orchestra consisted of thirty free-lance musicians, teachers, *Stadtpfeifer* and outsiders, with a handful of local amateur players. Wagner, accepted as a great figure in the musical world, with *Tannhäuser* going the rounds of the German opera houses, was in great demand as a conductor in Zürich, conducting the more ambitious works in the *Gesellschaft*'s programmes. His audience noted the difference between the results he obtained from the orchestra and those obtained by others, and he was induced to conduct three concerts of his own music there in May 1853, but despite a great success, Wagner had decided that music in Zürich needed a total reorganisation. The city was too small, he realised—it had some 33,000 inhabitants in 1850—to support separate orchestras for the opera and for the *Musik Gesellschaft*, so in 1855, as the most distinguished musician in the city, he drew up a plan as thorough, practical and generally advantageous as that for Dresden to rationalise Zürich's musical resources. The two orchestras should be united and the resulting ensemble used both for opera and concerts. This would provide players enough for the larger modern operas and an orchestra capable of doing justice to the concert works of Beethoven and his successors; he remembered that he had been compelled to collect players from far and wide for his concerts in 1853. These plans cut across vested interests in both organisations; their ambition was noted, but not their practicability, and they were never implemented. It was Winterthur, a smaller town than Zürich, which became the centre of Swiss concert life in the later 1850s, simply because there was no conflict there between the interests of an opera and those of a concert society; thus a group of mainly young enthusiasts were able to build a concert society which, after 1863, followed an entirely un-Wagnerian line, following the tradition of Mendelssohn, Schumann and Brahms.

German cities where opera did not traditionally dominate musical life developed concert organisations with greater ease than Dresden or Berlin. The wealth of Lübeck had enabled the city to equip itself with eight town musicians to undertake the traditional *Stadtpfeifer* duties. A secondary guild of twenty-one musicians, the *Rollbrüder* and *Kostendbrüder* existed to take part in church music and municipal ceremonial. In addition to these, there were the regimental musicians of Lübeck's own militia. The City

Fathers, realising that the musicians could not earn their livings simply by fulfilling their traditional duties, encouraged them to join with the theatre musicians to set up a *Liebhaber Konzert* Society, thus creating something which both in its organisation and its composition was more or less equivalent to a concert orchestra; it provided ten concerts each winter at a subscription of 20 marks a season. The exigencies of war in 1808 and 1809, and between 1811 and 1815, temporarily put an end to their activities, but the orchestra survived, and the Lübeck Senators themselves paid the fees of musicians qualified as *Stadtpfeifer*; there were ten in 1825, fifteen in 1829.[15]

Although the Senate insisted that the status of the *Stadtpfeifer* should be preserved, Lübeck had really created what to all intents and purposes was a City Orchestra which, because of the great simplification of church music and the meaninglessness of traditional *Stadtpfeifer* duties in the nineteenth century, functioned almost entirely as a concert orchestra before its civic organisation was officially brought into line with the facts of its existence in 1873.

Public concerts in Augsburg, comparable to those of Lübeck, followed a similar pattern. With twenty-seven musicians to carry out the duties of the *Stadtpfeiferei*, it was natural that the town musicians should involve themselves in any profitable or potentially profitable concert scheme, but it was not until the Free Cities lost their independence and Augsburg was incorporated into Bavaria in 1810 that the Augsburg musicians formed themselves into an orchestra with the principal purpose of giving subscription concerts under the aegis of the city Senate.[16]

The historically 'great' orchestras developed later to vindicate Wagner's conviction that any orchestra, for the sake of its quality and musical standards, should be involved in both opera and concert music. Vienna remained without regular, professional concerts until the success of the annual Pension Fund Concert—the 'Nicolai Concert' inaugurated by Otto Nicolai, conductor of the Court Opera from 1842 to 1847—led in 1860 to the organisation by the orchestra itself of the Vienna Philharmonic Orchestra, through which the members of the Opera Orchestra became a concert-giving organisation, self-governing and appointing its own conductor, at times when it was not engaged in the theatre. The consequent expansion of the orchestra's numbers was beneficial to both aspects of its work. The Philharmonic Orchestra remains the central and most respected Viennese orchestra, but its double life inevitably restricts its scope and led to the formation of ensembles free from operatic duties—the *Konzertverein*

[15] Eberhard Preussner: *Die Bürgerliche Musikkultur*, Bärenreiter, Cassell, 1950. p. 152.

[16] Ludwig Wegele: *Musik in der Reichstadt Augsburg*. Die Brigge, Augsburg, 1965. pp. 163–4.

Orchestra in 1900 and the *Tonkünstler* Orchestra in 1907. The two amalgamated in 1922 to form the Vienna Symphony Orchestra.

In Munich, too, the Musical Academy concerts, twelve a year, given by the Court Orchestra since 1810, proved insufficient to satisfy the public appetite for orchestral music, and lesser organisations added to the official concert season. In 1893 the piano-maker Franz Kaim formed an orchestra of seventy-five musicians who gave twelve concerts a year and evolved first into the Munich *Konzertverein* and eventually into the Munich Philharmonic Orchestra.

Berlin, too, owed its regular professional concerts in the nineteenth century to the initiative of its court musicians. Anton Bachmann, one of the players in the Prussian Court Orchestra, founded the first orchestra—a semi-professional organisation, to give public concerts in Berlin in the late eighteenth century, and amateur orchestras multiplied throughout the following century while the Court Opera Orchestra, as the *Königliche Hoforchester*, gave fairly regular symphony concerts. The Berlin Philharmonic Orchestra, free from operatic entanglements, was founded in 1882 and the Berlin Symphony Orchestra, the deliberately modernising force in a city where music had become conservative, in 1908.

The social composition of audiences had not bothered German concert-giving organisations. Just as music had traditionally been the solvent of social differences in Vienna, where Beethoven behaved with a sense of superiority to the nobles with whom he associated and who met musicians on terms of relative equality, so it was taken for granted in Germany and Austria that the artisan class would be no less comfortable at concerts than was the bourgeoisie; the availability of orchestral concerts at prices within the reach of the relatively poor prevented the development of a class to whom music was unfamiliar and intimidating. When Sterndale Bennett, the most notable English composer of the early and mid-nineteenth century, first played in Leipzig, 'he was prepared,' wrote his son, 'to find music more widely cultivated than in England', and he noted the greater respect paid by intellectual Germans to music. The affectionate filial biography continues:

> He also observed that in Germany a love for [music's] more advanced forms was to be found in all classes. On the evening when he made his début at Leipzig he espied the man who blacked the boots at his lodgings sitting in the gallery of the Gewandhaus.[17]

The boots later explained that attendance at the Gewandhaus Concert was a pleasure for which he saved his spare money and to which he eagerly looked forward.

Concert life in the nineteenth century, however, depended increasingly

[17] J. R. Sterndale Bennett: *The Life of William Sterndale Bennett*. Cambridge University Press, 1907. p. 101.

on the exploitation of a repertoire often restricted by limitations of taste either in the audience or on the part of the conductor. Neville Cardus remembered how the petition of younger members of the Hallé audience to Hans Richter, that the orchestra should pay some attention to the works of Debussy and 'modern French composers', was dismissed by the great conductor's sweeping assertion, 'There is no modern French music.'[18] Usually, however, the limitations were those of the audience; a very brief research into the concert statistics of almost any major orchestra, as well as the accounts of musical controversies, demonstrates the general resistance against new music which delays the acceptance of many composers into the repertoire.

For this reason, the development of orchestral concerts throughout Europe was of comparatively little direct help to the composer, who had to be popular before his music was played but who was denied the opportunity of popularity until his music was heard. Any symphony after the death of Beethoven was necessarily a major undertaking simply in the amount of time it exhausted; to produce the full score of a work lasting for more than forty-five minutes is a singularly time-absorbing task, and the composer who undertook it in the nineteenth century was compelled to do so, as often as not, with no certainty of earning any money from his labour; probably he had neglected more immediately profitable work in order to bring to birth a probable white elephant. The mere economics of the task, even more than the mystique of the symphony as in some sense the greatest, most profound and demanding of forms, probably inhibited the would-be symphonist. John Shedlock, the pianist and music critic who died in 1919, wrote of Brahms a month after the composer's death in 1897:

> There was, however, a higher step to take, and that was to write a symphony. Mozart, Schubert, and Mendelssohn, while yet boys, rapidly wrote off symphony after symphony, but when they grew to manhood they took longer over such works, and were far less prolific. Beethoven was more than thirty years old when he published his first Symphony in C, and before the C minor of Brahms appeared the latter had passed his mature age of forty.[19]

One of the usual facts about the creative mind in youth is its almost inordinate ambition: Wagner's first acknowledged work, when he was in his early teens, was a poetic tragedy with a huge *dramatis personae*, many of them dead and resurrected in the last act. Britten, we are told, wrote a huge oratorio, *The End of the World*, as a small boy at his prep school. What Brahms wrote as a child it is not ours to know. To speak of a form as the

[18] Neville Cardus: *Second Innings*. Collins, London, 1950. p. 127.
[19] J. S. Shedlock: *Brahms. Monthly Musical Record*, May, 1897. Quoted in Norman Demuth: *An Anthology of Musical Criticism*, Eyre and Spottiswoode, London, 1947. pp. 282–3.

most serious, intense and profound is to offer a challenge immediately accepted by the young. The symphony had no special quality when Beethoven worked for more than fifteen years before he composed one he was prepared to acknowledge; but he was a professional musician living upon his earnings; until he had a practical reason to compose a symphony, he did not bother to do so but composed what the world needed from him.

Brahms was well enough aware of the symphony as a challenge; his first attempts at Beethovenian intensity. But when he declared that 'a symphony is not a joke', he may not have been thinking of the spiritual and emotional depths of the task; it may have been the economic and practical aspects of the task, its long, time-consuming demands, that disturbed him: it can never be a joke to withdraw for a considerable length of time from the activities which enable a man to earn his living even if the result is as friendly, charming and companionable as the Second Symphony which Brahms composed within a year of the passionately intense First. This does not suggest that Brahms was inhibited from writing a symphony until he felt himself emotionally and spiritually capable of answering the Beethovenian challenge. The First Piano Concerto which he wrote in his twenties was a practical work; he earned a great deal from his appearances as a concert pianist, and it measures itself against a properly Beethovenian seriousness; he wrote a symphony as soon as his career was sufficiently advanced to allow him time to do so and to regard the work as a probable source of income. One of the difficulties of the nineteenth century was that it neglected to attend to, and still tends to prevent us from considering, the practicalities of musical life. Writers still prefer to give their attention to the imponderables of inspiration about which they cannot know, although mundane practicalities provide us with valid reasons for many of a composer's activities.

The composer had, one way or another, to secure a career in order to win a hearing for the work on which his career was to rest. The nineteenth century distrusted music composed on commission on the grounds that inspiration cannot be booked in advance. There was, too, so far as concert organisations were concerned, the danger of providing time in a programme for music which might antagonise patrons; the prospect of commissioning new music was even more dangerous than that simply of rehearsing and performing it. Thus, it may have been a sentimental wish of concert promoters to encourage young composers, but it was no essential part of their duty to do so. The purpose of an orchestral concert, even outside Britain and the United States, where concert finance was an insoluble problem and depended entirely upon what could be taken at the box office, was to play the music which most pleased the audience.

8

National Music

Until the nineteenth century, music was generally regarded as an international language. Its technical vocabulary was Italian, and from the time of the early baroque European music in general had evolved its styles and technical devices from the developments initiated by Italian composers. Court opera was opera in Italian both in Weber's Dresden and in Victorian London, no matter who composed it and where it was staged. In 1855 Queen Victoria suggested to Wagner that *Tannhäuser* should be translated into Italian so that it could secure a production in London.

French music had in one sense always been French; it had served the social and political purposes both of the Bourbon monarchy and of the revolutionary governments, and its styles had been determined by its subjugation to the French language and French prosody, so that its melodic idioms could barely survive the translation of libretti and lyrics into any other language. These facts did not prevent French music exerting a powerful attraction on German composers, among others, in the early years of the eighteenth century. English music, too, had its national idiosyncrasies. In England as in France Italian-type recitative sounded unnatural and either incongruous or simply ridiculous when applied to English words for any dramatic purpose. In England the tradition of consort music for a long time withstood the development among English composers of the Italianate sonata. Jenkins, in England, had published 'sonatas' before Purcell published his trio sonatas in 1683 with the declaration that by doing so he 'endeavour'd a just imitation of the most fam'd Italian masters'. Both Jenkins and Purcell were unable or unwilling to eradicate specifically English traits from their Italianate works; early English sonatas often move like fantasies, in free polyphony, use biting false relations in their harmony, as English composers for a couple of centuries had done, admitted modal flavouring to their harmony and interchanged expected iambs with trochees, or trochees with iambs, as, for example, the Agincourt Song had done in the early fifteenth century and as Purcell did innumerable times in his vocal music. But music, in spite of such local eccentricities, aspired, as Purcell's words show, to the state of an international language which might be legitimately spoken with a variety of local accents by members of different races. In the late eighteenth century the international idea had conquered; music was a European application of Italian techniques and styles.

The international idea began to collapse in the early nineteenth century. Embattled nations, or nations subjugated by a foreign invader, began to think of music as an expression of their own national personality, a way of voicing their own national aspirations. In the *Adieux* Sonata (*op.* 81a), Beethoven's *au revoir* to the Archduke Rudolf when in 1809 that most exalted of his pupils left Vienna to escape from the advancing French, Beethoven set out the first movement with the instruction *Adagio*, leading to *Allegro*; the second movement is *Andante*, with additional German instructions, *In gehender Bewegung, doch mit Ausdruck*; the third movement is *Vivacissamente, in lebhaftigen Zeitmasse*. The next sonata, *op.* 90, written in 1814, retains such Italian terms as *ritard., in tempo, crescendo, sempre diminuendo* and so on; its main instructions are in German: *Mit lebhaftigkeit und durchaus mit Empfindung und Ausdruck*; *Nicht zu geschwind und sehr singbar vorzutragen*. The 1816 and 1819 sonatas are the two for *Hammerklavier*, the generally accepted Germanism for pianoforte.

Beethoven's Italian was not always as fluent as it might have been, and as his primary instructions to a pianist become more detailed and complex, it might have seemed natural to him to set them out in his own language, although he had previously been happy enough with such conventional Italianisms as *con espressione* and *cantabile*; his German directions usually have an acceptable Italian equivalent which Beethoven had been happy enough to use in the past. The Napoleonic invasions which turned Beethoven from a simple revolutionary into a patriotic Austrian revolutionary seem to have made him feel that his own language was a perfectly satisfactory way of telling pianists how he wanted his music played.

The urge towards nationalism in German and Austrian music before 1815 appears in other *dicta* than Beethoven's. Weber, writing with little if any evidence beyond Bach's keyboard works, twenty years or so before the so-called 'Bach Revival', wrote:

> Sebastian Bach's characteristic attitude, in spite of its rigidity, was clearly romantic and fundamentally German.[1]

In the context of 1811, the date of Weber's remark, the later composer can hardly have been thinking of the melodic and rhythmic idioms suggested to an eighteenth-century German master by the language of the text which occupied him. 'Clearly romantic' and 'fundamentally German' are given as characteristics of the music itself, part of its special personality.

It was, perhaps, natural that, because Central European nationalism was prevented from finding any expression in political life, it expressed itself vehemently through the arts. For some years a considerable part of Germany had been given unity by Napoleon; there was, beyond and including that, a huge and potentially powerful area in the heart of Europe which used a

---

[1] Weber: *Ausgewählte Schriften*.

common language and shared most of the same aspirations; the complex which was to become the German Empire presented a more or less homogeneous state, united by language and culture but forced by political organisation into political disunity against the will of its people; even the idea of an Austro-German Empire uniting all German speakers seemed anything but unreasonable until the power and ambition of Bismarckian Prussia put such a union beyond the bounds of practicality.

The idea of German unity, however, had awakened before Napoleon's revolutionary rationalisation of the map of Central Europe. It preceded Beethoven's use of a German musical vocabulary and Weber's statement about the essentially German nature of Bach's music. The writers and thinkers of the Enlightenment in Germany, notably Johann Gottfried Herder (1784–1803) and Johann Gottlieb Fichte (1726–1814), had taught that nationalism manifested a unity of culture rather than any political situation. If, declared Herder, the German-speaking word achieved a unity of education and culture, these would inevitably generate political unity. It was the personality of the German *Volk* and their consciousness of a common culture which would create the less essential unity of political organisation. Then Fichte, treading in the footprints of Immanuel Kant, believed that a nation was not simply the aggregation of people living in a defined geographical area but a spiritual unity achieved by the creation of a shared culture and shared aspirations forged by the various pressures—religious, social, economic and political—to which they were subjected.

The collision of this cultural and idealistic nationalism with war and the political ambitions of Napoleon's France forced the German people if not to find political expression for their spiritual unity at least to justify the political endeavours of their rulers. As ex-members of Napoleon's empire, the German states came each to renounce not the political absolutism which was their political tradition but the supra-national ideas—of the Holy Roman Empire and even of the recent Napoleonic Confederation of the Rhine—which had lingered on as a sentiment even though eighteenth-century absolutism had largely destroyed their reality. Although during the years of French dominance the old German patchwork was largely reorganised and rationalised, and although many parallels to Napoleonic social and economic law were applied to the German states, an entirely unpolitical concept of nationalism made Germany return willingly to the pre-revolutionary *status quo*.

The refusal of the Congress of Vienna to allow Austria any foothold in Western Europe destroyed the last vestiges of the Austrian Emperor's traditional authority as Holy Roman Emperor and left the tangle of German states without a centre, creating a gap which remained until 1870 and the creation of the German Empire under Prussian leadership. The German cultural unity, existing despite differences of religion between the various German states, the unity of a national language, national folklore and national traditions, all of which Herder and Fichte exalted as the reality of unity, became realities looking for political expression.

From their foundations, the German choral societies found it natural to sing folk songs and songs in folk styles. *Des Knaben Wunderhorn*, the anthology of German folk poetry which provided texts for Mendelssohn, Schumann, Brahms, Mahler and Schoenberg, as well as numerous lesser composers, was collected by Ludwig Achim von Arnim and Clemens Maria Brentano and published between 1805 and 1808. Earlier collections of folk music, like that published by Herder in 1778 and 1779, had brought together popular songs from various nations; *Des Knaben Wunderhorn* is totally and exclusively German. Such anthologies, like Beethoven's choice of a German rather than an Italian musical vocabulary, indicate the national feeling that was eventually to force itself into political expression and find itself continually frustrated in the age of the reaction. To Hegel (1770–1831), the state, its policies and the order it enforces, were the only real embodiment of the national culture which to Herder and Fichte had been realities transcending any political expression. Hegel laid it down as the duty of the state to ensure the independence of art, philosophy and religion, but it must be the state itself, and not its incidental culture, which embodies the national personality. Thus, in the writings of the most decisive German philosopher of the early nineteenth century, political nationalism became a matter of urgency.

The outcome of this sense of national unity thwarted by a threadbare, repressive political system underlay the longing for national unity which persisted until the creation of the German Empire. The patchwork of German states, lacking a capital or any cultural, political or educational centre, seemed to express its individuality most effectively through music rather than through literature and the nebulous political structures which tacitly denied the unity its people felt; it created a potentially dangerous sense of national inferiority.

The much-travelled young Mendelssohn, on his first visit to Britain, found himself staying in Llangollen and so persecuted by Welsh harpists that he wrote a letter home violently rejecting the whole notion of 'national' music, a term by which he seemed to mean little beyond Welsh harps and folk songs, Scottish bagpipes, alphorns and Swiss yodelling. Conscious nationalism in music, he wrote to Zelter from Paris in 1832, was simply the intrusion of politics, which bored him, into art. The Germans talked interminably of politics because the disunity of Germany made them feel inferior to other nations, but it was their ceaseless grumbling which caused the sense of disunity of which they were so conscious.[2]

[2] Mendelssohn: *Letters*. Edited by G. Selden-Goth. Elek, London, 1947.

In this, Mendelssohn was for once out of tune with his times. Wagner, Mendelssohn's junior by four years, grew up with a childish prejudice against Mozart's music because most of Mozart's opera libretti are Italian: Weber's music he loved because it, and the libretti of Weber's operas, are German in language, style and atmosphere. It was a performance of Mozart's *Requiem* in Leipzig in 1828 which opened his eyes to Mozart's greatness. In 1834 Bellini's *I Montecchi ed i Capuletti*, in Leipzig, left him with ideas which he explained fully in the *Autobiographical Sketch* nine years later:

> Though I could see no great merit in Bellini, yet the stuff out of which his music was made seemed to me to be better suited to spreading the warm glow of life than the calculated pedantry with which we Germans, as a rule, achieved only a laboured make-belief.[3]

By this time, Wagner was convinced that he had been born to save German opera and had reached the conclusion that the way to do so might be learned from the Italians. In the June 1834 issue of a Leipzig magazine, the *Zeitung für die Elegante Welt*, Wagner turned to the plight of German opera, thinking in entirely nationalistic terms:

> We are too intellectual, too learned, to create warm, human figures. Mozart could do so, but he animated his characters with the beauty of Italian song. Since we have come to despise this, we have wandered further and further from the path that Mozart beat out for the salvation of our dramatic music. Weber never knew how to handle song, nor does Spohr understand it much better. But song is the organ through which a human being can communicate himself musically; and so long as this is not fully developed, he lacks genuine speech. This is where the Italians have an enormous advantage over us; with them, beauty of song is second nature.[4]

The fault of German opera composers, Wagner declared, was that none of them 'has known how to win for himself the voice of the people'.

The essence of Wagner's thought is national. German, French and Italian music each have their individual characters, and the character of German music had lost, not the learning for which it had always been celebrated, but the reality of its connection with German popular melody. But while it is fairly easy for a modern listener to isolate French, Italian or English music by their national characteristics, so much of the *lingua franca* of music in practice is German that its national character often escapes us. The use of an English, French, Spanish or Italian folk tune immediately advertises the tune's place of origin, we miss the profound nationalism advertised by Papa-

[3] Quoted in Ernest Newman: *The Life of Richard Wagner.* Cassell, London, 1931. Vol. 1. p. 110.
[4] *Ibid.* p. 111.

geno's arias in *Die Zauberflöte* or the closeness to folk song of very many of
Schubert's *Lieder*; *Die Zauberflöte* and even *Fidelio* seem to owe their
nationality to their libretti rather than to their music, and Germanism becomes a matter of various imponderables like attitude and atmosphere, not
of any specifically German tradition.

The nationalistic aspect of Wagner's *Rienzi*, like its political aspect,
therefore tend to escape us. It is, however, the musical statement of Wagner's political attitude. Rienzi, 'the last of the tribunes', rises from the
people to defend them against the tyranny of a corrupt aristocracy. The
libretto was written before Wagner abandoned his post in Riga and was at
least partly translated into French ready for exploitation in Paris when
Wagner slipped away from his creditors there. Neither Wagner's praise of
the popular liberator–leader nor various lines altered by the Saxon censor
for the work's first performance in Dresden would have ruffled a single
feather in Paris, but before the Dresden production the censors found it
necessary to insist on a variety of alterations. 'Not only Rome shall be free,'
cries Rienzi in the original version of the libretto, published in Wagner's
Collected Writings: 'All Italy shall be free. Hail to united Italy!' The censor
was not enamoured of either the idea of freedom or that of unification,
which could easily be applied to Germany; to prevent audiences from making that dangerous identification, not concern for Italy (which the censor,
like Metternich, may have regarded as no more than 'a geographical expression'), Rienzi's declaration was changed. 'Not only Rome is great!' he cried
in the Dresden production. 'All Italy shall be great. Hail to the ancient
greatness of Italy!'

Wagner's openly nationalistic occasional works, the *Huldigungs Marsch*
for his patron Ludwig II of Bavaria and the *Kaisermarsch*, celebrating the
Prussian victory over France in 1870 and the long-delayed unification of
Germany, are not impressive works; they celebrate the political nationalism
which has nothing much to do with the composer of *The Ring*, in which the
mythology of the German people becomes a means of universalising a
nationalism far deeper than its overtly political expression. *The Master-
singers*, in which the *Volk* themselves, richly and lovingly depicted, makes
the people the guardians of artistic tradition and artistic progress. Wagner
at his greatest became a mouthpiece of the doctrines expounded long before
by Herder and Fichte. Political considerations, which Wagner confused
with the progress of his own cause, and mixed up with memories that made
him loathe France and celebrate Prussia's victory in 1870 with mean-
spirited glee, always show Wagner at his least likable.

If the German national style is not, like other national styles, immediately identifiable through its musical expression, it nevertheless had
popular manifestations which now seem strange to us. In 1863 the *Gesellschaft der Musikfreunde* in Vienna awarded a first prize to Joachim Raff's

First Symphony, *An das Vaterland*. The composer provided the work with a fairly detailed programme:

> First movement: *Allegro*. Image of the German character; ability to soar to great heights; tendency towards introspection; mildness and courage as contrasts that touch and interpenetrate in many ways; overwhelming desire to be pensive.
> Second movement: *Allegro molto vivace*. The outdoors; through German forests with horns calling; through glades resounding with folk music.
> Third movement: *Larghetto*. Return to the domestic hearth, tranfigured by love and the muses.
> Fourth movement: *Allegro drammatico*. Frustrated desires to work for the unity of the Fatherland.
> Fifth movement: *Larghetto—Allegro trionfale*. Plaint; renewed soaring.

It is the naivety of this programme which makes the work sound at least faintly ridiculous, and there is no reason why Raff's symphony *An das Vaterland* should be any less musically valuable than a symphonic poem by Richard Strauss. Though it has meant nothing to the world for a century or so, its importance to our argument is that a composer born in Zürich but educated in Germany and spending his career in the latter country should choose a nationalistic subject for one of his first major works and should win a prize for doing so. In Raff's mind, it seems, 'The Fatherland' was a theme as important and stimulating as the struggle with fate, life and death, love or any of the other favourite subjects of nineteenth-century composition.

Nationalism in German music was never a conscious effort to find a national voice, for the national voice already existed. German music simply set out to express a national reality which its creators believed to exist in all aspects of their lives except the political. Brahms, born in Hamburg, where memories of the city's old independence as a member of the Hanseatic League seemed to have more influence than the struggle for unification and leadership in a united Germany, preferred to live in Vienna in spite of Vienna's complete dissimilarity from the earnestness and emotional sobriety of northern Germany. But the Austro-Prussian War of 1866 left him equally annoyed with both of the combatants because the question of whether Prussia or Austria should lead the inevitable united Germany seemed to him to be meaningless. Yet Prussia's victory in the Franco-Prussian War of 1870 stirred him to his foundations; he told Georg Henschel, the singer-conductor who was later to settle in England, that his first impulse on the outbreak of war had been to join the army. Count Bismarck, the architect of the German Empire, became his hero, and he greeted the victory over France with his *Triumphlied*, a choral and orchestral work with biblical words which identified the cause of German nationalism with Old Testament Hebrew patriotism.

The German conviction that the music produced by German composers has a certain national quality on which each individual composer of worth stamped his own individuality created new problems in the minds of some German musicians. The belief that German music is of its nature more intellectual than other music was old enough—Burney drew attention to it in the 1780s—before anyone began to think systematically about music as the natural expression of national character. By the 1830s, it seemed natural to ask if the musicians of other nations could ever truly understand German music. Wagner, during his first stay in Paris, was properly impressed by the performances of Beethoven's symphonies which he heard from Habeneck and the Conservatoire Concerts Society Orchestra, but there were questions to be asked, he felt, on a deeper level than that of the accuracy and injustice to the text of these performances; surprised by the quality of these French communications of Beethoven's essentially German spirit, he wrote:

> They love to admire and applaud things beautiful and unknown from abroad. As witness the reception that has been so quickly accorded to German instrumental music. Though, apart from this, whether one could say that the French completely *understand* German music is another question, the answer to which must be doubtful. Certainly it would be wrong to maintain that the enthusiasm evoked by the Conservatoire orchestra's performance of a Beethoven Symphony is affected. Yet when one listens to this or that enthusiast airing the various opinions, ideas and conceits which such a symphony has suggested to him, one realises at once that the German genius is very far from being completely grasped.[5]

It would, probably, have been anything but difficult to hear equally startling examples of incomprehension from German listeners to a German concert. Wagner himself wrote uncomprehendingly of Haydn's symphonies, and Schumann, like many of his contemporaries and successors, did not see a great deal in Mozart's instrumental music beyond its elegance and shapeliness, while Spohr, and many of his generation, could not come to terms with the later music of Beethoven.

Because German music was apparently more intellectual than the music of other nations, it was not difficult for German musicians to feel that they had grasped the totality of French or Italian music, for the difficulty faced by French audiences and musicians when confronted by Beethoven's symphonies was not simply the foreignness of different musical languages but the German habit of thinking in music more deeply than musicians outside Germany found it necessary to think. This is a point which has some validity, but it became a point to exaggerate at the time when music was the central unifying force of a politically disunited people. Music was the out-

[5] Robert L. Jacobs and Geoffrey Skelton: *Wagner writes from Paris.* George Allen and Unwin, London, 1973. p. 36.

ward and audible sign of the essential cultural unity of the German people; it was never in any sense a weapon in the political struggle for German unification.

In Italy the long story of the *Risorgimento* is given a musical commentary by the operas of Verdi. To what extent Rossini intended his Moses, leading his people from bondage to the Promised Land, or his William Tell, heroically confronting a foreign tyrant, to express the political realities of Italian life in the early nineteenth century, nobody can say. It was Honoré de Balzac who claimed that during Moses's prayer in the last act of the opera he was watching the liberation of Italy.[6]

The Italy of Verdi's youth makes Metternich's remark that Italy was not a nation but simply 'a geographical expression' not a mere gibe but a statement of fact. The Italian states spoke no central language but a number of related dialects; Italy had neither a central language nor a literary tradition of its own. In Naples and Piedmont the official language was French; in the Papal States it was Latin. The Austrian provinces—Lombardy, Venice, Parma, Tuscany and Modena—were governed in German. The Milanesi spoke in a dialect not immediately or completely comprehensible to the users of the Ligurian dialect in their north-west or to the Parmigiani, who provided Verdi with his mother tongue in Roncole and Bussetto, where he worked as a young man. Travelling from Roncole or Busseto to Milan as a student, Verdi needed not only a passport but also a language in which to make himself understood. Verdi was fourteen when in 1827 Alessandro Manzoni published his novel *I Promessi Sposi*, and sixteen when he read that masterpiece. *I Promessi Sposi* is to a large extent the beginning of modern Italian, moulded from the Tuscan of Dante and fitted out with acceptable new and compound words. Music, as Verdi inherited it from tradition, had a special position in Italian life because it was not a dialect but a national language which cut across the various local differences of dialect and custom. Italian music insisted, as did German music, upon a fundamental unity of style and spirit inevitably clamouring to become political unity.

Therefore Verdi, who by virtue of creative genius dominated Italian music for the last sixty years of the nineteenth century, could not stand apart from the political struggles of his age. Unlike Wagner, he made no effort to involve himself in political action and his membership of the Italian parliament, accepted to please Cavour, whom he idolised, seemed to him to be only a sardonic joke. His beliefs and aspirations were totally expressed in music, so that many of his works seem to be either a reflection in terms of romantic opera of the struggle for unification or of the political problems that were inescapably part of the struggle. Whilst Wagner could see in the

[6] Quoted in Francis Toye: *Rossini; a Study in Tragi-Comedy*. Norton, New York, 1963. p. 131.

elaborate vocal style of Bellini the essentially melodic Italian musical tradition, Verdi's melodies begin at a point closer to the music which might be sung in streets and taverns; even the superb choruses which mark climatic moments even in his early operas are in this sense the voice of the Italian people united in musical style though in nothing else. The problems which had to be solved by the *Risorgimento*—the impossibility of independence without unification, the futility of either under any absolutist rule—are reflected in the music of Verdi the liberal patriot. In a country with no literary tradition, Verdi and his music, in its patriotism, its sense of Italy as a musical nation, its enormous vitality and inexhaustible energy spoke for all Italians.

To Verdi, the divided group of states, many of them under alien control, which comprised a narrow Mediterranean peninsula were never a geographical expression; in his mind Italy was a nation. Its divisions existed without reason or justification as an attempt to deny its nationhood. To what extent he set out deliberately to write the music of the *Risorgimento* nobody knows; it seems that it was simply the music of the great chorus *Va, pensiero*, in *Nabucco*, which led his audiences to feel that the music of the ancient Hebrews in exile spoke really of a divided and suffering Italy; we do not know that Verdi, as he wrote the music, identified himself with the sorrows of his characters in their Babylonian captivity. His choice of subject matter often invited the audience to break into the patriotic ecstasies which greeted *I Lombardi* and *Attila* when they were new. If he did not intend to be the mouthpiece of the *Risorgimento*, he nevertheless chose subjects apparently motivated by his consciousness of Italy's sufferings, and neither he nor his librettists can have been unaware of the effect of such correspondences on his audiences. He was exploiting the political situation to win an audience if he was not inflaming it to advance and possibly secure his own political aims.

Nabucco was produced at La Scala, Milan, in March 1842. It was accepted as a revolutionary work—revolutionary less in its technique than in its early-Verdian quality of almost brutal directness and emotional intensity. In a country where political discussion and argument were stifled, the chorus of exiled Hebrews seemed to early audiences to be their own cry of pain. With Austrian help, a rising in Naples had been crushed in 1820; in the following year, rebellion had been suppressed in Piedmont. In 1831 the Pope had appealed for Austrian assistance to smash a rising in the Papal States. An abortive rebellion in Piedmont had failed in 1833. The music of the Hebrew chorus was the music of Italian liberalism conscious of the parallel between Sion and Italy; the parallel was no secret.

The situation seemed perhaps rather less dark in 1843, when *I Lombardi* was staged at La Scala. The battle cry of the crusaders—'Today the Holy Land will be ours?—was interrupted after early performances with shouts

of approval from the audience. The police were unable to prevent the giving of a number of encores, although encores were forbidden; everyone knew
that the Lombardian crusaders were the Italians of 1843 and the stage
Saracens were the Austrian troops on whom the disunity of Italy depended.

Before *Attila* reached the stage of La Fenice Theatre in Venice, in 1846,
a combined rising in Naples, the Papal States and Tuscany in 1843 had
failed and a revolt at Rimini been defeated. In *Attila* a Roman general
cried, 'You can have the Universe, but leave Italy for me.' Again the performance was interrupted with cries of enthusiasm. The struggles of 1848,
with the almost irrelevant conflict (in terms of Italian unification) of
monarchists and republicans and the defeat of a rising in Lombardy, seem
to be reflected in *La Battaglia di Legnano* in 1849. This was an immediate
and dangerous comment on the current situation, with the troops of the
Emperor Barbarossa defeated by an Italian army and its hero, imprisoned
in a tower, leaping to freedom to join his compatriots with a cry of *'Viva
Italia!'* which roused the audience to repeated cheers; at every performance
the fourth act, the battle and victory, had to be repeated.

It is not only the nationalism of the *Risorgimento* but also the doctrine
of liberalism in politics—Verdi's anti-clericalism does not appear much in
his work, except in *Stiffelio*, until *Don Carlos*, in 1867—which motivated
much of his writing. *Les Vêpres Siciliennes*, written for Paris in 1855 and
revised for Milan a year later, is about national liberation. *Un Ballo
in Maschera* justifies the assassination of a king although censors insisted on
reducing his rank. In 1849 Charles Albert of Piedmont had abdicated in
favour of his son Victor Emmanuel, so it was after *Un Ballo*, ten years later,
that the name 'Verdi' appropriately became an acronym for *'Vittoria
Emmanuele Re d'Italia'*, and the shout *'Viva Verdi!'* saluted more than a
patriotic composer. By the time that *Don Carlos* was composed for the Paris
Opéra in 1867, the struggle was all but won and only Rome stood outside
the Italy which Mazzini, Cavour, Garibaldi and Victor Emmanuel had
created. But Don Carlos harps still on the theme of liberation; the Nether-
lands, say its Spanish heroes, must be free, as Italians, we gather, must be
free. Because Verdi was a great dramatist, the tortured King Philip is
created with sympathy and compassion, but he is wrong, just as the
Church, in the awesome figure of the Grand Inquisitor, is wrong. More con-
sistently than Wagner's, Verdi's politics have moved along in parallel to his
work, adding to its vitality.

Beyond its effect as an expression of thwarted national will, music to
Verdi is national by virtue of the tradition to which it belongs:

> Our composers are not good patriots [he wrote in 1889]. If the Germans,
> stemming from Bach, arrive at Wagner, they are doing as good Germans
> should, and that is fine. But for us, descendants of Palestrina, to imitate

Wagner is to commit a musical crime, and we are doing something useless, even harmful.[7]

Verdi looks back to Palestrina, whose work was probably the earliest Italian music of which he was aware, as the beginning of the tradition which he himself served, the necessary foundation for the vocal style which is intrinsically Italian and which all Italian composers should serve:

> Palestrina cannot compete with the very daring harmonic discoveries of modern music, but, if he were better known and studied, we might write in a more Italian manner, and might be better patriots (in music, I mean.)[8]

Music in Germany and Italy reflected the struggle for unity of states divided by the will of the great European powers; in other states, notably Poland, Hungary and Bohemia, national music was the music of an unlettered, unpolitical class of peasants and artisans. National rhythms, harmonic and melodic idioms and tastes in instrumental colour were not features of the music of the educated Poles or Bohemians, let alone of the great generality of trained musicians. For the first time since Haydn, the idea of national resurgence after the collapse of Napoleon's empire again made it natural for the composer to look at and refer to idiosyncrasies of national style.

Such idiosyncrasies became increasingly important in the countries dominated by the Habsburg Empire, where educated culture was German in outlook and language, imposed on educated classes who saw in these essentially foreign attributes the only way to realise their ambitions; in Hungary and Bohemia the nobility, usually more at home in Vienna than in the territories from which they drew their titles, positions and wealth, German culture and German music, inevitably disregarded the plebeian music of the indigenous populations. Thus, inevitably, individual folk styles became symbolic of the national identities the subject provinces were determined to assert and the master races to forget. Poland, to Russia, Austria and Prussia, was simply a nuisance so long as Poles regarded it as a nation: the culture of Hungary and Bohemia, to the Austrians, was simply a crude irrelevance.

Thus, a composer like Chopin, who adopted and glorified national rhythms in polonaises and mazurkas, became a heroic patriot who, according to legend, travelled always with a precious cup full of Polish earth among his luggage, although he seems in reality to have preferred Paris to all other cities as a home. Politics impinged on his life, as they impinged on the lives of all nineteenth-century musicians. The Warsaw friends of his

---

[7] Verdi: *Letters*. Selected and edited by Charles Osborne. Letter to Franco Faccio, 14 July 1889. p. 206.

[8] *Ibid*. Letter to Giuseppe Gallignani, 15 November 1891. p. 249.

youth lived in a ferment of liberal revolutionary politics and, apparently, felt him to be indissolubly of their number. His departure to Paris was delayed by the nationalist rising in Warsaw in 1830, but Chopin's letters of that time seem to concentrate more on his need to explore wider musical worlds than to suffer for the agony of a native land which, since 1772, had been partitioned between Austria, Russia and Prussia, a division exploited after 1815 for the sake of Metternichian *Real-politik*. The fact that Chopin's nationalism was active only in his affection for the dances and musical idioms of his people, and that he took no active part in their struggle, cannot lessen the extent to which his work supported their political aims and won sympathy for Poland though his exploitation of what was naturally Polish in music. Moniusko, Chopin's contemporary, was a lesser composer and occupies a lower place in our musical awareness, but he was, in a sense, more consciously a mouthpiece of Polish nationalism than Chopin in the sense such a work as Vaughan Williams's *Hugh the Drover* and Kodály's *Hary Janos* are consciously English and Hungarian respectively. Moniusko's *Halka*, produced in Wilno in 1848, finds its inspiration in Polish life, legend and folk customs as it finds its musical inspiration in the idioms and rhythms of Polish folk music; in spite of amateurish dramatic construction, it opened the road to a distinctively national operatic style which neither Moniusko in his later works nor any of his successors have successfully trodden.

The real battle for musical nationalism was fought out in the Austrian subject provinces. 'The conflict between a supernational dynastic state and the national principle had to be fought to a finish,' writes A. J. P. Taylor, 'and so had the conflict between the master and the subject nations.'[9] Poland had been divided among greater powers—Austria, Russia and Prussia—in 1772 to insulate Austria against any Russian advance in Central Europe, only the core of the Polish kingdom remaining. Kosciusko's rising against Russia was crushed by the three great Powers although, according to Thomas Campbell,

> Hope for a season bade the world farewell
> And freedom shrieked when Kosciusko fell!

The rest of Poland fell with its would-be liberator, and naturally the Congress of Vienna ratified the destruction of Poland. Chopin's generation was close enough to the memory of a free and independent Poland to struggle bitterly against its subjugation, but it was harder in the Central European subject provinces of the Austrian Empire to find any sense of national individuality or national culture like that to which the discontented Poles could look back for inspiration. Any sense in which Liszt, a willing expatriate

[9] A. J. P. Taylor: *The Habsburg Monarchy, 1809–1918*. Hamish Hamilton. London, 1948. p. 7.

who towards the end of his life spent part of each year in Budapest, was a Hungarian nationalist can only have been very limited, but he wrote what he believed to be Hungarian works because the enjoyment of exotic national idioms was a new taste to be savoured for the sake of the expressive intensities which could be drawn from it.

Liszt in the *Vormärz*, the period before the revolutions of 1848, believed the gipsy music of Hungarian cafés and street bands to be the traditional music of the Magyar people; Brahms, about a decade later, made the same mistake. It was natural for them both to fall into error because any high culture in the Habsburg dominions was essentially Austro-German. Paul Ignotus describes what he calls the 'estrangement' of the Hungarian aristocracy from their national traditions:

> Their withdrawal from the intellectual life of the country, however, seemed total; at one time the chief patrons of Hungarian arts and letters, by the end of the nineteenth century they had lost absolutely all interest in them. . . . Some were well-versed in the philosophical trends of German-speaking Central Europe but hardly noticed those in their own country.[10]

The real centre of aristocratic life—Hungarian, Bohemian or in any of the subject provinces—was Vienna, as it had been in the days when Haydn, as *Kapellmeister* at Ezterhaza, had written music that would have come just as naturally to him—even when, for the sake of high spirits, he was writing *alla Ongarese*—in Vienna or London. Music and drama were what could be found in the capital, and the gipsy fiddlers of Hungary, bending over the supper table to play 'in the ear' of a fashionably dressed lady while his accompaniment second violin, viola, cello and dulcimer or cimbalon, kept time with him from a suitable distance, lacked metropolitan dignity, but the fierce, often fiercely melancholy music, the *czardas*, with its alternations of wild high spirits and wild melancholy, developed from earlier folk dances, was often far from genuine. It resembled the many Irish songs composed in New York for American singers and became, in spite of its dubious ancestry, a powerful nationalist propaganda. The stranger music of a Hungarian peasantry was left for Bartók and Kodály to discover in the twentieth century; Liszt, like his fellow countrymen and Brahms, accepted the gipsy music as the traditional idiom of his people.

If, as may well be the case, he exploited it for the sake of its piquancies and exoticisms rather than as the true voice of his native land, Liszt's fellow countrymen regarded his music as national, expressing their hatred of Austrian authority. After the creation of the Dual Monarchy (by which the Austrian Emperor took the title King of Hungary and gave Hungary some outward show of independence) it manifested their dislike for the pretence that simply masked the continuation of Habsburg dominance. In

[10] Paul Ignotus: *Hungary*. Ernest Benn, Ltd. London, 1972. p. 80.

Liszt's later years he was almost totally disregarded by the official 'establishment'. His *King's Song*, an attempt at a Hungarian national anthem, was not played at the opening of the Royal Opera House in Budapest in 1874 because, according to the Superintendent, Frigyes Podmowiczky, 'its motives are borrowed from a well-known revolutionary song'. To the people of Budapest, Liszt was Hungary's greatest composer and a national hero, and this slight against him led to a demonstration in his favour outside the theatre.[11] Liszt thought himself a nationalist composer in spite of his cosmopolitan way of life and his apparent inability to find a home either among or away from his fellow countrymen. Arguing backward from the discoveries of Bartók to the late piano works of Liszt, with its strange harmonic conundrums, it is possible to see in his work another nationalism quite different from his flamboyant delight in the pseudo-nationalism of Hungarian rhapsodies.

The position in Bohemia, and indeed throughout the provinces which were later to become Czechoslovakia, was more complex. The Bohemians, and the rest of the Czechs for that matter, had always been an extremely musical people; from the Middle Ages onwards, Bohemian musicians had supplied Germany and Austria with fine musicians. The Benda family had been prominent in Frederick the Great's Berlin; the Mannheim School, which had influenced Mozart, was largely the creation of a group of Bohemian musicians, and such composers as Dussek, Reicha (who after 1818 spent the last eighteen years of his life at the Paris Conservatoire and was possibly the most influential teacher of his day as well as an extremely prolific composer) to say nothing of Vanhal, Kozeluth, Gyrowetz and Tomascek, composers far from negligible but overshadowed, as every other composer working between 1770 and 1820, by the work of Haydn, Mozart and Beethoven.

None of these composers, however, owed his reputation to his work in his own country. The nobility of the Central European Slavonic lands was a largely artificial creation, owing its way of life, and often its origin, to the Empress Maria Theresa. Like Beethoven's patron Prince Lobkowitz, their homes were in Vienna and their culture the international culture of the eighteenth century. An absentee aristocracy, they concentrated their musical life on Vienna and were almost infinitely remote from the way of life and the folk culture of their homeland. Even the gifted musicians of Bohemia and the other Austrian provinces could not earn their living at home among their own people.

It was the success in Bohemia of *The Marriage of Figaro* and of *Don Giovanni* that began the renaissance of Bohemian music and encouraged musicians to exploit recent political reforms. Joseph II, the most enlighten-

[11] Bence Szabolski: *The Twilight of Ferenc Liszt*. Translated by Andras Deak. Hungarian Academy of Science, Budapest, 1959.

ed, it seems, of 'Enlightened Despots', had abolished serfdom, granted religious toleration, permitted the publication of a Czech newspaper and allowed the Czech language to become a subject for study at the Charles University in Prague, although Czech was never taught at any lower levels in the schools. More influential still was the growth of industry in the Czech provinces and the consequent rise of a bourgeoisie which took its culture from the way of life of the German cities. Napoleon's empire had created areas in the Austrian dominions where the native population found itself thrust by war and French conquest into contact with Germans and Frenchmen rather than with Austrians; naturally, the doctrines of liberal nationalism spread like an epidemic through Austria's subject provinces.

It was Germany and not France, however, which provided the model for emergent Czech nationalism. In 1807 a German Opera House opened in Prague, and in the following year the Prague Conservatoire was founded. It is significant that from 1813 to 1816 the *Kapellmeister* of the Opera was Weber, and that Weber also conducted the orchestra of the Conservatoire. For some reason, composition was not taught at the Conservatoire, which did nothing to stimulate interest in a national musical style, although it turned out a considerable number of virtuoso instrumentalists, perhaps as a consequence of the neglect of theoretical teaching and the study of ideas.

When Weber went to Prague in 1813 his determined effort to modernise the Opera's repertoire brought in not only his own works but operas by Rossini and the French composers, so that in the long run it was amateur opera companies and amateur concert organisations that started the exploration of Czech idioms and Czech life as a subject for libretti. The 'successful' works by Czech composers of Weber's day were operas like Weigl's *Die Schweizerfamilie*, which was so successful in Vienna that its composer became *Kapellmeister* of the Imperial Opera. But in spite of the traditional draining away of Czech talent towards Vienna or the northern European courts, the first steps towards an individual Czech style (itself an amalgam of various styles present in the folk and popular music of what became Czechoslovakia) came in the 1820s, and the failure of that style to develop any further for a quarter of a century was not the result of any lack of enthusiasm or even the lack of any central Czech musical tradition; it was the irruption into Bohemian musical life of an influence as powerful as that of Mozart.

> Before any real native voice could be heard, [writes Brian Large] Prague was invaded by a number of visiting artists, notably Berlioz, at the request of a dissatisfied clique forced to look abroad for inspiration. After Berlioz came Liszt, then Wagner. Music was reborn, but not by Bohemians—by French, German and Hungarian visitors whose influence began to stifle everything Czech.[12]

[12] Brian Large: *Smetana*. Duckworth, London, 1970. p. 25.

The inspiration brought by such visitors was influential enough, and eventually beneficial—the national schools which developed in the second half of the nineteenth century came into the world with a sense of the orchestra which they had learnt from Berlioz. It was the political ambitions of Bohemian musicians—they wanted and were prepared to work for independence outside the Austrian Empire, and saw the unifying effects of their national music as a weapon in their hands—which released them from their inhibitions by turning them to explore the possibilities of folk song and folk dance. Smetana, who was twenty-four when the revolutions of 1848 shook the European establishments and the Austrian Empire with them, saw Austria struggle to hold on to her Italian provinces and was stimulated by the sight to demonstrate his own sense of Bohemian nationality. Smetana's operas take their plots from Czech history, Czech national myth and Czech folk customs; *Libuse*, the essential national myth, became an opera he wished to see preserved for national occasions. But for twenty years or more, before his operas reached the stage, his choral orchestral and piano music exploits, as often as not, Czech idioms and rhythms. Occasionally they are written to openly nationalistic texts.

Smetana, perhaps, was more politically conscious than any other composer. His letters refer to such political phenomena as the growth of Czech influence on the *Reichrat* (the consultative assembly originally designed by Metternich and set up in 1851 to support the Emperor's absolute rule with a show of popular consent). The elections of 1859, Smetana declared, gave enough strength to national opinion for the Czechs (never, in Smetana's correspondence, Bohemians and Moravians but always members of a single nation) to insist that the demand for national independence be continually reiterated until official Vienna, which he saw as entirely destructive of the Czech way of life, was compelled to take notice.[13] Both to Smetana and to Dvořák, the fact of their Czech birth was a reality which gave a special national character to their music. The difference between the two is, perhaps, that Smetana wanted Czech music to be established for its own sake, while Dvořák fed national ideas into the European mainstream.

Musical nationalism in Russia had other than political sources. Russia, in what may have been a somewhat ramshackle way, was united, independent politically and ranked among the great powers; its musical revival was a matter of national pride rather than of any political demand. The Russian musical tradition, both in folk song and dance and in liturgical music, had lost whatever influence it might once have had because of the westernising policy adopted by the Czars since the seventeenth century. Czar Alexis Mikhailovitch, the father of Peter the Great, began the *rapprochement* with the West which was ruthlessly accelerated; Peter left Russia in 1697 for

[13] Frantisek Bartos: *Bedrich Smetana; Letters and Reminiscences.* Translated by Dorothy Rustridge. Artis, Prague, 1956. p. 113.

a year and a half's tour of the West and then set out to complete the
creation of a Westernised Russia from first-hand experience of Western
society, industry and customs. Western music, especially Italian opera and
Singspiele, became the models for Russian composers. The Empress Elizabeth Peter's successor, appointed the Italian Francesco Araja to direct
music in her court, and Araja held office continually until the murder of
Peter III and the usurpation of his wife, Catherine the Great, in 1762.
Araja, seven years before this, had composed the first opera to a Russian
text, a work representative of Westernising demands through its subject
matter, *Cephalus and Procris*.

The policy of westernising Russian music so far succeeded that, by the
time of Catherine the Great, every aristocrat had his own musical establishment performing Italian or German music.[14] Catherine was as resolute
a westerniser as any of her predecessors. She brought Galuppi, at the
height of his fame and influence, to St. Petersburg in 1766. Galuppi controlled the music of the Imperial Court Chapel as well as of the court's
secular events, and among his pupils was Dmitry Stepanovich Bortniansky,
who returned to Italy with Galuppi in 1768, to continue his studies
at Catherine's expense. In Italy he had three operas successfully produced
before he returned to Russia in 1779, where the court composers were suc-
cessively Paisiello and Traetta; Martin y Soler and Cimaroso followed in
their footsteps, and it was not until after the death of Catherine and the
reign of Paul I that Bortniansky, in 1796, found an official position in
Russia. Paul I made him director of the Imperial Court Chapel, a post in
which he wrote Italian style music for the Russian liturgy. Erstignei
Ipalovich Fomin, Mikhail Martinsky and Vassily Paskewitch, Bortnianski's
contemporaries, wrote opera equally Italianate in style, their training
having been no less Italian than Bortniansky's. Their models were the inferior Italian works of a period which is, to modern listeners, that of the
operas of Mozart. Vladimir Stassov, writing more than half a century later,
saw in these works some appetite for Russian national music crushed to the
conventions and tyranny of the court:

> The fact that we were so long in producing an art music of our own
> was due solely to the unfavourable conditions of Russian life in the
> eighteenth and nineteenth centuries, when everything national was
> trampled in the mud. Nevertheless the need for national music was so
> widespread that even during the time of Catherine the Great . . . one of
> our poor composers after the other tried to incorporate folk melodies
> into his poor operas.[15]

Nevertheless, not only the audience for such works, but the composers

---

[14] R. A. Leonard: *A History of Russian Music*. Jarrold, London, 1956.
[15] Vladimir Stassov: *Selected Essays on Music*. Translated by
Florence Jonas. Cresset Press, London, 1968. p. 71.

themselves, were wedded to an Italian style and Italian taste, accepting models considerably behind those acceptable in the Europe of Mozart, Beethoven and Rossini. In Russia, Gluck's reform operas apparently won little approval though his earlier, conventional works, were popular. The next model, after the assassination of Alexander I in 1801, was Boieldieu, who went to the Imperial Opera as conductor in 1803 and was succeeded by Daniel Steibelt, a German who had worked successfully as a conductor in Paris, in 1808; two years later Steibelt was promoted to become *Maître de Chapelle* of the Imperial Court. Among Steibelt's Russian pupils was Alexis Nikolaievich Verstovsky, the most successful composer yet to be produced by Russia.

Verstovsky, born in 1799, had a conventionally cosmopolitan training. The Irish John Field, the Italian Tarquini and the German Böhm were his teachers for piano, singing and the violin respectively. His own compositions began to attract attention in 1818; in 1824 he was made Inspector of the Imperial Opera in Moscow, and between 1828 and his death in 1862 he composed six operas, the third of which, *Askold's Tomb*, produced in 1835, became so popular that for some years it eclipsed even Glinka's *Ivan Susannin (A Life for the Czar)* produced a year later.

The composers who followed Verstovsky, Glinka among them, belonged to a class which had not previously been much occupied in the arts. The recent history of Russia, its encounter with the might of Napoleon in particular, had created a new sense of national pride and national purpose, especially among the growing middle class which provided the country's legions of bureaucrats and civil servants, its middle-class shopkeepers and business men who had previously been too few and too unregarded to have much influence on any aspect of Russian life. The shock of war had become the seed from which conscious patriotism grew among a class which was not involved with the court, and therefore with the deliberate Italianism which court music expected. The use of popular-style melodies in *Askold's Tomb*, the work of an official musician, suggested that at last a truly national music had been born, but Stassov, summing up the achievements of the National School in an essay written in 1883, almost sourly put Verstovsky's into perspective:

> Half a century ago the Russians firmly believed that they had achieved their own national, truly Russian, music. The reason for this was that they had a 'national anthem', which had been written on commission by Lvov and was being ardently disseminated, and also Verstovsky's opera *Askold's Tomb*, whose quasi-gypsy, quasi-popular melodies excited many listeners. But the belief that these constituted a national music was only an illusion. Neither the anthem nor the opera had any national character, and despite the expectations of the authorities and the public, they did not give rise to any national music or school of composition whatever.[16]

16 *Ibid.* p. 66

The real Russian nationalist school, with and following Glinka and Dargomiszky, were all, as Verstovksy had been, amateurs born outside court circles and therefore not indoctrinated with the Western tastes which they came to despise. Glinka, born in 1806, was a country gentleman who spent four years in the Ministry of Transport and Communications before retiring at the age of twenty-three. He had studied the piano and the violin, brought up on German music until, in 1830, he went to Italy, where he came to the conclusion that his future was to write opera, not in the Italian style but for his own people. His only formal study of composition was undertaken during a year's stay in Berlin, where he broke his return journey from Italy in 1834. *Ivan Sussanin* was produced in 1836; aristocrats in the audience, brought up on German and Italian music, dismissed Glinka's work, with its contrasting Russian and Polish melodies, as 'coachman's music', in other words, unfit for aristocratic ears. But the use of an episode from Russian history and the combination of Russian-style melodies with a conventional operatic technique, all written with vividly colourful or- chestration, persuaded the unaristocratic audience that at last a composer had found the real music of Russia. Glinka's second opera, *Russlan and Ludmilla*, its libretto pieced together by the composer himself from a poem by Pushkin, never won the same popularity.

Dargomizhsky, nine years younger than Glinka, was another country gentleman trained as an amateur pianist. His only consistent training in composition came from the notebooks in which Glinka had worked out the exercises set for him during his year of study in Berlin. After a series of minor successes in the theatre with works based on Russian subjects, he was close to fifty years old when, in the early 1860s, he came into the orbit of Balakirev and reformed his style according to the tenets of the deliberate, conscious nationalist school which owed its dogma to Balakirev. The result was Dargomizhky's last opera, *The Stone Guest*, based on Pushkin's treat- ment of the Don Juan legend and produced in 1872, three years after its composer's death. *The Stone Guest* became extremely influential because of the precision and accuracy with which it did justice to Russian rhythms and prosody.

Of the brilliant group who came together as '*The Kuchka*', 'The Mighty Handful' or 'The Five' in the generation after Glinka, none was academi- cally trained, all tended to despise academic training, none was originally a professional musician and all were provincials. This meant that though all of them were well-trained instrumentalists, their impressions of music as a living art came not from the operas and symphonies heard at court or in aristocratic circles generally but from the songs and dances of the serfs and peasantry on the estates where they grew up. The music they studied formed a second, more superficial, level of experience, less immediate and less personal to them than the music of their own countryside. The similarity of their backgrounds and upbringing made it natural for them to cluster together round Balakirev, the most prolific in ideas and the most unusual in personality; it was equally natural for them to look scornfully at the Russian Musical Society founded in 1854, and bringing more up-to-date Western music to St. Petersburg. Out of the Russian Musical Society the St. Petersburg Conservatoire grew in 1862; its staff and its pupils did not accept or for a moment take seriously Balakirev's conviction that tradition and saturation in the music of the past was the only training a composer needed. Nevertheless, the Russian Musical Society began to bring into its programmes the works of the Balakirev group, all of whom studied with their leader, who taught them only what he himself would have done with the materials of their compositions. Rimsky-Korsakov, as a pupil-disciple of Balakirev, lived to find that his hero's teachings were not sufficiently comprehensive to be fully useful to him. Balakirev, he wrote:

> should have given me a few lessons in harmony and counterpoint, should have made me write a few fugues and explained the grammar of musical forms to me. He could not do so, as he had never studied systematically himself and considered it unnecessary. As a product of the Conservatoire, Tchaikovsky was viewed rather negligently if not haughtily by our circle.[17]

Tchaikovsky, at various times, expressed similar uncertainties about the procedure of the Balakirev 'Mighty Handful' and its leader; their lack of training, he felt, and the absence of real mental discipline in their music, led often to the squandering of brilliant ideas and the crippling of remarkable talents.

The essential amateurishness of the 'Handful', from which only Rimsky-Korsakov escaped, did not prevent the creation of several indisputable masterpieces, although most of the members remained amateurs composing in the intervals of their extra-musical careers. For a time, the group dominated St. Petersburg music, as the Russian Musical Society fell into the hands of Balakirev, who, though he did not remove Western works from its programmes, never found it necessary to arrange for the performance of any works earlier than Beethoven's but regarded it as a point of principle to see that a Russian work was included in every programme. The only work by Bach to appear in the Musical Society's programmes during the years of nationalist control was, perhaps inevitably, conducted by the more academically-minded and disciplined Rimsky-Korsakov. Amateurishness was both a strength and a debilitating weakness of his colleagues and explains why so much of his time was spent in clearing up and making practical the works of his fellow nationalists.

Tchaikovsky, with his Europeanism and his unfashionable devotion to

[17] Rimsky-Korsakov: *My Musical Life.* Translated by Jonah A. Jaffe. Knopf, New York, 1942. p. 34.

Mozart, was never an official, exclusive nationalist, but it may be that, acting, so to speak, the Dvořák to their Smetana, he advanced the cause of Russian music by building the necessary bridges between it and the central tradition. He chose Russian subjects for some of his operas and found folk melodies and national rhythms valuable. But he never considered the wholesale rejection of European influences or sympathised with the excesses of the 'Mighty Handful'. It was with him, and with other composers who achieved the synthesis of the unmistakably Russian with the generally European, that the future of Russian music really lay, so that the symphonies of Glazounov, Prokofiev and Shostakovitch follow not from the exclusiveness of the Balakirev group but from the Tchaikovskyan synthesis. The greatest work of the 'Handful' is, it seems, that of Mussorgsky, greatest in songs and operas, reaching a style of melody which is the outcome of Russian speech, 'a reincarnation of recitative in melody'. But the outcome of that was that Mussorgsky's operas were known until the mid-twentieth century in the tidied, smoother versions prepared by Rimsky-Korsakov when he assembled their disorganised fragments.

Nationalism, however, was a nineteenth-century necessity, affecting music in Spain, in Britain, where the collection of English folk songs showed the way to Holst, Vaughan Williams and other refugees from an outworn European style, and eventually in America, after Charles Ives had used the music of his youth, revivalist hymns and popular melodies, to create the musical reality of the United States.

9

The Great Schism

Until the nineteenth century, the idea that 'light' music is something essentially different in nature from 'serious' music would have been meaningless. The professional composer of the eighteenth century had to be as willing, and ideally as capable, of providing music for amusement or for social relaxation as he was of writing a mass or a church cantata, and the specific gravity of his music ideally depended on the music that was expected from him for any particular occasion. Leopold Mozart, who never found life at Salzburg intolerable, wrote rather academic church music and a considerable number of light, humorous and occasionally freakish works because such music was expected of him. Dittersdorf, in spite of serious operas and oratorios, could be seen as a 'lighter' composer than Wolfgang Mozart because his various patrons required light-hearted music from him rather more often than they asked for serious works. Sets of dances by Mozart or Haydn seem to have occasioned neither composer any pangs of conscience, just as Schubert's dance music for piano seemed to him to be quite natural music to compose and to publish. Beethoven's sets of minuets, German dances and *Ländler* have all the essential character of light music. It was Chopin, Schumann and Brahms who refined dance music into abstraction, just as it was Lanner and the two Johann Strausses who decided never to venture beyond what is enjoyably light, though the younger Strauss sometimes gave almost symphonic emotional depth to the introductions and codas of his waltzes. But Chopin, Schumann and Brahms are accepted as invariably and incurably 'serious' musicians while Lanner and the Strausses were accepted as specialists in 'light' music who could not be expected to write 'light' sonatas, string quartets and symphonies, although earlier musicians had done so; they could not be expected even, in the way of Mozart, to write a Mass with its *Kyrie* in waltz-time.

This precise and now tidy distinction between music for amusement and what for the want of a better name passes now as 'serious' music (Malcolm Arnold's Second Symphony, because it is a symphony, is 'serious' in spite of its hilarities and the rhythmic jokes that it plays on the listener) asks questions which permit no simple explanation. The Marxist critic, noting the general decline in Viennese music, and to a lesser extent of Central European music generally, from the end of the Napoleonic Wars until the triumph of Wagner and the rise of Brahms, is inclined to see the decline of power as a result of the post-revolutionary reaction in politics. Serious thought about life and, consequently, about society was likely to give offence to governments. Therefore musicians turned to the great music of the past, rediscovering Handel, Bach and works of power and beauty which could no longer shock tender political sensibilities; or they spent their time with the romantic extravagances or glorious flippancies of Rossini, Bellini and Donizetti. Or there was the spectacular grand opera of Meyerbeer, emasculated, as was often necessary, into political conformity.

The move towards charming, easy-going dance music, as satisfying to listeners as to dancers, came first from Vienna. Weber and Schubert had composed waltzes before the first master of the dance, Michael Pamer, and his disciples Lanner and the elder Johann Strauss first set Vienna, and then the rest of Europe, dancing to the slightly distorted three-four time of the Viennese waltz. It was in 1814 that a disillusioned diplomat in Vienna, asked about the progress of the Congress of Vienna, said that Congress did not progress, it only danced. Lanner joined Pamer's orchestra in 1813, when he was twelve years old, and Strauss, three years Lanner's junior, played with it until, in 1819, he joined the trio—two violins and a guitar—which Lanner had formed two years before. The quartet thus formed had become an orchestra playing in the Prater before the two quarrelled in 1825 and Strauss broke away to form his own orchestra, eclipsing both his master and his friend.

The Viennese waltz was an offshoot of the Viennese musical tradition; though both Lanner and the elder Strauss were virtually self-taught both as violinists and as composers, they united the tradition of Austrian folk dance with the legacy of the Viennese classics. Elegance and taste, with sentimentality never denied its place but always kept under control, were as important as high spirits. Both Lanner and Strauss introduced their waltzes with a musical prologue, Strauss briefly with a flourish, Lanner often with a quasi-symphonic, poetically emotional introduction. The younger Strauss, who usurped his father's title, 'Waltz King', before the elder Strauss was prepared to abdicate, was a trained musician whose juvenilia include church music. The second Strauss took his orchestra, and his waltzes, to France, England, Russia and the United States. His father's music had intoxicated Wagner during Wagner's first stay in Paris, and Strauss the Second was greeted with critical approval by the critic Hanslick, Wagner's most irreconcilable enemy, but lost the critic's advocacy when he introduced Wagner's music into his Viennese programmes, which, naturally, demanded some occasional relief from dance rhythms. The younger Strauss showed in the introductions to some of his waltzes—*The Blue Danube* and the *Kaiserwaltz* for example—that he knew and loved Wagner's music, and understood Wagnerian orchestration, which he applied to his own smaller orchestra. More ambitious than his father, he composed operettas which, at their best, are great (if the concept of 'greatness' in music has any real meaning) in their unique expression of things which more serious masters have never really wished to express; no other music creates the alcoholic goodwill of a successful party so perfectly as the finale of act two of *Die Fledermaus* with a waltz which celebrates, if not the essential brotherhood of man, at any rate the temporary brotherhood of the good-naturedly tipsy.

If the cult of light music, started in Vienna, had been restricted to the German-speaking nations when they were condemned to silence by the Metternichian reaction, the Marxist explanation might stand as a complete account of its origins. But light music, often of genius, came from Offenbach (and from others) in Paris. From 1839 onwards, Offenbach was supplying the Paris stage with complete operettas, one-act plays with music, and cabaret sketches more than thirty years before the younger Strauss invaded the theatre. Among Offenbach's vast collection of stage works are several unique masterpieces like *Orphée aux Enfers, La Belle Hélène, La Vie Parisienne* and *La Périchole*, and, like the younger Johann Strauss, he was followed by an army of imitators. Strauss's disciples lack the refinement and inventiveness of his music, and its exact balance between sentiment and undue sentimentality, while Offenbach's imitators rarely possessed in any marked degree the technical finesse and elegance of his music, while no other composer has achieved the heartless, glittering frivolity of his finest scores; emotion he reserved for *Les Contes d'Hoffmann*, the final and technically unfinished work which he rightly described as an opera.

The need for light music in the nineteenth century, not only in Austria, Germany and France, in countries of great political agitation and upheaval, but also in countries where music was as free as the circumstances of commercial music-making would allow it to be, seems to need other than political and social explanations. The effect of Beethoven's work was to make unprecedented demands not only on instrumentalists but on their audiences. The *Eroica*, writen in 1803, lasts almost as long as any two symphonies by Haydn and Mozart; the Ninth Symphony lasts half as long again. The intricacy of such music, its demands on the resources of the average violinist or oboe player, its demand for more and more rehearsal time, tended to put this music in as much a class of its own as Mahler's Eighth Symphony or Schoenberg's *Gurrelieder* are in the late twentieth century; such works, before the days of the long-playing gramophone record, could not become familiar, and familiarity is a necessary ingredient of devotion to any music. But Beethoven also demanded an unprecedented concentration and development of the musical memory if the problems set in the early pages of his major works are to be heard to have a convincing solution at their end.

Chamber music, especially the companionable string quartet, played by amateurs in their homes, probably without rehearsal and intended simply for their pleasure, became the vehicle for Beethoven's most exalted thought and complex structures, not uningratiating to the ear but baffling to the traditional understanding of musical grammar, syntax and logic. Schubert, too old in the 1820s to be diverted from his own paths by the works of Beethoven's third period, was the last composer outside Italy not to feel the Ninth Symphony as an inescapable challenge and the late quartets as invitations to a world which he must enter; he was, with Mendelssohn, the last composer to invite the attention of amateur chamber musicians. However close to normal experience the chamber music of Brahms may be, however heartful and melodious that of Dvořák, the music of such composers demands a technical expertise beyond that of the amateur quartet. The popularity of the piano as everybody's all-purpose instrument meant a decline in the number of amateur string and wind players—the world ceased to be crowded with enthusiastic amateur flautists—and the number of amateur ensembles of all kinds decreased; the technical demands of the nineteenth-century composer kept at bay all but the most accomplished players.

In this situation, as a direct descendant of Beethoven, Wagner appeared as the composer who not only demanded unusually large orchestras exactly balanced, but also listeners who could hear the end of *Götterdämmerung*, late on Friday evening, as a fulfilling recapitulation of music heard early on the previous Tuesday evening. Beyond that, he imposed upon Europe an aesthetic which exalted music from the status of a delightful and moving art to a religion, to be treated with an invariable devotion and seriousness, with no room for pleasantry and relaxation. The music lover who could listen with pleasure, or even with a sense of revelation, to the symphonies of Haydn and Mozart could come to terms with Wagner only when he was able to recognise the final cadence of *Tristan und Isolde* as the necessary resolution of a harmonically baffling harmonic statement made in the work's opening bars. Listening, like playing, had become much harder, and whilst Wagner won the complete devotion of those who were capable of learning his ways, there were music lovers who could not do so. Light music, within the tradition which Europe had developed, was an alternative course to the ever more demanding works of the serious composers. It was, in addition, socially necessary; somebody had to write the music of relaxation and social enjoyment. If Beethoven, by the time that Strauss and Lanner had begun to delight audiences in Vienna, no longer felt disposed to enliven all and sundry with dance music, and Wagner bypassed that area of music altogether, less exalted composers had to fill the breach. As music became the romantic composer's substitute for religion and its most earnest composers became less and less willing to do anything which derogated from the divine dignity of their art, they ceased to regard it as belonging to a world which urgently needs music, however ephemeral, for social life and activity.

The worlds of light music and serious music are not, for all that, mutually exclusive. Brahms, for example, though for a long time he was regarded as a composer of almost unfathomable profundity and super-human intellect, was an admirer of the younger Strauss; Bruckner's scherzos usually stand in a clear relationship to Austrian folk music and Mahler could never, even in his most ecstatic moods, break contact with the music of the Vienna streets and inns, the Schrammel groups of fiddlers, guitarists and accordion players, the buglers and trumpeters of the barrack square. It has always been popular, even in a work as sophisticated as *Wozzeck*, to connect the opera house to the music of streets and dance halls, but the nineteenth century made the journey between diverse musical worlds far more difficult. It is not only that there will always be people who are musically underdeveloped, just as there will always be people to whom mathematics, beyond its simplest operations, is a matter of insuperable diffi-culty and those who seem by nature incapable of using any language but their own. The development of light music towards ever-increasing simpli-fication and of serious music into increasing abstraction and specialisation has created a schism so that it often easy to see the two as acrimonious armies engaged in hostilities across the divide.

The example of English music in the nineteenth century provides a clear demonstration of the development because, perhaps, by the 1820s English music had been more or less buried by the popularity, among the wealthy, leisured patrons of the opera and the London concert hall, of foreign musicians and European styles. Such English forms as the glee, music essentially for small amateur groups of singers, held their own and until the middle of the century provided music admirably fitted to its social and artistic purposes, while the English symphonies and oratorios of the period are no more than dutiful reflections of the style and ideas more pointedly used by Beethoven and Mendelssohn; Sterndale Bennett, a composer of considerable originality and technical expertise, who married the English tradition to the techniques of Mendelssohn and Schumann, was driven into teaching and administration while his music was forgotten. In Britain, how-ever, the development of an industrial working class, bred in towns created simply to satisfy the demands of industry or into poor areas of existing cities decayed into centres for industry, produced a whole population which for generations grew up divorced from any traditional standards of culture, general or musical. When Dickens, as a young journalist, reported the amusements of the working classes in the essays eventually published as *Sketches by Boz* in 1836, he found the London working classes preserving the manners of the well-to-do and aping their social superiors in the song and supper rooms with glees interspersed by solo songs, like the comfortable Bohemians of Thackeray's *Pendennis* and *The Newcomes*, novels of the 1850s. The early music halls, beginning in the middle of the century, provided at first opportunities for concerted singing of the same sort, with solo songs and occasional excursions into 'serious' music. The first London performance of Gounod's *Faust*, as a piece in concert form, was early in the 1860s at the New Canterbury Music Hall in Lambeth. But whatever the quality and zest of the concerted singing and the degree of public interest to be aroused by performances of opera, there was always Little Swills, the archetypal comic singer of Dickens's *Bleak House*, ready to attend the inquest on the mysterious suicide, held in the Sol's Arms; such material would enable Little Swills to entertain the habitués of the same pub later that evening with a topical comic song with a nonsense refrain. The song and supper rooms had their singers of often extemporary, topical comic songs, and while the music halls and their audiences were never averse to easy and directly melodious songs from opera, or to the more spectacularly acrobatic feats of *coloratura*, their strength eventually came to be the artists they created, for whom songs were written reflecting colourful, eccentric personalities, with easy sentiment or socially pointed derision, growing from, or creating, a folk tradition much further from the concert hall or the opera house than the waltzes of Strauss, which are never more than a stone's throw from the hall of the *Gesellschaft für Musikfreunde* in sentimental, music-obsessed Vienna. The music hall invented a style of popular song developed from the tastes, habits and manners of the industrial working class who grew up with no contact with the world of high culture except, perhaps, the language of the authorised version of the Bible.

The music halls eventually created their community, an entirely classless one, not through its music but through the startling, flamboyant and extraordinarily gifted people who became its stars. Their gifts were not, perhaps, primarily musical, although one of their central abilities was to be able to project songs, comic, satirical, pathetic or simply sentimental, with the maximum point. There was no essential way from the music hall to works which conveyed other, and perhaps even more important, aspects of life than the everyday experience of a working-class audience which understood why Marie Lloyd's old man, engaged in a moonlight flit, told her to follow the van without any undue waste of time. It is not that the wealthier patrons of the 'halls' necessarily became aware either emotionally or intellectually of the world in which a tandem bicycle became a more suitable wedding conveyance than a coach, or of the pathos of entering a workhouse where, after forty years of happy married life, they would be parted from their old Dutch. It was the 'star quality' of a handful of great entertainers whose gifts were often for satire—they lived in Trafalgar Square, with four lions to guard them, or watched the activities of Burlington Bertie, who rose at ten-thirty and walked down the Strand—which were the life-blood of the music hall. If offered membership of a classless community and created a social unity almost without attention to the music or poetry which it used.

The publication of *Hymns Ancient and Modern* in 1860 seems to have added the final ingredient to English popular music. The compilers of that anthology included in their collection a considerable number of hymns from the Latin liturgy, with their original plainsong melodies somewhat unsympathetically harmonised, but these seem to have made comparatively little impression on the congregations which used the book; it was the more stirring or more sentimental tunes which were most often heard and many of these were held in common with the nonconformists. Probably any enquirer looking, in the 1880s and 1890s, for music which was universally known to the English would have turned to the Victorian hymn tunes, which, close on a century later and in a period of religious decline, are still in the mind of almost every Briton. To strike chords in the average English heart, the composer need only turn, deliberately or unconsciously, to the idioms and harmonic procedures of Victorian hymn composers. The popularity of these melodies did not, perhaps, entirely depend on their being given week by week to a captive audience in church or chapel but because many of them seem to express, in sturdy if limited rhythms or in sweetly lachrymose melodies, certain essential English attitudes. *Hymns Ancient and Modern* became virtually a national possession perhaps twenty years before the greatest days of the music hall, and the music of the anthology (as the old habit of prefacing Football Association Cup Finals with the singing of the hymn 'Abide with Me' indicates) created a musical taste perhaps even more universal than the music hall. From the meditations of Mrs Waters, the heroine of Ethel Smyth's opera *The Boatswain's Mate*, to pop songs, the cadences of Victorian hymnology haunt English popular music.

In so far as music creates a social unity among its hearers, so that such composers as the two Johann Strausses and Offenbach preserved a corner of the central musical tradition, the development of English music into two largely antipathetic styles lessened the possibility of such unity. The Victorian hymn melody, sung with whatever sincerity or fervour, was not really a means of entry to any wider musical tradition, though the chorales of Lutheran Germany had opened doors to more extensive musical horizons. Hymns were the only contact which the huge and largely illiterate population of Britain outside the choral societies had with any type of musical experience.

Because of this, the English composer who can justly be classed with the Strausses and Offenbach achieved enormous, deserved popularity. Arthur Sullivan was in no way inferior to the continental masters of light music. It could be argued that in inventiveness and range of emotional expression he was possibly Offenbach's superior. While the 'Savoy Operas', in which he deals with the libretti of W. S. Gilbert, are not his only worthwhile music, the 'operas' maintain a remarkably high musical level; their elegance of melody, harmony and orchestration is rarely less than delightful, Sullivan's gift as a parodist is made all the more effective by its restraint, while his lyrical gift seems almost inexhaustible. But the Savoy Operas are the work of 'Gilbert and Sullivan', relegating the composer to a junior partnership in the enterprise; Gilbert was invincibly and almost arrogantly of the middle class, almost its laureate. The situation of the English theatre in the late nineteenth century insisted that the Savoy Operas were written for and enjoyed by middle-class audiences, by tradition the most eager theatre-goers; they became available to a wider public, of course, but the wider public of the theatre gallery and the amateur performance aimed at and implicitly accepted nineteenth-century middle-class values. This Gilbert and Sullivan opera reinforces the old-fashioned conviction that the upper-classes are amusingly effete, that foreigners are quaint and the working class unamiably funny; the coster, as a matter of course, jumps on his mother; middle-class spinsters past their first youth are, equally 'of course', a subject of unparalleled hilarity. The Savoy Operas perform the important incidental feat of creating a community out of a mere audience, but their influence is largely a narrowing one, offering membership to a small, closed world.

The brass-band movement in England and Wales was to reach a similar musical restrictedness. The bands rose in the areas, and among the class of people, who created the choral societies, so that band music was part of the early nineteenth-century appetite for self-help, for moral and material improvement. Like many of the choral societies, many of the brass bands grew out of nonconformity. The band formed at Stalybridge, in Cheshire, began its recorded history when it played as a reed band at the laying of the foundation stone of a local Sunday School on 24 June 1815. The members of the band had created it for their own pleasure and practised in the house of one of the members, but their understood allegiance to the chapel was marked by the membership of the son of the local minister who had himself blessed the organisation at its foundation.

The poverty of most of the members of the early bands restricted them to reed instruments, notably cheaper than brass, but employers were as quick to see the benefits of bands as they had been to encourage choral singing. In 1816 an employer, John Foster, became a member of the group which was later to evolve into the Black Dyke Mills Band while it was still restricted to reeds. Foster's took the band over, and in 1854 converted it into a brass band. The Besses o' th' Barn Band, equally celebrated in brass-band circles, began life as a string band in 1818; in 1854 it changed to brass. Because of their alliance with nonconformity, many brass bands added the adjective 'temperance' to their name; the Bramley Old Band, which began with reeds in 1828, took up brass instruments in 1836 and became the first such organisation proudly to describe itself as a 'temperance' band. At Brown's iron works, at Blaina in Monmouthshire, a brass band was created in 1832, the employers apparently buying the instruments, which were all imported.

William Gardiner, a Leicestershire hosiery manufacturer who died in 1853 (he made a pair of stockings for Haydn and wove the notes of the Emperor's Hymn into them), was an amateur editor of music, composer of religious music and translator of biographies of Haydn and Mozart. In his reminiscences he provides a splendid picture of a factory band in Derbyshire:

> The Messrs. William, George and Joseph Strutt of Derby, men of great wealth and acquirements, employ nearly the whole population of Belper. . . . To give a higher taste to the work people at Belper, Mr. John Strutt (the son of George) has formed a musical society by selecting forty persons, or more, from his mills and workshops, making a band of instrumental performers and a choir of singers. These persons are regularly trained by masters and taught to play and sing in the best manner. Whatever time is consumed in their studies is reckoned into their working hours. On the night of a general muster, you may see five or six of the forgemen, in their leather aprons, blasting their terrific notes upon ophicleides and trombones.[1]

Apparently as early as the middle 1830s a band had become a source of pride, prestige and, possibly, advertisement, to the workplace which sponsored or even created it. There are numerous other records of similar bands created, financed and encouraged by employers. The Strutts found that their better musicians were likely to be enticed away from the mills as soon as they were fully trained, either to jobs in mills with rival bands or to become teachers of their instruments. The poaching of good players to build up rival bands became common practice, as did the advertising of industrial jobs restricted to players of instruments in short supply at whatever mill offered the vacancy. The Strutts found it necessary to arrange that 'members of the orchestra are bound to remain at the works seven years'.

The organisation of brass bands rather than of any sort of concert orchestra was a matter of simple practicality. To train foundry men and other manual workers into reasonable string players would have been too time-absorbing a scheme to have been of any great value; string players are unlikely to emerge from among men who undertake heavy work with their hands, and it takes less time, even with the most promising material, to create effective brass players who can enjoy themselves by playing than to make violinists and cellists.

The nineteenth-century centres of adult education in England, the Mechanics' Institutes and Lyceums, planned originally to increase the

[1] William Gardiner: *Music and Friends*. London, 1838. Vol. 2. pp. 511–13.

efficiency of workers, and their chance of escape from the most degrading work by increasing their basic knowledge, found themselves rapidly answering demands for a variety of what would now be called 'cultural' subjects. Musical teaching, in singing classes and the teaching of brass instruments, became extremely popular additions to the austerely practical aims of the educators. At first, the bands played arrangements of glees and of music from operas and oratorios. As the century progressed, they became increasingly satisfied to live in a world of their own in which the popular selections from popular operas, and the popular overtures, joined works written for bands competing in the various local or national competitions which tended to become the real purpose of the bandsmen's efforts. Since 1853, when the first National Brass Festival was held in the Belle Vue pleasure gardens in Manchester, the bands have followed a path some distance from either the developing tradition of popular music or the world of orchestral concerts, paying comparatively little attention to works composed for them by such musicians as Elgar, Vaughan Williams, Holst and Bliss (among many others) active in wider musical worlds. For all that, a considerable number of brass bands can be regarded as virtuoso ensembles, and any effective band makes music with a splendid, extravert panache.

The nature of light music is to offer simplifications and dilutions of styles and methods which are presented with due and natural weight in the opera house and the concert hall, but while Sullivan, for example, was rarely contented with clichés or banalities in his early orchestral works or his operettas, in his writing for a popular audience, which inevitably included the church audience of hymn singers, he could descend to the level of 'Onward Christian Soldiers' or 'The Lost Chord'. The divorce of the popular audience from any music which could stir its imagination, since the music hall abandoned the glee and their forays into opera, together with the absence of music from upper-class education in Britain, and the inanity of what was presented as musical education for the state schools established in the days of compulsory education, made a decline in standards as inevitable as the eventual rooting of English popular music in hymnology.

The rise and enormous popularity of the drawing-room ballad presented to British audiences, round about the first ten years or so of the twentieth century, prove the existence of composers who could plug like telephone operators without difficulty into customary channels of popular sentiment and whimsy, producing some works to which we can listen with an indulgent smile and others which we find intolerable. Every age produces its music, of all degrees of weight in considerable bulk and, if it is lucky, manages to achieve a handful of masterpieces. The production of ephemera is natural and necessary; what ultimately became depressing about so much English light music was the way in which it unerringly found its way to the lowest common denominator of taste and sentiment. The result is that music-hall songs, the best of which were created to exploit the voice, style and personality of a particular star who was often concerned to make a social rather than a purely musical point, often had not only a far greater vitality of style and rhythm but also, in their own way, a far more convincing musicality.

Thus English popular music came to inhabit a backwater from which it was difficult to reach any mainstream. The story of American popular music echoes that of English light music until it reaches the late nineteenth century, when the music of American negroes became not simply quaint but intellectually and socially acceptable. Ragtime became an international style; it reached England before the first World War, and jazz, its development, with an intellectual structure of its own, followed without any interval. Part of its appeal was the fact that it grew out of a clear social situation and expressed social realities; the high spirits, humour and ebullience of the jazz style matched the natural optimism of an America which, until the 1920s, could think of little reason for pessimism; after the first World War, when the United States for the first time learnt what were to be the realities of twentieth-century life, the pathos of American negro music found its place in the jazz-oriented style which became the world's popular music for not only the social amusements of the Western world at large but also for such works as the operas in which Kurt Weill found music for Berthold Brecht's vision of the final paroxysms of capitalism. This music, which occupied the dance bands of the United States and Europe, was in itself another simplification; it diluted the Afro-American music which demands a receptiveness which the listener to popular music is usually disinclined to reach; it was the music of black America simplified for white Americans.

Light music is invariably a simplification of things current, or recently current, in other musical spheres, and the jazz-orientated music which became an international style for the twentieth century was a reaction against the negative politeness and lack of vitality which had befallen the descendants of the Strausses, of Offenbach and of Sullivan. It succeeded a music of unexciting mildness and effete good manners—the good manners which are entirely negative and not a refinement of passion and energy. In the United States the new style was always a natural way of musical speech, and it can be listened to with pleasure in songs that are its classics; it was more exclusive than the domestic Wagner of the younger Strauss and opened no doors into more extensive musical worlds, so that it trapped lesser composers into routines of composition which diluted its basic African style with nothing stronger than water, so that whilst a composer like Kurt Weill could use the American popular style with point and wit, the bulk of mid-twentieth-century light music offered nothing to reflect any social reality, to engage the mind or even to startle the listener. Jazz itself demands attentive listening; it has its forms and its musical order as well as its open spaces for often outrageous instrumental virtuosity. What came to replace it in the 1960s was a popular style far more undernourished than any of the earlier dilutions of more demanding styles. 'Rock' and 'pop', the 1950s reaction and its 1960s offspring, are styles in which every other element of expression is sacrificed to the often spurious vitality of mechanical rhythms.

This music became the music of adolescence, a fact which gives it unusual social significance. The American cult of youth is probably a natural result of the development of a society built by immigration from all the European countries of adults who cling to their own languages and national traditions in the land which they adopted only to find that their children, born or at least educated in the United States, speaking the language of the new homeland and mastering its culture, become the guides and leaders of their parents. If a 'generation gap' (to use today's cant phrase) is an inevitable, naturally unobjectionable though sometimes irritating part of the business of 'growing up', it became in the United States an unnatural situation in which adult experience tended to yield to youth's mastery of new linguistic and social ways, a mastery too easily exploited by advertisers, politicians or anyone who found advantages in the exploitation of inexperience. It created an attitude—as twentieth-century attitudes tend to spread from the United States—which became international.

Thus pop, in its various manifestations, came to balance the attitude of those serious composers who found their natural speech in music too far removed from that of their hearers to win a reliable audience and who therefore ceased to regard musical life as a tripartite agreement between composer, performer and audience; as much of what might appeal to the young because of its novelty, its daring and its brilliance in the concert hall became too complex for assimilation, the music of the young became increasingly elementary, undernourished in style and limited in vocabulary.

Therefore pop tends to have a restrictive influence on its natural audience. It began as a reaction against the tepid, jazz-orientated style of the 1930s and 1940s, which, by the 1950s, had very little vitality left with which to appeal to the young. The successful composers in the style (they deserve, perhaps the epithet-begging term, 'great'), Gershwin, Jerome Kern, Cole Porter and a few others, were either dead or reaching the end of their careers, and though many of their songs have survived them, light music lives on novelty succeeding novelty. The weariness of their style opened the door for the mechanically rhythmic style of 'Rock 'n' Roll' in 1954 and 1955, and for the musically more interested period of 'skiffle', in which the young made music for themselves with whatever instruments—home-made if necessary—were available. The piano, for the first time since jazz had become respectable, ceased to count, for even a poor piano is not only a relatively costly instrument but also one not easily transportable to concerts or easily mastered by a musician whose contribution to any event depends on enthusuasm rather than training.

Skiffle was, by the nature of its performers, a return to a more lyrical style than rock, and it asked for a very small instrumental group: guitars, one for melody, one to provide the bass and one to join a percussionist in marking the rhythm, together with whatever instruments could be available in the style of primitive jazz, like a tea chest bass and a corrugated washboard in the 'rhythm section' became the source of a music meant for its own performers rather than for an audience; it was a style through which enthusiastic young amateur performers could explore and expand their own musicality. Any material simple enough appealed to the performers and turned the attention of many groups of young and almost self-trained musicians towards folk music, creating a passion that grew, bifurcated and survived its division. There were, among folk musicians of the new generation, those with whom music went hand in hand with social and political dissatisfactions; they saw in many folk songs an attitude to life and to society which could be applied to the present and suggest a style in which the ills of twentieth-century life could be expressed; both in Britain and in the United States, for many folk-song enthusiasts, the term became one which combined a genuine love for old music with an adherence to pacifist, left-wing, generally 'progressive' political and social beliefs often naive but admirable in their sincerity and dedication. Whilst most of the music of the young celebrated nothing beside the experiences of youth, and these in often pathetic simplification, the enthusiasm for folk song created a large number of young musicians whose music was closely related, even if naively related, to social realities. Other folk-song enthusiasts turned to extreme puritanism, rejecting any modernisation of their chosen musical way by accompaniment or adaptation. Whilst skiffle was trodden underfoot in the 1960s by the triumph of pop, the new folk-song revival, both in Britain and in the United States, continued to hold its broad front—from the singers whose concern is social protest to those who maintain a strictly purist attitude—throughout the pop period.

Rock 'n' Roll was unremittingly noisy music, utilising the brass of the standard 'dance band' as well as percussion. Skiffle and pop slimmed down the band to a group with the guitar as its standard instrument; the skiffle group was content with 'acoustic' guitars, but pop demands the electronic instrument which compensates in the eyes of young players and their audiences for its limited range of colour and effect by its capacity for filling any auditorium with overwhelming sound. It is loud, simple, appealing in its concentration upon elementary music and elementary words. In the hands of the Beatles, who for a time were not only the most celebrated musicians to rise to power through this style but also its most resourceful musicians (a fact which has led many authorities to exaggerate their attainments to the point of silliness), these elementary musical facts created a harmonic style which enriched what was essentially old-fashioned and never very far from the harmonic processes of Victorian hymnology with passing notes, or passing chords, which provided the sophisticated listener with a pleasant surprise.

The style, however, is international. The fact that the Beatles spoke and sang in a regional English accent no more impeded their success in the United States than an American accent reduced the appeal of popular translantic stars, and Europe seems to breed groups whose natural language for performance is English or Americanised English. Part of the appeal of the Beatles was that they appeared on any stage simply as four unexceptional young men who did nothing beyond the capacity of anybody who put his mind to such achievements; there was nothing obvious in their performance (their talent being kept carefully undercover) to indicate that these were hardly four ordinary young men with whom the audience could not completely identify.

The Beatles' original rejection of performance gimmicks died, perhaps through shrewd management, perhaps as a result of the adoration of their 'fans', until, since their departure, tricks of performance are probably more important than the quality of a song within the idiom in deciding any group's success. Pop is the first music to depend on gramophone and tape recording rather than on live performance for its success; thus it is forced to become a part of a complex business and financial world and to run the risk or face the consequences of commercial exploitation. One historian of the 'pop scene' (it is worthy of note that pop needs its own verbal as well as musical language) noted that pop is largely determined by changing fashions.[2] Pop not only created fashions in dress, hair-style and externals; it creates and discards musical fashions in a determination always to have something different that can be applauded by an audience inexperienced enough to believe that 'latest' is necessarily synonymous with 'best'. Nevertheless, while maintaining the illusion that this is any young person's music, shorn of the difficulty and the mystique of traditional musicians, the Beatles' later, more ambitious and often attractive records co-opted the services of orchestral musicians playing instruments usually outlawed by the basic principles of pop. A number of admirable instrumentalists took part in such recorded performances without acknowledgement, adopting an anonymity which seems at times to be a deliberate attempt to cheat the young.

The creative and performing world of pop music is dominated by the 'charts' which, week by week, estimate the most popular songs available by a calculation of their commercial success through sales. The charts in themselves suggest that what is most popular is often most widely advertised and

[2] Richard Mabey: *The Pop Process*. Hutchinson Educational. London, 1969. p. 38.

most frequently heard by radio from the stations which exist to provide the
young with a ceaseless flow of their music. There was a period in the late
1960s when, for more than a month, the charts in Britain were headed by an
innocuous and undistinguished waltz tune, sang unusually 'straight', celebrating the 'good old days'. 'Those were the Days', the song in question, delivered
a message dogmatically unsympathetic to most pop songs and their audiences
in a style which adolescents normally deride; but it was extremely popular
for a considerable length of time. More recently, a Welsh hymn tune has
held pride of place, played not by a conventional 'group' but by a military
band; if such phenomena suggest that conditioning by advertising has not
been totally successful among the pop audience, it also suggests the reverse
proposition—that the pop audience accepts whatever advertisers insist that
it enjoys. At the same time, the advertising of pop music suggests to an inexperienced young devotee that whatever happened before or happens outside the closed and inevitably commercial world of pop is irrelevant to the
lives of those who accept exploitation.

Thus the attractive idea of pop as an international style which has its
audience among the young and will develop with them is made doubtful
by the methods used to promulgate the music. Pop has not been a static
form, and it has created players and composers whose ambitions are not
satisfied by its strict conventions. Its development, however, has led to
the emergence of a 'progressive' pop which depends on relatively un-
trained composers with little experience of music outside their own
speciality; the liveliest and most imaginative pop music comes from the
world of the groups working directly for audiences within a convention
which, like all conventions, can be strictly observed or cleverly expanded.
Nevertheless, those whose primary concern is the quality of music and its
communication cannot but be anxious about the commercial pressures on
pop music. 'Is it, or was it,' writes Richard Mabey, 'a spontaneous
creation at all? Or has it been skilfully manufactured by an adult world
that wants as much as possible of its offspring's £1,000,000,000-a-year
spending money?'[3]

As long ago as 1934, in *Music Ho!*, Constant Lambert predicted the
death of the listener who, in the terminology of the time, he described as
'middle-brow' as distinct from the devotee of jazz and jazz-orientated
dance music on the one hand and the concert and opera-goer on the other.
He was prophetically envisaging a world in which music and musicians were
driven into one or other of two camps—the totally undemanding and
usually uncreative on the one hand and the increasingly remote and 'serious'
on the other, with no means of communication between the two. Recent
developments have left no space in life for salon music, for the palm court
orchestra or the cinema organist; there is no twentieth-century, post-

[3] *Ibid*. p. 35.

World War Two equivalent to the Victorian ballad in any country of Western Europe. In so far as this disappearance is the consequence of the commercialism which seems likely to prevent the liberation of pop from its commercially profitable conventions, the present situation is sinister; our light music is tied to commercial interests while the *avant-garde* musician eagerly accepts the notion of a divorce between the composer and the audience with whom it is his duty, as it should be his pleasure, to communicate.

10

Music in the United States

Because the bulk of the earliest settlers in what became the United States were British, the pattern of music-making among Americans at first followed the pattern created by musicians in English cities. By 1750, some sort of concert system was growing in a number of American cities; perhaps Charleston, in South Carolina, was musically the most advanced of them simply because it was closest to England in manners and social customs; life in South Carolina offered more leisure than life in the New England colonies, and none of the southern states developed the intolerance to any form of public entertainment which had to be combated in Massachusetts and which spread throughout the northern colonies. Concerts in Charleston, and subsequently in the other major cities, were semi-amateur events in which music teachers and the orchestra of the theatre collaborated with enthusiastic amateurs. Charleston, though small, with some eight thousand people in 1750, was the wealthy 'gateway' to the richly agricultural south. Before it developed any orchestral organisation its citizens founded a St. Cecilia Society for the performance of choral works, and the town's musical pre-eminence, perhaps, explains why Theodore Pachelbel, son of the great Nuremberg organist, who emigrated to America in 1733 to become organist at Newport, Rhode Island, and was responsible in 1736 for organising the first concert in New York of which any record remains, moved to Charleston a year later, when he was given a benefit concert there, and remained for the rest of his life.

New York's music was, apparently, waiting for someone like Pachelbel to bring it to life. The size of its population, the extensiveness of its business interests and its growing wealth made it a good city for immigrant musicians who realised that, whatever other possibilities might open up for them, the essential foundation of their American careers would be a teaching practice as extensive as they could make it.

Puritan Boston, too, had at least occasional concerts from 1731, and even Quaker Philadelphia, where music was at first distrusted as merely a worldly amusement, began to regard music as permissible in 1757. Twelve years later, an opera house had been opened there and the gentlemen of an amateur orchestra began to play with the theatre's professional orchestra on opera nights.[1]

[1] Gilbert Chase: *America's Music*. McGraw Hill, New York, 1955. p. 84.

Semi-professional music-making continued in a growing number of American cities, as it does in the United States to this day in many community orchestras which flourish in cities which cannot support a completely professional orchestra: European visitors to the concerts of the Fort Worth Symphony Orchestra as recently as 1969 would probably have been startled to find three nuns, properly habited, among the orchestra's violinists; further investigation of the orchestra would have revealed that while many of the players earned their living as teachers of their instruments —no other regular musical work is available to them—many of the players are completely amateur. The structure of such orchestras, except for the presence of a salaried music director-conductor, has hardly changed since the early days of music in the United States. It was in a relatively few cities of the industrialised, commerically active and affluent states of the north-east that completely professional orchestras arose in the second half of the nineteenth century and brought with them a new and often fruitful form of patronage.

Boston, for example, has a musical history which reaches back to the early eighteenth century. The first regular, professional orchestra to be heard there grew up round the German Gottlieb Graupner in 1810; it followed in the footsteps of a predominantly amateur Euterpe Society. In 1815 the Handel and Haydn Society, an amateur choral society with its own orchestra, began a long and fruitful history, devoted to 'cultivating and improving correct taste in the performance of sacred music'. University music at nearby Harvard, first effectively organised in 1808, grew into the concert-giving Harvard Musical Association. The Handel and Haydn Society, in 1823, commissioned an oratorio from Beethoven, who took the offer seriously enough to note it, although he never began the composition.

In 1842, however, the professional musicians of New York, most of whom played in the orchestras of the city's theatre, decided to establish their own orchestra and concert society on the model of the Philharmonic Society in London. Less than fifty years before this date, New York, for all its financial and commercial importance, had counted for less in commercial prestige than Boston and for less as a business centre than Philadelphia. But since the Erie Canal had been opened to traffic in 1825, New York had grown enormously and had some four hundred thousand inhabitants by the 1840s. Its growth had attracted immigrant musicians eager to establish themselves in regular employment, so that a large number of theatre musicians, most of whom were also teachers, were looking for ways of satisfying musical ambitions and of augmenting their salaries by organising regular orchestral concerts. The death in 1838 of Daniel Schlesinger, a musician popular in New York, had been the occasion of a memorial concert given by an orchestra of sixty instrumentalists gathered mostly from the New York theatres. Despite what seems to have been the barest minimum of rehearsal, the concert was successful enough to demonstrate an appetite for such events. By 1842, the Philharmonic Orchestra, a co-operative body, had been built, and it gave its first concert in the December of that year.

The original members of the orchestra created a self-governing organisation, employing a salaried conductor whom they elected, and paying a librarian; the members divided the profits of the concerts among themselves at the end of each session, all members taking equal shares. Thus the concerts were necessarily a spare-time occupation of the players, who continued to depend for their livelihood on their work in the theatres. The orchestra met only at rehearsals or concerts, and necessary business discussions consumed the exiguous rehearsal time, so that players not attracted by business discussions often did not bother to attend. Naturally, when members found themselves facing a clash of engagements, it was the Philharmonic Concert, the less profitable of any two engagements, which took second place. The orchestra originally gave membership to any musicians who wanted it—twenty-two violinists and four cellists, for example, at one stage of its early history. Its audience, most of the members subscribers whose advance payments made the whole operation possible, was both fashionable and generous, but it did not provide sufficient money to entice good players from Europe. Nor were the musical ambitions of the audience as high as those of the orchestra, so that the quality of the programmes had to be diluted to win audiences sufficient to support the concerts. In addition, distances in the United States militated against any comparison of one orchestra with another, and, therefore, of any comparison of standards. Though there was considerable musical activity in both Boston and Philadelphia, there was no competition between orchestras and no improvement evolving from comparison of standards and methods; the United States did not, therefore, at that time create patrons exigently demanding the highest standards of performance.

In 1848 a group of central European musicians, exiles from the revolutions of 1848, reached the United States and banded themselves together as the Germania Orchestra. As unsuccessful revolutionaries or sympathisers with unsuccessful revolutions, their music did not stop at Beethoven and Mendelssohn but went on to Wagner and Liszt; they had been members of efficient European orchestras and, beginning from Boston, they toured the United States, reaching as far from the east coast as St. Louis, suggesting orchestral standards at that time out of reach of any American orchestras. Eventually the members of the Germania Orchestra went their individual ways, joining existing American orchestras to the orchestras' advantage. Carl Bergmann, one of the Germania's cellists, became conductor of the New York Philharmonic and, in the words of Theodore Thomas, the first American conductor to impose high standards on his players; Bergmann, said Thomas in an address when he left New York to take charge of the new

Chicago Symphony Orchestra in 1891, was 'the first conductor to give us an insight into our great composers'.[2]

Louis Antoine Jullien, if he did nothing quite so high-minded as Bergmann, showed American audiences what a really well-drilled, thoroughly rehearsed ensemble of good players was capable of. Looking for fresh worlds to conquer and another wealthy audience to enthrall, in 1853 Jullien took the key members of his London orchestra to play to American audiences recruiting American instrumentalists as he arrived to tour the United States from Boston to New York with divers concerts on route, travelling as far as New Orleans. During a two-month stay in New York he conducted nightly concerts with programmes perhaps rather less ambitious than those his London audiences had come to enjoy; he had visited the United States to create the sort of audiences he had found and educated in England, and succeeded in doing what he wanted. Those who attended his concerts were struck by such everyday matters as the fact that his violinists bowed together—some indication, perhaps, of the standards of orchestral playing which his visit disturbed.

It was Theodore Thomas, the son of German parents who arrived in the United States in 1845, when he was ten years old and who played in Jullien's orchestra when he was eighteen, who did more than anyone else to raise American musical standards. In 1863 he formed an orchestra with which he gave regular concerts in New York and *al fresco* light music concerts in Central Park. The orchestra was his own, founded, organised, paid and trained by Thomas himself with the support of wealthy sympathisers. Because his orchestra was paid a regular salary and not simply working for a share of the box-office takings, its players rehearsed and played together with a regularity the New York Philharmonic could not achieve. Thomas and his orchestra, moreover, toured indefatigably, creating an audience for regular concerts in Cincinnati and Chicago as well as playing in musically conscious centres like Boston and Philadelphia.

Thomas had joined the New York Philharmonic Society in 1852, and in 1877 was elected its conductor; the following year he became Director of the Cincinnati College of Music, an institution inspired by the annual festival concerts he gave there. In 1879 he returned to New York to conduct the Philharmonic and to revive his own orchestra. In 1891 he became conductor of the Chicago Orchestra, which changed its name to the Theodore Thomas Orchestra, and then, in 1902, it became the Chicago Symphony Orchestra; Thomas kept the conductorship until his death in 1905.

Thomas's own orchestra had created a specifically American form of musical finance. His concerts could not be supported to his own satisfac-

[2] John H. Mueller: *The American Symphony Orchestra.* John Calder, London, 1958. p. 33.

tion simply by the proceeds of the box office, although he played to large audiences, and as a professional musician, popular and well paid though he was, he could not afford to finance it himself; the money he needed came from wealthy patrons of music who were prepared to back their faith in music, or in the abilities of Theodore Thomas; or in both.

When Thomas was offered the conductorship of the New York Philharmonic in 1877 the offer was an attempt to rescue an ailing institution which had come to depend for support on its prestige rather than on the quality of its performances. Members who had for the sake of their livelihood to regard the Philharmonic as a mere second string, and a weak one at that, could not attain the standards imposed by Thomas on his fiercely drilled players; absenteeism alone was enough to ensure that. Nor was the Philharmonic Orchestra's repertoire, designed not to startle old-fashioned audiences whose attitudes were as much social as musical, sufficient to maintain the level of excitement and interest which other concerts had reached. The result was the creation of the New York Symphony Orchestra in 1878. Not only did it seem that a city of well over a million inhabitants could happily support two orchestras; the Symphony Orchestra's motive power was its founder, Leopold Damrosch, German by birth, who had found his way to New York as conductor of the Arion Männersanverein after some conducting experience in Breslau. Damrosch was a friend of the 'progressive' school in German music and believed that he could find not only finance for a rival orchestra to the Philharmonic but also audiences for more adventurous concerts than the Philharmonic presented. The acceptance of the Philharmonic conductorship by Thomas meant that the admirably trained instrumentalists of the Thomas Orchestra were mostly unemployed—Thomas had taken the best of them with him to the Philharmonic—so that Damrosch had the foundations of an orchestra from the players whom Thomas could no longer occupy. With the financial guarantee of men who were great powers in American finance, and the adherence of New York 'Society' won by his natural geniality and friendliness, Damrosch set out to enliven New York's music in spite of the enmity of Thomas, who explained to Damrosch that it was his habit to 'crush' anyone who ventured to oppose him.

The infirm Philharmonic suffered another severe blow in 1883 with the establishment of the Metropolitan Opera House; the greater glamour of opera and a determination that it would bring the greatest European stars to New York, so that opera in America should have the same prestige as opera in Milan, Vienna or Dresden, created excitements beyond those of the concert hall, and New Yorkers who had felt that their social position had been kept up by attendance at the Philharmonic—after all, it had the prestige of being one of the world's oldest concert societies—was overshadowed by the social glamour of the opera, which drew audiences, publicity and funds from the wealthy within a considerable area round New York.

The splendour of the Metropolitan overshadowed all earlier attempts to provide New York with opera, and crushed all later operatic ventures for a long time to come. The repertoire of the 'Met' was always popular; new or controversial works were resolutely avoided, while those which had won the adoration of audiences everywhere were produced with the greatest possible lavishness not only in the quality of singers but in costumes, décor and all the ancillary services of opera. Efforts to provide opera at prices which the average New Yorker could afford failed, in spite of determined efforts, until 1944, when the New York City Opera presented its first short season and succeeded to so marked an extent that it has grown to create its own stars and to follow a policy far more adventurous than the Metropolitan dared to implement until the lesser house had shown that tastes were less circumscribed than the Metropolitan's tradition had imagined.

Damrosch's early days with the New York Symphony Society were not easy, and membership of the Symphony Orchestra, like membership of the Philharmonic, necessarily occupied only part of a player's time, so that the new orchestra had many of the problems of absenteeism which weakened the old. The final departure of Theodore Thomas from the Philharmonic Society in 1891, when the veteran conductor moved to Chicago to establish the Chicago Symphony Orchestra, enabled Damrosch to secure the financial backing of several of the legendary rich of the United States who had previously supported Thomas during the days of his independence. With Carnegie, Vanderbilt, Rockefeller and Morgan ready to finance a more ambitious policy, Damrosch brought Adolf Brodsky from England to lead the orchestra, established daily rehearsals and announced his new ensemble as 'the only permanent orchestra in New York'. Unfortunately, despite the fabulous wealth of his patrons, by 1898 the guarantee fund they had established was exhausted, and for four years the Symphony Orchestra's concerts were abandoned.

By this time, however, the Boston Symphony Orchestra was established on a firmer basis than either of the New York ensembles. In 1881 Henry Lee Higginson, the son of a wealthy Boston financier, decided to organise a permanent orchestra of sixty musicians to whom he would pay a regular yearly salary while subsidising the concerts they would give. He anticipated a deficit of $50,000, to meet which he was ready to provide a capital of $1,000,000. There was a considerable audience for music in Boston, a city which regarded itself as the cultural capital of the United States, and in the surrounding centres like Harvard; concerts in Boston and in Harvard were anything but infrequent, and the Handel and Haydn Society operated on a guarantee fund created by wealthy Bostonians. Higginson, originally a would-be concert pianist who had studied in Vienna, created a new system of patronage; like an Esterhazy prince he would completely support the orchestra, employing its personnel on a permanent basis to give weekly concerts of 'the highest type' of music; admission prices were to be low and the conductor himself was to be solely responsible for the ensemble's artistic policy. Unlike an Esterhazy, Higginson stuck scrupulously to the rule he had established and never sought to usurp the conductor's artistic primacy. He took care of the financial and extra-musical administration even when, in the orchestra's early days, Wilhelm Gericke (whom Higginson brought from Vienna to be its second conductor) followed a policy of dedicated, Mahlerlian ruthlessness in his determination to achieve the highest musical standards, dismissing unsatisfactory players and replacing them with instrumentalists brought from Germany and Austria.

Gericke's predecessor, the baritone–conductor–composer Georg Henschel, had been thirty-one when he conducted the Boston Symphony Orchestra's first concert, and though he lacked the experience needed to achieve standards comparable to those which Gericke pursued, his enthusiasm, panache, dedication and likable personality made the concerts popular. It was Gericke who made a real, disciplined ensemble out of players who often played for other organisations under a variety of conductors and were unaccustomed to severe orchestral discipline; Higginson supported him by refusing permission to his orchestra to play for any other concerts except those of the Handel and Haydn Society. Having worked himself into a breakdown by 1889, Gericke was replaced by Nikisch for four years, and then by Emil Pauer. In 1898 Gericke returned, and in 1900 a new concert hall, Symphony Hall, was built by public subscription. Until Higginson's death in 1919, not only did he remain totally responsible for the increasingly huge expense of the orchestra but ensured that the conductors, whom he personally selected, were musicians of the highest calibre. Influenced by the anti-German feeling aroused by the first World War and a political scandal which rose around Karl Muck, conductor from 1906 to 1908 and again from 1912 to 1918 (Muck found himself in a controversy over the demand that he should play the American National Anthem before concerts), Higginson, whose personal tastes were almost exclusively for the German classics, appointed Henri Rabaud in 1918 and Pierre Monteux in 1919, supporting their widening of the orchestra's repertoire in a city where music, to most listeners, meant German music and where Monteux's delight in works by Debussy and Stravinsky was anything but immediately popular and where his undemonstrative, bandmasterly style disappointed audiences who wished to see a conductor expressing and visibly shaping the music by gesture.

Higginson was able to leave no endowment for his orchestra; its maintenance had left him with little money to leave as he had been forced, during the last few years of his life, to face annual deficits of about

$100,000. Since his retirement from business, he had recruited three hundred guarantors to ensure the orchestra's continuance and the maintenance of its high standards, but their guarantee was not sufficient to face the huge annual deficit, and it was left to the very wealthy to fill Higginson's place.

In 1895 the Cincinnati Symphony Orchestra came into being. It was the indirect offspring of Theodore Thomas's earlier tours in a city which had a considerable German population with the usual vocal groups—*Liedertafel*, *Liederkranz* and *Männerchor*—which were the result of German-American nostalgia for a lost fatherland. Since 1873, Cincinnati had been the scene of regular biennial festivals given by Thomas and a stalwart patron, Mrs Maria Nicholas Longworthy. In 1878 a College of Music was opened, financed by a group of extremely rich citizens, and for its first two years Thomas was appointed its director at a salary of $10,000. Among Thomas's great qualities seems to have been a stubborn intractability which had made him a magnificent musical pioneer incapable of compromise; he was also apparently incapable of working under direction, and after two years he was replaced by a virtual nonentity.

Naturally, Cincinnati had had regular concerts before 1895, mounted by orchestras which rose and failed to survive. The most notable had been a Philharmonic Orchestra, inaugurated in 1857, on the same co-operative lines as the New York Philharmonic and sharing with its model the difficulties which naturally afflict any orchestra whose members are compelled to earn the bulk of their livings by other activities and therefore to sacrifice it whenever they are faced by a clash of interests. A private patron organised an orchestra and choral society in 1865, building it a small concert hall; other patrons, led by a Mr. Springer (who himself paid $200,000 towards the cost), built a larger hall for concerts and festivals in 1875. The permanent orchestra eventually founded in 1895 was planned by a group of women who organised its finance by private benefactions. In 1909 pledges of support to the extent of $50,000 a year for each of the next five years were secured, the players were offered contracts holding them for a complete season and the young Leopold Stokowski, who had arrived in the United States from England in 1904 and was quite literally at the beginning of his exciting conducting career, was appointed conductor.

The next of the major orchestras to appear was that at Philadelphia, another city which had a musical history antedating the American War of Independence. Philadelphia had never been without an orchestra, though it had never employed musicians who rivalled the prestige of those of New York and Boston; the formation of a Musical Fund Society in 1820 had led to regular concerts and performances of opera, mounted to 'care for decayed musicians and their families'. In 1856 the Germania Orchestra, another self-governing ensemble organised on the lines of the New York

Philharmonic, was as active as the Musical Fund Society; neither body, however, had any financial organisation or the ability to reach the standards set by Damrosch with the New York Symphony Orchestra and Gericke with the Boston Symphony Orchestra, both of which visited Philadelphia regularly. Local patriotism, a considerable force in American life in the nineteenth century, was outraged and in 1900 the President of the Musical Fund Society called a meeting to raise funds to establish a permanent orchestra, and guarantors contributed $15,000 to support an inaugural season of six concerts to be conducted by Hans Scheel, who had been assistant to Hans von Bülow in Germany and had already made an American reputation in Chicago and San Francisco. Like Gericke, Scheel created a new orchestra, dismissing players and replacing them with experienced instrumentalists from Europe. Money continued to be supplied by the guarantors, satisfied by the response to the first season, and a Women's Committee, formed in 1904, undertook the task of raising funds and persuading the public to regard the orchestra as a social necessity. Scheel died in 1907, and after an unimpressive interregnum of five years, Stokowski was appointed conductor. Stokowski, by a combination of musical brilliance, ruthlessness, charm, good looks, expert knowledge dressed up as eccentric charlatanry, and remarkable organising ability was able to make the orchestra the most famous in the United States if not in the entire world and to mould it into a superb virtuoso instrument. He secured endowments substantial enough to allow ample rehearsal for novelties and for familiar works and to recruit the finest players he could find. For the first performance in America of Mahler's Eighth Symphony, in 1916, Stokowski found additional funds to the extent of $15,000 and, by skilful publicity, was able to make a profit on nine repeated performances in Philadelphia itself and in both Boston and New York. Stokowski's twenty-four years with the Philadelphia Orchestra were full of excitements whipped up to keep the orchestra in the public eye, to make it newsworthy, to attract attention; Stokowski made the orchestra a regular broadcasting attraction in the early days of radio, took it into the television studios for the first television symphony concert in the history of American broadcasting, gave ambitious seasons of opera—the one area where his enterprise and flair failed—and became a film actor in order to take his orchestra into the world of cinema in the sentimental little film *A Hundred Men and a Girl*. In Walt Disney's *Fantasia* he lent the orchestra to cartoon treatments of Bach, Beethoven and Stravinsky, amongst other music, only to find when the film was completed that the visual interpretations which were a counterpoint to his performances were not entirely sympathetic to his view of the works involved.

Stokowski proved that an American orchestra, given a Stokowski to conduct it, could survive financial storms and flourish. But for all the sensationalism of his work in Philadelphia, the apparent charlatan was a superbly sensitive expert in sound quality and tone colour, an undaunted champion of new music who refused to surrender his right to experiment both in repertoire and in the organisation of the orchestra.

But by the time that Stokowski was demonstrating to Philadelphia that the musical life was a matter of irrepressible excitement, the self-governing orchestral financing itself from box-office receipts could no longer hope to survive in the climate which had brought Nikisch to Boston and Arthur Seidl and Gustav Mahler from Leipzig and Vienna respectively to New York; Stokowski's career in Philadelphia was an object lesson to all American concert organisations in the art of establishing a symphony orchestra, building its repertory and integrating it into the community it served. It proved, too, the importance of finding conductors who would create an atmosphere of almost dangerous excitement and vitality.

The want of a sufficiently compelling conductor forced the New York Symphony Orchestra into silence between 1898 to 1903, and in 1907 falling attendances and the visits of the secure Boston Symphony Orchestra almost destroyed the New York Philharmonic. In 1901 Andrew Carnegie had become President of the Philharmonic Society, and Walter Damrosch, Leopold's son, had accepted its conductorship in 1902; together the new President and the new conductor worked to reorganise the now historic orchestra; Carnegie established a fund which would guarantee the Society $25,000 a year for four years on condition that the orchestra would reorganise its establishment and enlarge its governing body of fifteen players to include seven representatives of the new financial powers who would assist them, make changes in personnel and give more and more thoroughly rehearsed concerts; the established board of governors, determined to remain masters of their own orchestra, refused, Damrosch withdrew his acceptance of the conductorship and revived the New York Symphony Orchestra. The Philharmonic carried on with the support of John D. Rockefeller and relays of guest conductors, and with the adventitious excitements such changes of personality and style inevitably bring. Most of the concerts of 1906 and 1907 were conducted by Vassily Ilyitch Safonov, whose brilliant handling of Russian music at first created a deserved sensation but eventually showed Safonov's limitations in the works of the German and Austrian repertoire to which the Philharmonic subscribers were wedded. The 1907 concerts were badly attended and the orchestra at last realised that its co-operative, democratic methods could not survive in the new, high-powered world of American twentieth-century music.

In 1908 Mrs. George R. Sheldon, the wife of a banker and republican politician, assembled representatives of 'the best families in the city' to save the Philharmonic and raised a fund of $90,000 for three years; among the contributors were Carnegie, Pierpont Morgan and Joseph Pulitzer. The conditions of this subsidy were harsher than those originally offered by

Carnegie five years before. The self-governing status of the orchestra, its right to frame its own policy and to elect conductors were all to go; old players were to be replaced by new; a board of control would be established by the financial powers on which the orchestra would be represented and more concerts, all more thoroughly rehearsed, would be given. Safonov was to be replaced by Mahler, who had conducted the German repertoire at the Metropolitan Opera for the previous two seasons and whose mastery in the opera house had dazzled New York. When Mahler died, in 1911, after storms and disillusionment, Pulitzer also died, leaving almost a million dollars to the Philharmonic on condition that it established itself as a permanent orchestra, created a list of a thousand contributing members, reduced its prices of admission and kept its programmes 'not too severely classical'. A new, still rather obscure but thoroughly efficient conductor, Joseph Stransky, was appointed. Stransky, with programmes weighted towards Liszt, Wagner and Dvořák (composers of whom Pulitzer thoroughly approved), played to standing room only.

As the basic conditions of twentieth-century music put an end to the orchestral democracy of the New York Philharmonic, the retirement and death of Higginson ended the era of individual patronage. Higginson had spent a vast fortune to support the Boston Symphony Orchestra for more than thirty years, maintaining an ensemble of the highest class while following a policy of musical non-interference. Unlike the great patrons—the Frederick the Greats and the Prince Nicholas Esterhazas of eighteenth-century Europe—and unlike Joseph Pulitzer too, he had never demanded the inclusion in programmes of music he liked and the exclusion of music which did not appeal to him. By the time of his death, not even his dedication and determination could preserve financial autocracy; the supply of instrumentalists from Europe had dried up as a result of the first World War and the American Musicians' Union, strengthened by the new demands for American players, fought a long-drawn-out and ultimately successful war against the concert organisations for rates of pay which themselves defied the individual generosity of the greatest of patrons. Though patrons whose wealth, like that of Carnegie, Rockefeller, Morgan and others, is belittled by the use of the adjective 'wealthy', provided vast sums for the support of American orchestras, the task of financing music in the United States was a job for committees of millionaires, not for single men of great wealth working alone.

With the development of group sponsorship came the growth of Ladies' Committees formed by the wives of wealthy patrons who tended to represent culture and 'Society' as their husbands represented finance; such committees tended to become thorns in the flesh of conductors and musical directors. Alma Mahler described with some eloquence the way in which her husband's originally indulgent amusement at the activities of the

Ladies' Committee of the New York Philharmonic Society turned to rage
when he found that the Committee tried to limit his authority as musical
director, attempting to control his programme planning and backing its
wishes by appeals to the governing body of the orchestra.[3] A Ladies' Committee which, in times of crisis, would be both persistent and effective in
raising funds and which kept the orchestra in the minds of the most affluent
and influential members of 'Society' was not an organisation to be treated
with Mahlerian disrespect. Mahler, whose refusal to compromise in Vienna
had led him to disregard the wishes even of members of the imperial royal
family, found that he lacked the qualities necessary for dealing effectively
with a Ladies' Committee; the young Stokowski had them, and moulded a
Ladies' Committee in Philadelphia into a powerful source of financial and
other support for his orchestra.

But the intensely competitive organisation of American music, especially
of its orchestras, insisted always on the finest performers directed by the
most spectacular conductors, even when the spectacular element in the conductor's work was the almost complete, calm immobility of a Fritz Reiner.
Mahler, Toscanini and Mengelberg conducted in New York, with the young
John Barbirolli and Rodzinski. In Boston Karl Muck was succeeded by
Monteux, Koussevitzky and Charles Munch; Rodzinski and Kubelik conducted the Chicago Symphony Orchestra and when, after twenty-four
legendary years, Stokowski left Philadelphia, he was succeeded by the almost equally glamorous Eugene Ormandy. The Cleveland Orchestra,
founded in 1918 as a reliable second-rank, provincial ensemble, in 1946
found the formidable Georg Szell to raise it to a place among the great
orchestras of the world. In America a conductor had to be flamboyant,
romantic, eloquent, extravagant in one way or another; he had to dominate
not only an orchestra but also its audience. The triumph of the Nazis in
Germany and Austria sent not only Schoenberg and Hindemith to teach in
the United States and to exercise a momentous influence on American taste;
Klemperer, Reiner, Szell and Bruno Walter were America's profit from the
Nazi revolution. The situation in twentieth-century America was like that
of nineteenth-century England until the second World War persuaded the
United States audience that native talents were not to be neglected or de-
rided, but the United States provided the cream of the musical profession
with possibilities of the richest rewards and the greatest adulation. As early
as 1892, the critic Eduard Hanslick had sourly written in his journal:
'America may not be the promised land of music, but it is the promised land
of musicians.'[4]

The consequences for the American composer were rather similar to

³ Alma Mahler: *Gustav Mahler: Memories and Letters*. John Murray,
London, 1946. p. 115.
⁴ Hanslick: *Aus dem Tagebuch eines Musikers*. Berlin, 1892. p. 58.

those which had arrested the development of English music a century before. The New York Philharmonic Society, at its inception in 1842, included among its rules an attempt to encourage the work of native composers:

> If any grand orchestral compositions, such as overtures or symphonies, shall be presented to the Society, they being composed in this country, the Society shall perform one every season provided a committee of five appointed by the Government [of the Society] shall have approved and recommended the composition.[5]

The rule, of course, makes no mention of the nationality of the composer, but only of the place of origin of the work, so that the encouragement to American music was no more than minimal. Anyhow, the first conductor of the New York Philharmonic Orchestra who seems to have paid any real attention to the possibilities of American Music was Mahler, who in 1910 conducted concerts of English and American compositions.

Protests against the German hegemony exercised over New York concerts had come long before. In the 1850s William Henry Fry and George Bristow, the first American-born composers to handle nineteenth-century orchestral forms convincingly, protested intemperately about the exclusion of American works from the Philharmonic Society's programmes, forgetting the occasional minor work which had won a hearing at Philharmonic concerts. Bristow resigned from the Society and its orchestra, in which he played as a violinist, to show his condemnation of what he called 'the systematised effort to extinguish American music'. In the first forty years of its life, the Philharmonic had made itself responsible for single performances of three of Bristow's symphonies and two of his overtures, but for all that Bristow and Fry (a critic as well as a composer who joined in Bristow's protest) were more successful than most of their contemporaries in winning something of a hearing; other organisations did less even than the New York Philharmonic Society to foster American music, and apart from the five works heard at Philharmonic Concerts, Bristow's opera *Rip van Winkle* ran for four weeks in New York, and as conductor of the amateur choral society, the Harmonic Society, he was able to conduct his cantata *Eleutheria*.

Fry was born in Philadelphia in 1915, studied composition with a French musician and, though he began composing in his early teens, became a journalist and critic. In 1846 he began a six-year stint as a European correspondent to various papers in the United States, returning eventually as music editor of the *New York Tribune*. His opera *Leonore*, based on Bulwer-Lytton's *The Lady of Lyons*—a large-scale work in what at the time was the latest and most flamboyant Italian style—was played at Philadelphia in 1845; a production in Italian by an Italian company was heard

[5] John H. Mueller: *op. cit.* p. 266.

in New York in 1858. His four symphonies, each written to a programme of considerable naivety, were taken up by Jullien, apparently to attract American audiences.

After Bristow and Fry, the most successful American composers were Bostonians, or musicians educated at Harvard and indoctrinated by the German classicism which dominated Boston music. They studied in Europe and several of them, like Daniel Gregory Mason, George W. Chadwick and Horatio William Parker, wrote works which were heard here and there in Europe and were not totally neglected in the United States. Edward MacDowell not only studied at the Paris Conservatoire, at Stuttgart and at Wiesbaden, but lived in Germany for four years after his studies ended; he taught the piano at Darmstadt. His compositions won some attention in Europe, and he returned to America with a higher prestige among his fellow countrymen than any earlier American had achieved among his own people. His works, too, were given occasional performances but they did not become part of the repertory.

If, in the first forty years of its life, the New York Philharmonic played only half a dozen works by American composers and found no place for any of them in its repertoire, the Boston Symphony Orchestra, between its foundation and 1914, when its history was written, played thirty-two works by native composers though none of them, not even those by Mac-dowell, found a regular home in its programmes, though the composers favoured by Boston were followers of the German classical tradition, far more Central European than American in their outlook. Between its creation in 1892 and its thirty-third birthday in 1925—precisely as long a period as that which measures activities in Boston—the Philadelphia Orchestra had given first performances to only four American works, although Stokowski, after his appointment in 1912, had tormented conservative Philadelphian ears with a large number of new European works and works by European expatriates to America, although much of the music he fought for seemed to his audiences almost offensively obscure.

The appetite for American music which first developed in the 1850s was part of the general agitation that established Americans began to feel at the mass immigrations which began with thousands of victims of the Irish potato famine who arrived in the United States in 1846; it continued with the flood of refugees from the abortive revolutions of 1848. The White, Anglo-Saxon Protestant settlers, faced with a flood of Roman Catholic Irishmen, and followed by an influx of Central Europeans many of whom were also Roman Catholic, noticed that immigrants tended to settle together and to maintain the culture and habits of their homelands rather than to assimilate and become native-born Americans by some act of will; in the face of so much immigration, what had become American national tradition seemed to be at risk and unlikely to survive, so that music which might be called American because of the nationality of its composer, whatever his stylistic preoccupations, seemed to be one of the possible lines of defence against European encroachments. But music composed in America could not sufficiently grip the affections of American listeners to replace the un-American works on which Americans, however proud of their Anglo-Saxon traditions, had grown up. The American music which won American hearts is better represented by the songs of Stephen Foster (the archetypal 'light' composer of mid-nineteenth-century America) than by the serious efforts of more intellectual American composers. Foster listened to the music of black Americans and refined it into a style compounded of Victorian balladry and negro folk music. Somehow, and not with any abundant sense of logic, this itself seemed to be a weapon in the service of the apparently endangered national heritage. Foster died in 1864, before either Bristow or Fry; his work predates the American Civil War, but it has retained its hold in affections in the United States and beyond.

Daniel Gregory Mason was the most determinedly classical of the classical school which developed in mid-nineteenth-century Boston, partly as the result of the traditional intellectual climate of Boston and partly the result of Higginson's choice of conductors for his orchestra. Mason, born in 1873, suggests in his opinions a representative of his parents' generation. On Thanksgiving Day, 1895, he wrote in his Journal:

> Thank God Wagner is dead and Brahms is alive. And here's to the great classical revival of the twentieth century in America.[6]

In *Music in my Time* he expressed his antipathy to 'excess, unbalance and romantic exaggeration' in the works of composers like Wagner, Tchaikovsky, Liszt and Strauss whose greatness he could not deny.[7] Mason, nevertheless, wrote that what he called 'the Anglo-Saxon element' in American life had become a 'minority element' in American national character.[8] But that belief did not alter his love of the minority element or prevent his realisation that American culture must inevitably adopt some degree of eclecticism. It is such an eclecticism in its earliest stages which is the strength of Foster's relatively unambitious music: the basic style comes from an undemanding European manner, but to it is married a semi-negro style. It is, in Foster's work, alive and native while its European background is simply acquired after a time-lag. At the same time, the New York Philharmonic in its early days had been as busy in its exploration of Beethoven's music as the London Philharmonic Society had been in its early days, and the audiences it

---

[6] Quoted in Gilbert Chase: *op. cit.* p. 101.
[7] Daniel Gregory Mason: *Music in my Time.* Macmillan, New York. p. 101.
[8] Daniel Gregory Mason: *Tune in America.* Knopf, New York, 1931. p. 160.

had won put up a resistance to new music—that of Brahms as well as that of Wagner—even more conservative than that of any European audience. In nineteenth-century America music belonged to the past, and only music from the past was regarded as serious and important.

While the importance of Foster is that he created a synthesis of Afro-American music with a tradition of European light music, both elements in his style were considerably diluted, but all the same he hit upon a style intrinsically American, though his highest motive for doing so seems to have been only to give refinement and respectability to what most of his contemporaries would have considered to be the music of rough, uncultivated entertainment. As negro music became a matter of more sympathetic interest and greater understanding, it added itself to the extensive stock of American raw materials at the composer's disposal, though, until the end of the century, he was disinclined to use them and unable to see their value for any purpose beyond that of easy-going entertainment: Puritan hymnology, both European and the work of early American composers who made the European hymn tradition into strangely primitive harmonic structure, transplanted folk song, especially English folk song, transatlantic song of every sort, including the indigenous styles of the United States, even American Indian song and dance, and Afro-American styles learned especially from negro religious music, with its idiosyncratic attitude to rhythm: it was the task of the American composer to find a style embracing as many of these remarkably disparate elements as possible, and the most influential of the available styles rapidly became jazz, which, because it was the most immediate, vital and inescapable, became part of the American musical atmosphere from the beginning of the twentieth century. Jazz in Europe, in the hands of composers like Kurt Weill, was an exotic importation, appearing always like a sort of quotation introduced when special points had to be made, but in the United States it was almost the only indigenous music which could be heard everywhere and belonged to the States and not to one of its various ethnic groups.

Thus, Charles Ives's creation of a personal style from the popular music of his youth, the music of white New Englanders—patriotic songs, revivalist hymns and so on—all treated with a total disregard for academic tradition and fortuitously discovering principles and ideas that European composers like Schoenberg were to reach through a painstaking reappraisal of first principles, wrote works which for more than fifty years was dismissed as the eccentricity of a musician who no one needed to take seriously. Even the Third Symphony, composed in 1911, with its beautifully treated if basically unsymphonic evocation of traditional American puritanism through its moving use of revivalist hymns, made little impact. It was the development of music which synthesised jazz and the European tradition which persuaded Americans to take their own music seriously.

Gershwin's *Rhapsody in Blue*, given its first performance in 1924 by Paul Whiteman's jazz orchestra and not by a team of musicians dedicated to 'serious' music, made 'symphonic jazz' respectable. Gershwin's Piano Concerto and Aaron Copland's *Dance Symphony*, heard in halls dedicated to the symphonic tradition, won interest rather than respect and acceptance when they were both heard for the first time in 1925. At the I.S.C.M. Festival of 1931 in London, Gershwin's *An American in Paris* won only disapproval, though it was greeted with enormous acclaim when it met its natural, American audience; thirty years later a dead Gershwin could expect the approval of international audiences who no longer dismissed jazz as a strange and musically illiterate dialect; the work was helped, of course, in the United States because it had the prestige which came from a performance by the Boston Symphony Orchestra and the conducting of Serge Koussevitzky.

Americans themselves were slow to accept American music:

> In the twenty-five-year period 1925–50 the names of 280 American composers appeared on regular subscription programmes of the ten oldest major symphony orchestras. Of these, 136, or fifty per cent, have been played by only one orchestra each, while only eighteen composers, or six per cent, have been heard in nine or ten orchestras. It is therefore apparent that most of the quota of American composers is consumed in purely token performances of local and regional interest.[9]

These were the circumstances which led Aaron Copland to complain as recently as 1941:

> I have no quarrel with the masterpieces. I think I revere them and enjoy them as well as the next fellow. But when they are used, unwittingly perhaps, to stifle contemporary effort in our own country, then I am almost tempted to take the extreme view and say that we should be better off without them.[10]

One of the effects of America's participation in two world wars was an increased self-confidence which affected attitudes to the arts as well as to politics; the music composed in the United States by American composers for American audiences seemed at last to be as worthy of attention as any other music. In the years before the second World War the most frequently played American composer was Charles Martin Loeffler, Alsatian by birth, trained in Paris, naturalised American in 1887 when he was twenty-six and totally French in his attitudes. Loeffler died in 1935. Second to Loeffler, John Alden Carpenter, born in 1876, was a pupil of Amy Fay, herself a pupil of Liszt; for a time he studied with Elgar. He was a graduate of Harvard and properly influenced by Bostonian classical ideals. He died

[9] Mueller. p. 176.
[10] Aaron Copland: *Our new Music*. Whitlesey House, New York, 1941. p. 134.

in 1951. The third favourite among American composers was Ernest
Schelling, born in New Jersey in the same year as Carpenter; Schelling
made a sensational reputation as a *Wunderkind* pianist in Philadelphia,
studied under Bruckner and Leschitizky, among others, and wrote decently
traditional music which owes nothing to its American origin.

After the second World War, however, the most popular—in the sense
of widely performed—American composers were Copland, Barber and
Gershwin. In common with many British composers of their generation,
Copland and Barber did not study in Germany but in Paris, with Nadia
Boulanger, opening themselves to a range of influences more susceptible to
novelty and experiment than their predecessors. Copland and Gershwin
both wrote overtly American music, although Copland's 'national' style
represents only the more 'popular' side of his work and is matched by more
difficult and learned works. Barber, whose reputation began in Europe
before it was established in American concert halls, is not in any direct
sense a musical nationalist. Statistics like those of Mueller quoted above
do not, of course, explain whether it was Copland's American music which
won audiences or whether his more austerely abstract music gained an equal
response.

The activities of Schoenberg, Hindemith and other established European
refugees to the United States naturally met the rising confidence of American composers and created an appetite among them—and to a lesser extent
amongst audiences—for 'advanced' styles. Schoenberg and Hindemith were
both inspiring and inspired teachers whose influence made 'advanced'
music intellectually respectable, while Weill, working in the American
theatre, influenced both opera and the elaborate, sentimental American
'musical', the United States' equivalent to Strauss operetta, to Offenbach
and to Gilbert and Sullivan. If there is something a little dubious about the
libretto of the greatest of all post second-World-War successes, *Oklahoma!*,
with its mystique of the Land and the Folk, the athleticism and spareness
of its music might not have been possible if Weill had not found a refuge
in the United States. Only Bartók, driven from Hungary to America, seems
to have been able to exert no direct influence upon the course of musical
history in his new homeland.

If American composition became respectable in the 1950s, the American
orchestras have been unmistakably American since the end of the first World
War, with a brilliance that is strictly national and a virtuoso quality that
European orchestras have rarely tried to achieve. This style is in part the
gift of conductors, for until after the second World War any major
American orchestra looked for a conductor who, having won a great
European, preferably German, reputation, was given a degree of authority
uncurbed, as conductorial tyranny is normally curbed in Europe, by a
variety of imponderables of custom and orchestral tradition; nowhere else

had a conductor had so free a hand to make what he wished of an orchestra, so long as he was supported by the committee which manages the orchestra's business affairs, and the adherence of orchestras, as he is in the United States.

In one point at least American concert organisations have shown a fore-sight not often in evidence elsewhere. The Children's Concert, unknown in Britain until the 1920s, when Sir Robert Mayer brought the idea home with him from the United States and the Children's Concerts of the New York Symphony Orchestra, is as old-established in the United States as the orchestras which perform such concerts. Children's Concerts have an influence exerted in many directions. With relatively few orchestras, and therefore little live music for most American children, a conductor capable of holding the attention of children while amusing them and winning their respectful admiration, could, in the person of Leonard Bernstein, become a television star presenting not only children but adults as well with an in-sight into the delights and excitements, as well as the intellectual founda-tions, of music. In Europe, where habits of concert-going and respect for music are traditional, such concerts may be of little importance. In Britain and America no work has been more valuable.

The finances of American concerts and opera, for all their dependence on the generosity of very rich Americans, are no more free from strain than comparable English organisations, and are equally concerned about success at the box office. Music in the United States benefits from the support of powerful trusts and foundations, like the Ford Foundation's huge grants to opera in New York, Chicago and San Francisco to support productions of American operas,[11] and the patronage of individuals, but little public money is used in support of the arts in America though municipalities often help by providing auditoria and with them the necessary rehearsal facilities. The Federal government helps through fiscal regulations which, while exempting donations to charity from income tax, regards money given to any cultural purpose as a donation to charity.

This does not prevent American orchestras from the necessity of work-ing to an exhausting schedule; the programmes of the New York Phil-harmonic Orchestra, for example, are each repeated on four successive eve-nings. Erich Leinsdorf, interviewed in London on his appointment as con-ductor of the Boston Symphony Orchestra, quoted the Bostonian witticism that the orchestra's schedule of work is 'all right for three orchestras and six conductors'. In Boston the audience likes to see its principal conductor in action at most concerts, and Leinsdorf's tenure of office bound him to conduct twenty-one concerts in the first six weeks of his first season. The Boston season, at the time of his arrival in 1962, included twenty-four sub-scription concerts played on Saturdays and repeated on Sundays, Tuesday

[11] Wallace Brockway and Herbert Weinstock: *The World of Opera.* Methuen, London, 1963. p. 388.

subscription concerts played in Cambridge, Massachusetts, and Sunday and Monday series of concerts.[12]

A multiplication of orchestras to lighten the burden on the musicians who carry it is made impossible not only by the money that is available for music but also by a shortage of players. There is no extensive pool of American musicians available in any of the major cities on which an orchestra could be based, so that except for the great established orchestras, music is necessarily served by community orchestras of amateurs with professional stiffening because no totally professional orchestra can be created without financial guarantees which are still impossible to maintain. When Toscanini, the idol of audiences in the United States, retired from the direction of the National Broadcasting Company Orchestra, created for him in 1936 when he left the New York Philharmonic, his players were naturally reluctant to disband an orchestra with a great international reputation and attempted to form themselves into a self-governing organisation on the lines of the London Symphony Orchestra. They were totally defeated by the facts of American financial life which left them with no funds except those which could be received from subscribers and the box office.

[12] Erich Leinsdorf: interviewed in *The Times*, London, 14 March 1962.

Music in a Fragmented Culture

The nineteenth century created the musical environment in which twentieth-century musicians and listeners have grown up. The opera and concert organisations, the system of chamber-music performances and recitals, and the alternative attractions of musical comedy, variety, popular music on all its various levels and the 'pop' music which is unlike all other forms of music in that it is addressed to a particular age-group although it claims listeners outside its special, selected audience: all these are developments of musical phenomena which first manifested themselves in the nineteenth century.

The twentieth century has modified the system without changing or substantially adding to its essential nature. The late nineteenth-century orchestra of Straussian or Mahlerian dimensions has lost much of its attraction for composers, who have found their way to smaller ensembles depending more often on contrasts of tone colour than on the blended colours of the late nineteenth century, but this development had already begun in the works of Mahler. As early as 1906, while Richard Strauss was still writing operas on a more than Wagnerian orchestral scale, Schoenberg had composed his first Chamber Symphony in E major 'for fifteen solo instruments', and Stravinsky followed during the first World War with *The Soldier's Tale*, first produced in 1918. In his autobiography Stravinsky explains his choice of instruments—violin, double bass, clarinet, bassoon, trumpet, trombone and percussion—as forced on him by the exigencies of wartime, which had dried up his resources and made it impossible for him to recoup them through the composition of the sort of large-scale work on which his reputation was based. Nevertheless, it is possible to see *The Soldier's Tale*, after more than half a century, as a liberation from the large orchestra, which became increasingly less important to many composers. Mahler's orchestras—and Mahler died in 1911—may have been numerically huge, but Mahler was an honorary member of the future in that his scoring is selective and often enough two or three contrasted instruments playing in counterpoint to each other convey everything he wishes to say.

Stravinsky's explanation of the small, selective chamber group of *The Soldier's Tale* became incomplete because even Stravinsky himself wrote increasingly for smaller orchestras, often unusually constituted, and the interest in smaller ensembles grew after the first World War had ended.

From the composer's point of view, smaller ensembles offered the possibility of more performances, and therefore greater financial rewards than the nineteenth-century orchestra, as well as the musical profits of new and attractive styles. The full weight and saturated tone of the post-Wagnerian orchestra became a matter often for special occasions and seemed to leave little new for the composer to do; the great masters of the orchestra in the twentieth century have been disciples of Mahler, who used the orchestra selectively for the sake of contrasted colours and not simply for the sake of its overwhelming power.

Thus the large orchestra ceased to be the natural, all-purpose ensemble it had been for nineteenth-century composers. The French composers of the 1920s, and English composers of the same period, like Bliss, spent as much time writing for oddly assorted *ad hoc* groups—like the soprano, flute, clarinet, bassoon, viola, harp and double bass of Bliss's *Madame Noy*—as with the full orchestra. In one sense, such music, like that of the original version with reciter of Walton's *Façade*, is a virtuoso composer's music for virtuoso players. In Germany Hindemith was composing *Gebrauchtmusik* ('utility music') for whatever group of players might find themselves together and need something to play, including not only sonatas for all the wind instruments, except tuba and piano, a concerto for piano and twelve solo instruments and one for cello and ten solo instruments.

When Britten, after the triumph of *Peter Grimes* in 1945, turned immediately to chamber opera with *The Rape of Lucretia*, he advanced practical and economic reasons for his decision to use an orchestra of twelve—five solo strings, five wind, percussion and harp, with no chorus. Opera on this scale would not be tied to large theatres in which complete orchestras can be accommodated, with stages large enough to permit the deployment and movement of a large chorus; chamber orchestras of Britten's dimensions could fit into almost any theatre in comparatively small towns and thus reduce the expense of producing opera while adding to the social relevance of the art by seeking, and possibly winning, new audiences. Chamber opera was not a totally new conception; Holst's *Savitri* and *The Wandering Scholar* were twentieth-century precursors of *The Rape of Lucretia*, and a considerable number of forgotten works from the late eighteenth century could fall within any reasonable definition of the form, but Britten and other contemporary composers have provided a growing repertoire of modern works within the not entirely rigid limits which Britten has observed. But however practical the original aims of *The Rape of Lucretia* and succeeding chamber operas were, the imaginative scoring and the originality and beauty of the effects that Britten has gained from his small ensembles suggest that whatever his primary motives may have been in reducing the scale of opera, his achievements in the form leave the listener to suppose that, perhaps unconsciously, the real motive may have been an artistic one. In any case, the extent to which Britten's chamber operas have widened the appeal and the subject matter of opera, and the distance over which they have carried it to new audiences, are not easy to calculate.

The interest in smaller orchestras of possibly mixed constituents was shared by many concert-goers. The success of the Boyd Neel Orchestra after its foundation in England in 1932, and of similar continental groups— I Musici in Italy, the Moscow Chamber Orchestra and the Stuttgart Chamber Orchestra, as well as a considerable number of similar orchestras all over Europe—meant the exploration of a new repertoire; by the end of the 1940s, almost forgotten composers like Vivaldi had won a place in modern concert programmes and, equally significantly, in gramophone record catalogues; the precise orderliness of the baroque concerto took its place in general musical experience. The unity of musical outlook, which had been shared by musicians and their audiences throughout the nineteenth century, was further broken by the revival of the baroque to add to the confusion caused by the Great Schism which had taken away from the musical centre those whose taste was for the purely entertaining.

At the same time, the situation of the composer had to some extent become easier than it had been. Though the social vacuum into which he had been compelled to live throughout the nineteenth century still existed, and though he was still virtually compelled to silence until he found a willing audience, society became increasingly ready to pay him for whatever work he did which gave pleasure.

Attempts to reward the composer, and other artists, through copyright laws have been made since the seventeenth century. The music of Heinrich Schütz, for example, was protected through copyright throughout Saxony, and George I granted Handel a copyright in 1720. But Handel's music could legally be issued in pirated editions though he had the King's 'licence for the sole printing' of his work for fourteen years, after which each passed in its turn into the public domain. Schütz's music had found its way into the hands of unauthorised printers as soon as published copies were available to be bought. Any special licence of this kind was so indefinite and poorly drafted, from any modern point of view, with no clear notion of how a work could be given real protection, that neither Schütz nor Handel, for all the century which passed between the grants in their favour, had any real safeguard against the pirating of their published work. George I's special grant to his favoured composer afforded Handel no more protection than he would have had from the general copyright act which was introduced in Queen Anne's reign.

As country after country introduced increasingly effective copyright arrangements, the problem came to be that of protecting works from exploitation in foreign countries. The English composer and publisher George

Smart, for instance, made business trips to Europe after the Napoleonic Wars, visiting publishers to buy from them, not from their composers, music which he believed would have a good sale in England. It was this situation that led Beethoven to sell limited rights to his publishers, reserving to himself the right to dispose of music already sold to German or Austrian publishers, exploiting his work in other countries to his own, if limited, advantage.

Foreign copyrights were a composer's headache. In 1855 Verdi, whose works were invariably published by Ricordi, in Milan, discovered that England had granted foreign composers the right to profit from the publication of their works in England, so that Verdi had been able to sell scores to English publishers. Then a case in the House of Lords had decided that this right was accorded only to those foreign composers whose countries had copyright agreements with Britain; Milan was not one of them, and the decision made it possible for British publishers to issue Verdi's scores without even consulting, let alone paying, him.

> During my two visits to London [he wrote in September 1855] it was suggested that I should apply for citizenship of either England or France, or even Piedmont (because France and Piedmont have international agreements with England), but I prefer to remain what I am, that is to say, a peasant from Roncole, and I prefer to ask my government to make an agreement with England. The government of Parma has nothing to lose in an agreement of this kind, which is purely artistic and literary[1]

The situation was not brought under control until the decisions of the Berne Convention of 1886, which decided that all the signatory countries should grant internal copyright protection to their nationals, and that foreign works should be protected within every country which subscribed to the Convention. Neither Russia nor the United States of America, however, did so, and Russian publishers of serious music proceeded to protect their composers—in the case of authors, whose work needed a translator, protection was a more difficult business—by setting up branch houses in France and Germany. The United States was satisfied by making bilateral arrangements with countries which had accepted the Berne Convention.

The protection given by a genuinely international system of copyright depended on the sale of works published. Composers of songs and piano music which caught public attention and could be sold as sheet music profited immensely; in England publishers promoted 'ballad concerts' at which popular songs composed to safe formulae with words that appealed to the popular sentiments of late Victorian England were sung by admired, and often justly admired, vocalists who were paid a royalty on each performance for their assistance in promoting sales. Ivor Newton wrote of the legendary Dame Clara Butt:

[1] Verdi: *op. cit.* p. 100.

Her mastery of ballads was doubly profitable for her. Her audiences loved them as she did, and she contracted with publishers to sing them, receiving a royalty on the sales of those she made popular; I believe that every copy sold of 'Abide with me' brought her threepence. When I asked her why she had dropped one highly popular song from her programmes, she explained that she had made a contract with its publishers for a royalty on sales which continued for seven years; the contract had now expired, and she was not prepared to go on advertising the song.[2]

Exploitation of this kind could produce sales of vast quantities of songs which won popular acclaim and were consequently a welcome source of income for the composer, who himself received a royalty of from ten to fifteen per cent on every copy sold. The publisher regarded it as his duty no less than his profit to sell as many sheet music copies of a composer's songs or small piano pieces as possible.

But though the composer of operas, symphonies, concertos and so on was at last protected so far as publication of his work was concerned, obviously he was in a far less favourable position. Even if an opera or a symphony rapidly became popular (and 'popularity' is a relative term; it rarely means for a symphony what it means for an undemanding song which any amateur can sing for fun), it could be expected to sell only a limited number of copies. An aria which could be published separately, as sheet music, with a piano accompaniment, would sell far more copies than a complete vocal score, just as a vocal score, or a piano transcription of an orchestral work, could rightly expect to sell more copies than its orchestral score. As the bulk of performances of any extensive new work, or relatively new work, are given not from published parts bought by a concert organisation but from parts hired from its publisher, the necessity for the composer's prosperity was payment not so much by the number of copies sold as by the number of performances given for so long as the work is protected by copyright.

The French had realised this as early as the late eighteenth century. In 1776 Beaumarchais was largely responsible for the creation of a *Société des Auteurs et Compositeurs dramatiques*, the members of which permitted performance of their plays and operas only by managements who paid them a royalty on each performance; this became a standard arrangement for composers in France. Berlin adopted a similar system early in the nineteenth century, and the Austrian and other German theatres followed suit. A similar recognition of performing rights in all music arose in France after 1850, brought about by a composer of light music who, hearing music of his played in a restaurant where he was dining, refused to pay for his dinner on the grounds that he had not been paid for the use of his music; the case came to court and the composer won it. The right of the composer, after this, to control the performance of his music, and to expect to profit

[2] Ivor Newton: *At the Piano*. Hamish Hamilton, London, 1966. p. 83.

from that performance, led to the setting up, in May 1850, of the *Agence Centrale pour la Perception des Droits des Auteurs et Compositeurs de la Musique*. Richard Strauss, more than anyone else, was responsible for the creation of a similar society in Germany in 1903, and international copyright acts were revised to recognise the right of composers to authorise the performance of their works in exchange for a fee.

English publishers operated the system of royalties on sold copies of music more extensively than other European companies so that they were at first unhappy about the principle of a performing right. Such a system, they felt, would be likely to reduce the number of performances of any new or relatively new work by throwing performers back, for the sake of economy, on works in the public domain and thus indirectly injuring the sale of copies from which the successful composer of popular works could expect to earn a valuable sum and the publisher a no less valuable profit. It was the development of recorded music which persuaded William Boosey, himself a music publisher, that the composer's situation had radically changed by virtue of technical and scientific progress. He wrote:

> I was beginning to be aware that probably, eventually a composer's performing rights might be even more valuable than his publishing rights.[3]

In 1911 a new Copyright Act added to the composer's rights that of controlling reproductions of his work by any mechanical means, and his right to authorise performances. Towards the end of 1913 composers and publishers (whose own rights might be threatened by unauthorised performance) began to discuss the creation of a society which would protect copyrights by controlling performances and preventing those that were unauthorised, with the result that the Performing Rights Society was registered in March 1914, the publishers involved in the Society having vested in it the performing rights of a large number of works of all kinds. Naturally, much of its time and energy was spent in ensuring that copyrights in the most popular kinds of music were not infringed, but 'serious' composers too benefited from its operation. Copyright in mechanical reproduction had been reorganised in 1908 and 1909 in all the countries which accepted the Berne Convention; these agreed to safeguard performers' rights in mechanical reproduction, so thus the actual player was in a stronger financial position than he had ever been before.

Recording, however, had other than financial effects on the composer; Edison's phonograph, which made its first recognisable sounds in 1877, had originally been nothing but an ingenious toy. The invention in 1888 of a shellac disc in place of Edison's cylinder as the recipient of the recording, revolving on a turntable to transmit the sounds imprinted on it, led to a

[3] William Boosey: *op. cit.* p. 175.

great multiplication of recordings. Before the first World War Adelina Patti recorded 'Home Sweet Home'; Calvé made records, as did Melba from 1904 onwards. Tamagno and Maurel, the first Otello and Iago of Verdi's opera, can still be heard. In 1905 Jean de Reszke recorded two discs, but permitted the release of neither, although even in those early days voices could be recorded with tolerable fidelity while instrumental tone was not satisfactorily captured until the development of electrical recording in the 1920s, by which time a considerable library of Melba and Caruso records already existed. Both Melba and Caruso made considerably more money from the recording of passages from Puccini's operas than did the composer himself.

The early gramophone record was an expensive pleasure: to listen to a sixty-year-old Patti sing 'Home Sweet Home' cost £1. But mass production and skilful advertising succeeded in lowering prices by increasing demand until in the 1930s Woolworth's sold seven-inch records for sixpence each, while to listen to Chaliapin, Paderewski, Kreisler and Casals and the great singers and instrumentalists, or to Toscanini and Stokowski, Weingartner and any of their peers on ten- or twelve-inch records cost only a few shillings for up to ten minutes' music. Electrical recording and reproduction conveyed instrumental and orchestral tone accurately enough to satisfy ears that were more concerned with the music played or sung than with concepts of 'high fidelity'. The gramophone became not only a source of easy-going entertainment but an invaluable tool in the hands of the musical historian and a means to knowledge for the student. Elgar conducted his own works; so did Rachmaninov and all composers who had won recognition in the concert hall since the technique of recording had developed sufficiently to allow a trustworthy account of their performance. Of equal historical value are many recordings of music of all kinds which preserve performances by the great interpretative artists of the past and those which present the evolution of popular styles from ragtime through jazz to the dance music of the 1920s and 1930s and on to the pop of the 1960s and 1970s.

The gramophone record, however, introduced a new style of advertising into our musical life. Any artist, soloist, or conductor, who catches the public imagination can be exploited by publicity machines simply to sell records. As the public interest almost inevitably precedes the records of any 'serious' musician, it is in the realm of 'popular' music that performer's reputations are likely to be established through the skilful advertising of records before they have made any genuine appeal to the public; the recording of any pop group may not precede the group's first, exploratory appearances in public, but recording and a position in the 'charts' of each week's most popular discs is the way to, and not as it is for 'serious' musicians the consequence of, celebrity.

The growth of recording, which by the 1930s was producing complete versions of the more popular and manageable operas, the still admirable recordings of the Mozart Opera Society, recorded versions of the standard symphonies and concertos, the offerings of the Sibelius Symphony Society and the Beethoven Sonata Society, as well as quantities of choral, chamber and solo instrumental music, naturally aroused the pessimism of many musicians. Why, it seemed natural to ask, travel to hear a work played by X, Y or Z in some discomfort and the price of a seat when for no more than the cost of a ticket you could obtain a more or less permanent recording of the work in an interpretation by Schnabel or Kreisler, Toscanini, Furt-wängler or Walter, or sung by the finest singers of the day? The pessimists, of course, undervalued the atmosphere of the concert hall, the appeal of participation which is the concert hall's special quality and the sense that live performance is an important communication to listeners delivered from the composer through the performers.

Actually, the effect of recording and later of broadcasting was to extend rather than diminish the attractiveness of 'live' musical events. Neverthe-less, after the doubtful advantages of recording, the advent of broadcasting in the 1920s was greeted with dismay, especially in England, where the concept of broadcasting as a public service dedicated to providing every-body with the best of everything flooded the air with music of all sorts available all the time. While conductors like Sir Thomas Beecham and Sir Hamilton Harty prognosticated the end of the public concert, Constant Lambert was moved to write in 1934 about the stultifying effects of what he called 'the appalling popularity of music':

> In the neighbourhood where I live, for example, there is a loudspeaker every hundred yards or so, and it is only rarely that they are tuned in to different stations. If they are playing the foxtrot I most detest at one corner of the street, I need not think that I can avoid it by walking to the other end. At times there is a certain piquancy in following a tune in two dimensions at once, so to speak—to buy one's cigarettes to the first subject of a symphony, to get some scraps of development as one goes to the newsagent, and to return home to the recapitulation—but the idea of the town as one vast analytical programme, with every paving stone a bar line, soon palls.[4]

The misuse and cheapening effects of music, which Lambert noticed, turned out to be side effects of the musical policy of broadcasters. Actually, if there were (and still are) those who conduct the trivia of their lives while radio or record player offer them the Ninth Symphony or *Tristan und Isolde*, the late Beethoven quartets or the *Art of Fugue*, if a balance sheet of the good and ill effects of broadcasting could be drawn up, it might

[4] Constant Lambert: *Music Ho!* London, 1934. Pelican Books, Har-mondsworth, 1948. p. 169.

easily show that both the record and the loudspeaker have served music faithfully and well, although both have made it possible to use great music as a negligible accompaniment to other activities. It is perfectly reasonable to think of works like (in the words of W. H. Auden):

> Those divertimenti which
> He wrote to play while bottles were uncorked
> Milord chewed noisily, Milady talked.[5]

as background to a meal or the completion of a crossword puzzle, but it is too easy now for the vacant corners of minds to be made receptacles for the late Beethoven quartets, or *Cosi fan Tutte, Don Giovanni* or *Die Meistersinger*. If every cloud has a silver lining, it has been justly pointed out, every silver lining had a cloud.

Furthermore, the permanent availability of a vast 'serious' repertoire through the radio, the long-playing gramophone record and, more recently, the tape recorder has robbed too much music of the sense of occasion which is part of the experience of great works. The question of how often we should hear the Ninth Symphony or the *Missa Solemnis, Götterdämmerung* or *Tristan und Isolde*, Mahler's Eighth Symphony, the Mass in B minor or the *St. Matthew Passion* is subjective; but it is a real and difficult question; huge works, some of the greatness of which is imparted by their sheer size, should perhaps always be events rare enough never to lose their power from over-familiarity. There is, too, an equally real question to be asked about the continuing validity of a record player's unvarying reproduction of the same performance; in the realm of 'live' music performances cannot be unvarying and identical, just as no 'live' performance can be expected to reach the state of unnatural perfection achieved by recordings constructed piecemeal from the splicing together of innumerable short lengths of tape; it is significant that many of the most communicative recorded performances are faulty and less than perfectly balanced preservations of particular performances played in the presence of a less than perfectly silent but usually excited audience. A performance can never do more, and perhaps should never do more, than represent its player's response to music at a particular time, in a particular hall, with particular colleagues on a particular occasion.

The coming of the long-playing record, which appeared in the United States in 1948 and in Britain a year later, containing up to or even more than half an hour's music on each side, was probably responsible for the greatest expansion of the repertoire ever achieved. It is natural enough that there should be a multiplicity of recording of important and popular works, all of which are capable of a variety of valid interpretations which may vary in tempo, dynamic scale, accentuation and phrasing. But together with the

5 W. H. Auden: *Metalogue to the Magic Flute.*

natural multiplication of great music has come the exploration of works rarely if ever heard in the concert hall and the opera house. The *Tristia* of Berlioz, for example, are, like many other works known by name rather than by actual performance, recorded when a conductor with an established reputation (and therefore the ability to attract buyers) shows a special sympathy with their composer's style. The popularity of Mahler's music in England since the early 1950s probably owes a great deal to the discovery that a fine and much-admired singer, Kathleen Ferrier, had a special sympathy for *Das Lied von der Erde* and the *Kindertotenlieder*. But it is equally arguable that recording companies, looking for new works to catch the record buyer's ear, found that Mahler's orchestral style exploited the record's technical qualities effectively. At the same time, the record has fanned a minority interest in medieval music into something already large with unexpected repercussions on popular music. A good deal of the most extremely radical music of the 1960s and 1970s is, too, given a wider audience by recording.

Recording under modern conditions and with modern techniques, however, fosters an appetite for a type of perfection which is not only capable of creating a liking for performances which win total exactitude of performance at a cost in communicative vitality, thus becoming inimical to music itself. The record collector is too often asked to concentrate on qualities of reproduction which in the context of a moving performance in hall or opera house would not capture our attention but would be subsumed in our response to the music as communication. There are record-makers and record-buyers for whom music exists only as an adjunct to the exercise of the techniques of the recording studio.

To draw any final balance sheet of drawbacks, to consider 'the appalling popularity of music' (which means, as Lambert pointed out, that music is heard without being listened to) and the pressures of advertising applied to what might be great and with equal vigour to what might be merely trivial, and to set these things against the enrichments brought by recording and radio, is impossible. Broadcasting, perhaps more effectively in Britain than in most countries, has led to the commissioning of works from both established and young struggling composers looking for their audience. Some of the music thus created has been important and interesting; some has been artistically successful; some of it has been deservedly forgotten. But any composer develops by composing, so that every commission is important, whatever the result it produces might be. If an unascertainable number of radio listeners and record-buyers misuse the music that is available 'on tap' (and there is, perhaps, a degree of unjustifiable superiority in claiming that any use of music is a misuse), an equally unascertainable number has found the same music to be a valuable enrichment of their lives. The 'appalling popularity of music' of all kinds, from the most exalted to the most trivial, has made it possible for large numbers of musicians of all sorts to live by their art and to contribute whatever they have to contribute to general pleasure and enrichment. Music as a profession is a more rewarding way of life for musicians than it was in the past.

The development of broadcasting led the BBC, in 1930, to create its own Symphony Orchestra on terms which would have seemed normal to the members of major continental orchestras but which were, in the Britain of the early 1930s, not only new but almost ideally benevolent. Musicians in the various BBC orchestras—for regional symphony orchestras were formed after the establishment of the major London orchestra—were granted not seasonal but annual employment on contracts which made music as safe a profession as any other, with the possibility of more than adequate rehearsal time and regular studio work interspersed with regular public concerts. The BBC could afford to organise an orchestra on these, for England, lavish lines while the Hallé, the Liverpool Philharmonic, the Bournemouth and Birmingham Orchestras and the Scottish National Orchestra could afford to give their players contracts only for the season and the London orchestras had never completely thrown off the deputy system. The London Symphony Orchestra, founded by dissidents from Sir Henry Wood's policy of no deputies allowed, prided itself, as a players' co-operative formulating its own policy and electing its own conductor, on the freedom its players maintained to avoid the compulsions of a policy which gave the players security at the price of freedom. It led a hand-to-mouth existence, never far from financial disaster, as did the London Philharmonic Orchestra established by Sir Thomas Beecham in 1932, collecting many of the finest players in Britain and establishing standards of virtuosity rarely achieved in the days before the second World War by any British orchestra. Box-office finance and the support of wealthy patrons left every British orchestra except those of the BBC to struggle for survival.

By the end of the second World War, the appetite for music and for all the arts in Britain, which up to that time had been as effectively self-supporting as they could, more than justified the creation of the Arts Council, created to organise and disburse government subsidies to artistic enterprises. Together with this, local governments were empowered to raise and spend money to support the arts. The result was that the provincial orchestras could be organised on the same effective lines as those of the BBC or, for that matter, the continental orchestras. Though the provincial orchestras are not left to serve audiences simply in their own city but play in wide areas around them, and though subsidies both from local government and the Arts Council are parsimonious when compared to those offered in support of opera companies and orchestras in Europe, they have helped to make music far more available, and far more widely attended, than it was when broadcasting first offered the listener his choice of music.

G*

The same experience is, to some extent, that of the United States, though radio in America has not felt itself very conscious of any duty to win audiences for the arts; its commercial basis meant that from the start concert and opera broadcasts were a matter of prestige rather than of artistic or social duty, but the introduction of music to audiences otherwise deprived of it had the same effect as it has had on the eastern side of the Atlantic.

At the end of the 1920s the cinema too found a voice and by doing so plunged the entire musical world into consternation. Wherever the film became popular—and that is almost everywhere in the 'civilised' world—it had employed musicians. If, in any local cinema, an indefatigable pianist accompanied each film with a musical commentary made up of works and pieces which seemed appropriate to his or her mind, larger and more expensive cinemas employed orchestras which not only accompanied the film on show but proved to be popular enough to occupy the stage and make music on its own account. Naturally, like restaurant orchestras, cinema orchestras varied both in quality of performance, quality of repertoire and in composition. But the conductor Eugene Goossens gives an account, in his autobiography, *Overture and Beginners*, of conducting sixty-five members of the London Symphony Orchestra throughout a performance of *The Three Musketeers*, the work of the fantastically popular Douglas Fairbanks Senior, when it was screened at Covent Garden in 1922. Seven years later the music critic Edwin Evans explained:

> It is estimated, on the basis of union statistics, that picture theatres, great and small, are now providing between three-quarters and four-fifths of the paid musical employment in the country. . . . For about fifty-nine hours weekly, music is being performed in upward of three thousand cinemas, and for shorter periods in perhaps a thousand isolated halls. Setting aside all aesthetic considerations in favour of a purely objective view, one may say that the cinema is at present the most important musical institution in the country.[6]

Cinema orchestras, the more or less resident musicians of many cinemas, created their musical commentary on the films (working out two programmes a week in most suburban and provincial cinemas) which consisted of either their leader's or their conductor's compilation and adaptation of familiar melodies from light music, popular symphonies and overtures or whatever seemed to convey the substance of the episode with which they were linked; occasionally a score was composed specially for the film to be seen, but such specially composed scores were rarely more stimulating than the usual arrangements by local musicians. Only in Russia, and for such special prestige films as Eisenstein's *Battleship Potemkin*, were the scores of particular musical value.

[6] Edwin Evans: 'Music and the Cinema'. In *Music and Letters*. Vol. X. January 1929. p. 69.

The destruction of 'live' cinema music by the talkies was a disaster for all cinema musicians, especially dire in England and the United States. But the musical influence of such orchestras had rarely been powerful; it seemed to mean little to audiences. The film score itself was gradually to have a considerable influence on 'serious' composers through the money it brought them. Originally love scenes often decided that their point of departures, musically speaking, was some special intensity from *Tristan und Isolde*; moments of extreme dramatic tension looked back to Tchaikovsky, horror and terror moved the film composer, if not towards the structures of Schoenberg and his followers, at least to their vocabulary of extreme dissonance.

By the 1930s, composers from the concert hall and the opera house were beginning to be called in to provide suitable music for films. In England Walton wrote his first film score, for *Escape Me Never*, in 1934. Bliss composed the score for the film of H. G. Wells's *Things to Come* a year later. Walton went on to deal with another ten films in scores that rightly yielded music for concert suites. Vaughan Williams found a rewarding discipline in working to a rigid time-table of the film shot. Shostakovitch had written film scores since 1928, Prokofiev found himself working for the cinema in 1924 and went on to a splendid partnership with Eisenstein in *Alexander Nevsky* and the *Ivan the Terrible* trilogy. In the United States Copland and Vergil Thomson have provided memorable music for films; French composers—Milhaud, Auric, Sauguet, Honneger, Ibert among them—composed for the cinema in the great days of the French film.

For the successful film composer the cinema provides a very profitable field of action, and the composer who is regularly demanded by the cinema finds himself pleasantly removed from the anxieties and uncertainties which are an inevitable part of the freelance composer's normal lot without, necessarily, cheapening his style or making unwilling concessions to audiences which cannot listen to his music in the concert hall.

But the protection of a composer's now multiplied rights, though it is elementary justice, depends upon the extent to which he can win a hearing. A composer of any nationality can live by composition provided that he becomes successful enough to receive commissions from films and from other sources, especially if he can feel confident that a work can look forward to a second and third performance. An enquiry into the situation of the British composer[7] in 1974 suggested that out of five hundred composers of all ages and all kinds in Britain, ten could afford to live by the proceeds of their work. The rest were compelled to earn money outside music or, more appropriately, as orchestral musicians or teachers of music; some worked as editors of music, wrote criticisms or undertook any musical hackwork they could find. A questionnaire submitted to five hundred and seventy-five com-

[7] *Observer Magazine*, 6 January 1974.

posers in 1971 revealed that their average earnings from composition for the previous year had been £357; the 'serious' composers among them earned an average £185.[8] A similar enquiry into the composer's ways and means in the United States revealed that a similar situation existed across the Atlantic. Though there is no available study of the economics of composition in Europe, a study of programmes in continental countries suggests that the 'serious' composer in Europe is in a position similar to that of his British or American contemporary. The conductor, the successful player and the teacher are all more than likely to earn more money from teaching than all but the few composers whose work proves popular enough to win frequent hearings and recordings. This, however, can hardly be regarded as a serious flaw in our musical system; the composer is properly occupied with the practicalities of music and gains from his struggles with them.

The distance between modern 'light' and entertainment music on the one hand and the work of such composers as Stockhausen, Cage, Boulez and Maxwell Davies on the other, together with the large spectrum—from Henze, Britten, Shostakovitch, Malcolm Arnold and Walton (remembering that while critics are inclined to regard Walton as a Grand Old Reactionary there are still devoted listeners and concert-goers who find his music too radical and 'modern' for their taste) almost defies the composer to win an audience along any wide front. The old attitude to music, acceptance of a tradition perpetually expanding under the pressure of every major composer's personality and aims, no longer has any wide authority. The criteria which we can apply to more or less all the music that has survived from, say, the age of Dunstable in the early fifteenth century and persisted until the music of composers whose activities began in the 1930s no longer applies to much of the new work we hear; to apply those standards to much of the music of Messiaen and most of that of Boulez and Stockhausen would be to invite invalid judgements, leaving aside the deliberate limitations of style and vocabulary adopted by composers like Gershwin. The traditional criteria apply more effectively to Rock 'n Roll and to pop, for example, than they do to much of the *avant garde* work of the '60s or '70s; the criteria by which we judge, or should judge, electronic music are not those we should apply to music by Britten, Orff, Penderecki or Shostakovitch, diverse as their music is. There are few composers who have Britten's gift for writing melodies which can be immediately accepted and enjoyed together with the self-discipline which leads him to simplify and refine whatever he composes until it comes as close as it can to its audience for all its originality of sound and style. The enormous amount of music permanently at the disposal of the modern audience, whatever individual tastes exist within that audience, makes it unnecessary for the listener to come to terms

[8] Alan Peacock and Ronald Weir: *The Composer in the Market Place*. Faber, London, 1975.

with any type of composition with which he is unfamiliar, so that musical conditions themselves assist in the separation of musical society into a multitude of coteries variously overlapping.

Music, however, creates societies. Any audience which undergoes a similar experience through a performance is welded, however temporarily, into a community, so that the attraction of such events as the carnival 'last night' of a London Promenade Concert season is only partly musical, though it is music which makes the carnival possible despite the fact that much of the music heard appeals to traditions only partly musical in themselves; these traditions are often worn, but music raises them to a power which restores their validity. This social power of music is exemplified over and over again in works of all periods: Bach's use of Lutheran chorales in his church music and the popular gaiety of the last movement of Berlioz's *Symphonie Funèbre et Triomphale* are examples from far extremes of musical style and aspiration. A similar unifying power is felt in the hysterical adulation which is poured out over some outstanding performers, from Maria Callas to Leopold Stokowski, from Frank Sinatra to the Beatles. But that is a power which 'serious' Western music has all but lost in the second half of the twentieth century.

Any attempt to organise music on behalf of society and set it to serve social ends make little appeal to musicians and to music lovers. In our state of shattered culture what concept of 'society' should music be organised to serve? By forbidding this or that manifestation of music as 'decadent' (a Hitlerian notion) or 'formalistic' or 'socially divisive' (two terms close together in political thought) is not, in the aftermath of the liberal age, a pleasant or a tenable idea. A work like Britten's *War Requiem*, for example, manifesting an inherited tradition and a common hatred of war, creates unities which may possibly be temporary but which are nevertheless consciously held; but performances of Mahler's Eighth Symphony or Schoenberg's *Gurrelieder* or, almost certainly, Havergal Brian's *Gothic* Symphony, indeed of any massive work which ends in a blaze of triumph, creates the terms under which we listen to them and thus imposes unity on us. The atheist and the agnostic, the unitarian, the quaker, the protestant and the catholic all respond to, say, the Mass in B minor or the end of *The Dream of Gerontius* more or less as Bach and Elgar compel them. Such responses operate infallibly so long as the audience shares some musical awareness with the composer and recognises the tradition of thought in which he has written so that it, so to speak, grasps the basic terms of the composer's vocabulary: music is self-sufficient with this one proviso, that it can be a foreign language and therefore exclude those who have no fundamental grasp of its grammar and vocabulary. Possibly music cannot create but only serve the society which it needs and which needs it. The young listener whose musical awareness is restricted to pop is not sure to respond to Bach any more than would be the listener, if such a being exists, who had heard no music except electronic compositions.

It is natural that absolutist government should wish to win the voice of the arts. Jewish music virtually ceased to exist in Hitler's Germany, in so far as music by Jewish composers within the European tradition can be validly classed as 'Jewish', just as all the musical styles and organisation of the Bourbon court in France was harnessed to serve the purposes of Napoleon's empire. In the same way, music in Soviet Russia is, so far as it can be, harnessed to clear social purposes evolved from a clear political philosophy. Russian music should be 'realist', objective not subjective, expressing the voice, ideals and nature of the people, not an unrestrained, solitary individualism; it is the voice of the state, the state existing ideally as the embodiment of the people and their will. As the aims of a Communist government are, as a matter of political dogma, correct and therefore certain to succeed, music must express not only natural individual experience— happy or sad—great intensities of individual emotion are not in the Communist sense 'natural'—but also the society in which the composer lives, its historical tragedies, its struggles and the inevitable final triumph to which it will lead. Obviously in the works of Shostakovich, often regarded as a dangerously subjective individualist by Soviet authorities whose attitude the composer (with what inner reservations we do not know) shared, and in that of Prokofiev, Communist doctrine no more precludes the writing of masterpieces than does any other dogma religious or political.

Nevertheless, the philosophy of Socialist Realism which orders the official life of Russian music is by nature restrictive, though it can be applied with varying degrees of rigour. The offences of Shostakovitch and Prokofiev were condemned at various times since the 1930s as 'formalism' and 'subjectivism'; that is to say, they treated music as an end in itself and not as an instrument of social development. The way to avoid 'formalism' and 'subjectivism', notoriously bourgeois faults growing from the bourgeoisie's misuse of the leisure it unjustly appropriates to itself, is to use traditional, comprehended forms and to fill them with materials which are somehow related to national or regional folk song, rooted in the music of the people. The fact that in the 1970s the dogma is used with more enlightenment (so far as the evidence of Shostakovitch's poignant Fourteenth or enigmatic Fifteenth Symphonies, which have not been condemned, can take us), does not alter the fact that freedom to explore not only techniques but states of mind is only given to composers of Shostakovich's genius and persistence. In the same way, Soviet Russia is prepared to be more open to other music than it was, so that a composer like Benjamin Britten can find not only popularity within Communist Russia but an honorary status as a 'realist' composer based on the fact that he expresses himself melodically and in terms traditional enough to make his originality acceptable. But pop music, apparently popular with Soviet youth which accepts it as the international style of youth rejecting old and imperfect societies, is still condemned though it is not actually forbidden; the difficulty of governments in the second half of the twentieth century in actually banning anything which can be heard on radio, bought on records or collected on tape are all but insuperable.

> Ideology and politics [writes Nicolas Slonimsky] are integral parts of Russian musical life. . . . The gigantic experiment of directing the language of music according to a set of philosophically formulated principals is unprecedented in history.[9]

In reality, of course, the doctrine has changed little since Plato first propounded the necessity of having the poet bound to the service of the state, and it is not intellectually disreputable. It was the doctrine of the catholic and Calvinist churches at different times in their history. The unacceptable and essentially restrictive elements in it are that it contains a doctrine of what is socially relevant to the needs of the world, and such a doctrine is no less subjective than any other, and music is capable of transcending the doctrines which it is set to serve; it can create its own relevance to individual life and to society, at least in those countries which have developed away from the classic Platonic view of social necessity. Music deliberately set to limit its appeal ultimately becomes catch-penny and boring even if it comes to life in a society where the necessity of catching pennies is not a pressing preoccupation. The Western music of a fragmented society is a result of the situation created by the nineteenth century, which divorced entertainment music from serious music and promulgated the doctrine of the artist as a personality innately superior to the rest of the race and therefore under no social compulsion to discipline his work to communicate with the widest possible audience. The greatest composers are those who communicated in this way, but since the nineteenth century they have been held in some suspicion; the acceptance of Elgar by the world at large is proceeding more than forty years after his death, at a time when advanced thinkers are developing their suspicions of Britten in spite of the demonstrable fact that whatever Britten communicates is stated with facinating originality, musical intelligence and certainty of effect.

It is possible now to win intellectual acceptance for works which have abandoned the notion that music is a discipline, that it has, in a not painfully strained analogy, a grammar and a syntax. Simplifications of the language of music until only a single element remains—rhythm or texture more often than melody or harmony have become confused with originality, as though Britten's *The Turn of the Screw*, making new sounds in

---

[9] Nicolas Slonimsky: Foreword to *Prokofiev*, by Israel V. Nestyev. Stanford and Oxford University Press, 1961. p. vii.

traditional ways, is somehow more old-fashioned than the attempts of Stockhausen to make electronic music out of the unco-ordinated improvisations
of a group of players who individually produce little of any moment. The
pessimist, sadly conscious of music dissipating its power, its capacity to
mould societies, may feel that as Western society is either crumbling away
or moulding itself into something new and probably inimical, can comfort
himself with the historical knowledge that there have been earlier ages of
musical disruption which have eventually synthesised themselves into musical
styles broadly based enough to contain the explorations of a J. S. Bach and
the cheerful prattle of a Telemann at his least exciting, to hold together
Wagner and Brahms and Bruckner. Any new synthesis will belong to the
society in which it is formed, to be a reflection of its character and purpose.
A reflection, after all, is not the most flattering of possible images, and music
in society reflects—with all a reflection's power of candid criticism—the real
face of the society to which it belongs.

A Note on Currencies
referred to in this book

In 1850 the £1 sterling had the following equivalents among the various European currencies:[1]

In France: 25.2 francs.

In Germany: Berlin: 6.85 thalers. 1 thaler = 30 silver groschen. 1 groschen = 12 pfennigs.

Frankfurt am Main: 6.49 Reich dollars (thalers). 1 Reich dollar = 90 kreuzer. 1 kreuzer = 4 pfennigs.

Hamburg: 13.4 marks banco. 1 mark = 16 schillings. 1 schilling = 12 pfennigs.

Leipzig: 6.5 Reich dollars. 1 dollar (thaler) = 24 bon-gros. 1 bon-gros = 12 pfennigs.

Lübeck: 16.4 marks. 1 mark = 16 schillings. 1 schilling = 12 pfennigs.

Munich: 11.7 florins (gulden). 1 florin = 60 kreuzer. 1 kreuzer = 4 pfennigs.

In Austria: Vienna: 9.7 florins (gulden). 1 florin = 60 kreuzer. 1 kreuzer = 4 pfennigs.

In Switzerland: Zürich: 10 florins. 1 florin = 60 kreuzer. 1 kreuzer = 6 keller.

In Holland: Amsterdam: 11.9 florins. 1 florin = 100 cents.

In Italy: Milan: 28.9 Austrian francs. 1 franc = 100 cents.

Naples: 5.9 new ducats. 1 ducat = 10 carbini.

Rome: 4.7 scudi. 1 scudo = 10 paoli.

Russia: St. Petersburg: 6.3 roubles. 1 rouble = 100 kopeks.

Subject to the normal fluctuations of value, these figures provide the most reasonable indication of such salaries, costs, etc., earned or faced by musicians.

Other information of value in considering the status and earning power of the nineteenth-century musician:

1813: Weber's salary in Prague: 2000 gulden.

1821: Weber's salary in Dresden: 1500 thalers (c. £220, says Grove).

1823: Weber was offered 2500 thalers to become *Kapellmeister* at Cassel.

1826: Weber's fee for the production of *Oberon* at Covent Garden, £1000.

[1] Isaac Slater: *Universal Money Table and Commercial Exchange Standard.*

1826: Weber's dinner for two in London: 6s. 0d. = 21 groschen 4 pfennigs.

1822: Spohr's salary at Cassel: 2000 thalers; after 1829, 2500.

1836: Berlioz's commission for the *Requiem*, 3000 francs, out of which he was responsible for the payment of copyists and all costs of rehearsal and performance.

1838: Paganini's present to Berlioz: 20,000 francs.

1840: Berlioz's commission for the *Symphonie Funèbre et Triomphale*, 10,000 francs, out of which he was responsible for payment of copyists and all costs of rehearsal and performance (four additional performances sponsored by the managers of the Salle Vivienne made the work unusually profitable to the composer).

1844: Festival of Industrial Products: Receipts: 32,000 francs. Tax: 4000 francs. Berlioz's net profit: 800 francs.

1832: Wagner's salary at Würzburg: 10 gulden per month. At Riga: 800 roubles. At Dresden: 1500 thalers.

1842: Nicolai's salary as *Kapellmeister* of the Vienna Imperial Opera: 2000 gulden.

1847: Nicolai's salary as *Kapellmeister* of the Royal Opera, Berlin: 2000 thaler.

1883: Mahler's salary as Second Conductor of the Opera at Cassel: 1000 marks and living expenses.

1888: Mahler's salary as Director of the Royal Opera, Budapest: 10,000 florins and various subsidiary benefits.

1897: Mahler's salary as Director of the Imperial Opera, Vienna: 6000 florins + 2000 florins for conducting + 2000 for expenses.

Bibliography

W. J. Argent: *Philharmonic Jubilee: Half a Century of Music in Liverpool.* Liverpool, 1889.

Richard Batka: *Die Musik in Böhmen.* Bard, Marquardt, Berlin, 1906.

Frantisek Bartos: *Bedrich Smetana; Letters and Reminiscences,* translated by Daphne Rustridge, Artis, Prague, 1955.

Jacques Barzun: *Berlioz and his Century.* Meridian Books, New York, 1956.

J. R. Sterndale Bennett: *The Life of William Sterndale Bennett.* Cambridge University Press, 1907.

Hector Berlioz: *Memoirs,* translated by David Cairns. Gollancz, London, 1969.
  Correspondance Gènèrale, edited by Pierre Citron Vol. 1. Flammarion, Paris, 1972.
  Evenings in the Orchestra, translated by C. R. Fortescue. Penguin Books, Harmondsworth, 1963.
  La Musique et les Musiciens. Colman Lévy, Paris, Gregg International, New York, 1969.
  On Conducting. Translated by John Broadhouse. London 1917.

Heinrich Bihrle: *Musikalisches Akademie München.* Munich, 1911.

Werner Bollert (ed.): *Singakademie zu Berlin.* Berlin, 1966.

William Boosey: *Fifty Years of Music Publishing.* Benn, London, 1931.

Wallace Brockway and Herbert Weinstock: *The World of Opera.* Methuen, London, 1963.

Maurice J. E. Brown: *Essays on Schubert.* Macmillan, London, 1966.

Hans von Bülow: *Letters,* selected and edited by Richard, Count of Moulin-Eckhart. Translated by Hannah Waller. Knopf, New York, 1931.

Adam Carse: *The Orchestra from Beethoven to Berlioz.* Heffer, Cambridge, 1948.
  The Life of Julien. Heffer, Cambridge, 1951.

Algernon Cecil: *Metternich.* Eyre and Spottiswode, London, 1933.

Gilbert Chase: *America's Music.* McGraw Hill, New York, 1955.

A. E. Cherbuliez: *Die Schweiz in der deutschen Musik Geschichte.* Verlag von Huber, Frauenfeld and Leipzig, 1932.

Chopin: *Letters,* collected by H. Opienski, translated and edited by E. Voynich. Desmond Harmsworth, London, 1932.

Henry F. Chorley: *Music and Manners of France and Germany.* 3 vols. London, 1841.

John Clapham: *Antonin Dvorák.* Faber, London, 1966.

Aaron Copland: *Our New Music.* Whitlesey House, New York, 1941.

Peter Cornelius: *Ausgewählte Schriften und Briefen.* Berlin.

J. E. Cox: *Musical Reminiscences.* London, 1872.

William L. Croston: *French Grand Opera; an art and a business.* King's Crown Press, New York, 1948.

A. Dandelot: *La Société des Concerts du Conservatoire.* Paris, 1923.

Otto Erich Deutsch: *Schubert: a Documentary Biography,* translated by Erich Blom. Dent, London, 1946.

Alfred Einstein: *Schubert,* translated by David Ascoli. Cassel, London, 1951. Panther Books, London, 1971.

John Ella: *Musical Sketches.* 3 vols. London, 1878.

Carl Fuchs: *Musical and other Recollections.* Manchester, 1937.

Hans Gal: *The Composer's World.* Thames and Hudson, London, 1965.

A. W. Ganz: *Berlioz in London.* Quality Press, London, 1956.

Wilhelm Ganz: *Memories of a Musician.* John Murray, London, 1913.

William Gardiner: *Music and Friends.* 3 vols. London, 1832.

Joseph Gmelch: *Musikgeschichte Eichstätts.* Eichstätt, 1912.

Henry-Louis de la Grange: *Mahler,* vol. 1. Gollancz, London, 1974.

Susanna Grossman-Vendrey: *Felix Mendelssohn-Bartholdy und die Musik der Vergangenheit*. Gustav Bosse Verlag, Regensburg, 1969.
Donald Jay Grout: *A History of Western Music*. Dent, London, 1962.
Heinrich Habel: *Das Odeon in München*. Walter de Gruyter, Berlin, 1967.
C. E. and M. Hallé: *The Life and Letters of Sir Charles Hallé*. London, 1896.
Eduard Hanslick: *Music Criticisms, 1846–99*, translated and edited by Henry Pleasants. Penguin, Harmondsworth, 1956.
Alec Harman, Anthony Milner and Wilfred Mellers: *Man and his Music*. Barrie and Rockliff, London, 1962.
Fritz Henneberg: *The Leipzig Gewandhaus Orchestra*. Dennis Dobson, London, 1966.
J. Hennings: *Musikgeschichte Lübecks. Band 1, Weltliche Musik*. Bärenreiter, Cassel and Basel, 1951.
Ferdinand Hiller: *Aus dem Tonleben unserer Zeit*. 3 vols, Leipzig, 1868.
George Hogarth: *Musical History, Biography and Criticism*. London, 1835.
Hajo Holborn: *A History of Modern Germany*. 2 vols. Eyre and Spottiswoode, London, 1965.
Edward Holmes. *A Ramble among the Musicians of Germany*. London, 1828.
Edgar Holt: *Risorgimento*. Macmillan, London, 1970.
M. A. de Wolfe Howe: *The Boston Symphony Orchestra: a Historical Sketch*. Houghton, Miflin and Co., Boston, 1914.
Paul Ignotus: *Hungary*. Ernest Benn, London, 1972.
Charles F. James: *The Story of the Performing Rights Society*. P.R.S., London, 1951.
Harold F. Johnson: *Sibelius*. Faber and Faber, London, 1959.
Jubiläum der Hessischen Staatskapelle. Cassel, 1960.
Michael Kennedy: *The Hallé Tradition*. Manchester University Press, 1960.
Helmut Kirchmeyer: *Das Zeitgenossiche Wagnerbild*. Gustav Bosse Verlag. 3 vols. Regensburg, 1972.
Georg Knepler: *Musikgeschichte des 19 Jahrhunderts*. 2 vols. Henschelverlag, Berlin, 1961.
Karl Kobald: *Alt-Wiener Musikstätten*. Amalthea Verlag, Vienna, 1919.
Henry Krehbiel: *The Philharmonic Society of New York*. Novello, Ewer and Co. Ltd., London and New York, 1892.
Herbert Kupferberg: *The Fabulous Philadelphians*. Charles Scribner's Sons, New York, 1959.
Constant Lambert: *Music Ho!* Faber, London, 1934. Penguin Books, 1948.
Brian Large: *Smetana*. Duckworth, London, 1970.
Karl Laux: *The Dresden Staatskapelle*, translated by Lena Jaeck; Dennis Dobson, London, 1864.
Hugo Leichtentritt: *Music, History and Ideas*: Harvard University Press, 1938.
R. A. Leonard: *A History of Russian Music*. Jarrold, London, 1956.
Benjamin Lumley: *Reminiscences of the Opera*. London, 1864.
C. A. MacCartney: *The Habsburg Empire, 1790–1918*. Wiedenfeld and Nicolson, London, 1968.
E. D. Mackerness: *A Social History of English Music*. Routledge and Kegan Paul, London, 1964.
Alma Mahler: *Gustav Mahler: Memories and Letters*, translated by Basil Creighton. New edition, introduction by Donald Mitchell. John Murray, London, 1968.
Daniel Gregory Mason: *Music in my Time*. Macmillan, New York.
Tune in America. Knopf, New York, 1931.
Wilfred Mellers: *Music and Society*, Dennis Dobson, second edition, 1950.
Music in New Found Land. Barrie and Rockliff, London 1964.
Felix Mendelssohn: *Letters*, translated and edited by G. Seldengoth, Elek, London, 1947.
Erwin Mittag: *Aus dem Geschichte der Wiener Philharmoniker*. Gerlach, Wiedling, Vienna, 1950.
Stephen Mizau (editor): *Frederic Chopin, 1810–1849*. Kosciusko Foundation, Macmillan, New York, 1949.
Rena Moisienko: *Realist Music*. Meridian Books, London, 1947.
Gotbert Moro and Ambros Wilhelmer: *Aus dem Musikgeschichten Kärnterns*. Klagenfurt, 1956.
Charlotte Moscheles: *Life of Moscheles*, translated by A. D. Coleridge. 2 vols. London, 1873.

John H. Mueller: *The American Symphony Orchestra*. John Calder, London, 1958.
Israel V. Nestiev: *Prokofiev*, translated by Florence Jonas, introduction by Nicolas Slonimsky. Stanford and Oxford University Press, London, 1951.
Ernest Newman: *The Life of Richard Wagner*. 4 vols. Cassel, London, 1933–6.
Musical Studies. John Lane, the Bodley Head, London, 1905.
Joseph d'Ortigue: *Le Balcon de l'Opéra*. Paris, 1832.
Alan Peacock and Ronald Weir: *The Composer in the Market Place*. Faber Music, London, 1975.
Eberhard Preussner: *Die Bürgerliche Musikkultur*. Bärenreiter, 2 vols. Cassel, 1950.
L. Ramaan: *Franz Liszt, artist and man*, translated by E. Cordery, London, 1882.
Nikolai Rimsky-Korsakov: *My Musical Life*, translated by A. Jaffe. Knopf, New York, 1942.
Alec Robertson and Denis Stevens (editors): *The Pelican History of Music*. Penguin Books, Harmondsworth, 1968. Volume 3.
Roland-Manuel (editor): *Histoire de la Musique*. Encyclopédie de la Pleiade. 2 vols. Paris, 1960, 1963.
Ernst Roth: *The Business of Music*. Cassell, London, 1965.
John F. Russell and J. H. Elliott: *The Brass Band Movement*. Dent, London, 1936.
Walter Salmen (editor): *Der Sozialstatus der Berufmusikers von 17 bis 19 Jahrhunderts*. Bärenreiter, Cassel, 1971.
Friedrich Schmidt: *Das Musikleben des bürgerlichen Gesellschaft Leipzig. Musikalisches Magazin Heft*. Hermann Beyer und Söhne, Langenzenn, 1912.
Arnold Schoenberg: *Letters*, edited by Erwin Stein, translated Eithne Walker and Ernst Lain. Faber, London, 1964.
Harold C. Schonberg: *The Great Pianists*. Gollancz, London, 1964.
Willi Schuh: *Schweizer Musikbuch*. Atlantis Verlag, Zürich, 1939.
Georg Schunemann: *Geschichte des Dirigierens*. Breitkopf und Härtel, Leipzig, 1913.
Karl Senn: *Der Innsbrucker Musikverein*.
G. Bernard Shaw: *The Perfect Wagnerite*. London, Constable, 1898.
London Music, 1888–89 as heard by Corno di Bassetto. Constable, London, 1937.
Music in London, 1890–94. 3 vols. Constable, London, 1932.
H. Sievers: *Die Musik in Hannover*. Sponholz Druckerei, Hanover, 1961.
Otakar Sourek: *Antonin Dvorák: Letters and Reminiscences*. Translated Roberta Finlayson Samsour, Artis, Prague, 1954.
Georg Sowa: *Anfänge Institutioneller Musikerziehung in Deutschland. 1800–1843*. Gustav Bosse Verlag, Regensburg, 1973.
Louis Spohr: *Autobiography*. English translation, London, 1878.
Vladimir Stassov: *Selected Essays on Music*, translated by Florence Jonas. Cresset Press, London, 1965.
Vladimir Stepanek, Bohumil Karasek and Ladislav Sip: *Zur Geschichte der Tschechischen und Slowakischen Musik*. Orbis, Prague, 1959.
Bence Szabolski: *The Twilight of Ferenc Liszt*. Hungarian Academy of Science, Budapest, 1959.
A. J. P. Taylor: *The Habsburg Monarchy*. Hamish Hamilton, London, 1970.
Alexander Wheelock Thayer: *The Life of Ludwig van Beethoven*, edited by H. E. Krehbiel, New York, 1921–5. New edition, introduction by Alan Pryse Jones, Centaur Press, New York, 1960.
Francis Toye: *Giuseppe Verdi*. Heineman, London, 1931.
Rossini, a Study in Tragi-Comedy. Heinemann, London, 1934.
Giuseppe Verdi: *Letters*, selected, edited and translated by Charles Osborne. Gollancz, London, 1971.
Richard Wagner: *My Life*. Authorised translation. London, 1963.
Wagner writes from Paris, edited and translated by Robert L. Jacob and Geoffrey Skelton. George Allen and Unwin, London, 1973.
Letters from the Burrell Collection, translated and edited by John N. Burke. Gollancz, London, 1951.
Ernest Walker: *A History of Music in England*. Oxford University Press, 1907. Third edition, revised by J. A. Westrup, Oxford University Press, London, 1952.
Frank Walker: *The Man Verdi*. Dent, London, 1972.
John Warrack: *Weber*. Hamish Hamilton, London, 1968.

Carl Maria von Weber: *Ausgewählte Schriften*. Edited by W. Altmann, Regensburg, 1928.

Hildergard Weber: *Das Museum; einhundertfünfzig Jahre Frankfurter Konzertleben*. Verlag Waldemar Kramer, Frankfurt-am-Main, 1958.

Ludwig Wegele: *Musik in der Reichstadt Augsburg*. Verlag Die Brigge, Augsburg, 1965.

Felix Weingartner: *On Conducting*, translated by Ernest Newman. Leipzig, 1925.

Herbert Weinstock: *Donizetti*. Methuen, London, 1964.

Alexander Werth: *Musical Uproar in Moscow*. Turnstile Press, London, 1949.

Pamela Weston: *Clarinet Virtuoi of the Past*. Robert Hale, London, 1972.

David Wooldridge: *The Conductor's World*. Barrie and Rockliff, London, 1970.

Percy M. Young: *The Concert Tradition*. Routledge and Kegan Paul, London, 1965.

Index